Population Pattern and Urban Development

Population Pattern and Urban Development

(*A Case Study of Patna*)

Urvija Shanker

RAJESH PUBLICATIONS
NEW DELHI-110 002

First Published : 2001
ISBN : 81-85891-25-7

Published by :
M. L. Gupta
RAJESH PUBLICATIONS
1, Ansari Road, Darya Ganj,
New Delhi - 110 002
Phone : 3274550

Lasertypesetting by :
Sanjay Gupta
SANJAY ENTERPRISES
New Delhi - 2

Printed at :
Samrat Printers, Delhi - 2

FOREWORD

Cities since ancient times have been administrative centres and have acted as a reservoir of material goods and culture. They have, in the modern age become centres of commerce and industry. With the concentration of power, both administrative and economic, the cities all over the world are growing in their population size and areal extent. This has created a greater awareness among geographers to study urban geography and to examine the character of towns and cities both temporally and spatially. Urban geography today has thus become a major branch of the discipline.

Urban growth and development are the concern of not only urban geographers but also sociologists, regional planners and architects. The population of a city mostly grows by immigration of people from the surrounding countryside. The influx of people leads to not only an areal expansion of the urban landscape but also to a diversification in land use and urban functions. As the process continues, there is an increase in housing density, accommodation density and traffic density, particularly in the core areas. Uncontrolled urban sprawl may engulf a number of rural settlements, while extreme pressure of population on land may lead to degeneration of built up landscape. Both result in the creation of slums, shortage of civic amenities and decrease in health and hygiene. Such conditions can be witnessed all over the world particularly in the developing countries where haphazard unplanned growth of towns is the rule rather than the exception. This is also true of India.

Many Indian cities had acquired the character of twin towns during the last two centuries. These were : a medieval city core and a modern civic centre. In the post-independence era, uncontrolled growth and haphazard addition of numerous housing colonies have created slums and confused the functional structures of these towns. Unbridled commercial expansion and the resultant snarl in traffic have compounded the problem. Lack of adequate finance has handicapped the town planners while political interference has prevented the implementation of town plans. The city is an excellent example of the incompetence of authorities in the face of unprecedented population explosion. Although Patna is an ancient centre of civilization, the present chaos in civic life is to be seen to be believed. The question now is not one of planned development, but of renewal, reconstruction and redevelopment.

The author has tried to analyse the temporal and spatial patterns of urban population and functions in the city of Patna. She has suggested strategies for control and development of the urban landscape through appropriate policies as well as physical planning efforts. The study is based on original research and field work which are well documented. The study should be useful in the wider context of urban analysis and planning in the country.

L. N. Ram
Ex-University Professor and
Head of the Department of Geography
& Pro-Vice-Chancellor,
Patna University, Patna

CONTENTS

PREFACE

Cities the world over are growing, both in population and in areal extent. The urban geographer is concerned with the city as a functional as well as a physical unit. He is therefore, concerned with the problem of guiding urban growth and development into such forms and patterns as will further the attainment of a better way of life.

The guidance of population density in cities through control of land use and the provision of instruments by which the character, density and distribution of housing and residential areas can be made better to serve the need of the population are important objectives of an urban planner. The securing of better relationships spatially and functionally among the various forms of land use in cities, the reduction of time and energy-wasting journeys between home and work; the securing of a better physical urban environment through guidance of city growth into forms more acceptable than the sprawl which now characterizes most urban areas-these are the obvious challenges before the urban geographers.

The cities of the colonial period suddenly came out of their constricted urban area and opened up for unrestricted urban expansion. The result has been inevitable unplanned and uncoordinated growth of the major towns. Cities in India have been expanding by uncontrolled urban sprawl engulfing a large number of rural areas, giving shelter to innumerable unemployed and under employed people, creating numerous problems of housing and transport, while the basic civic amenities have failed to grow correspondingly. The result has been an immense pressure of population on land and development of slums with an unhealthy urban environment.

There is thus a need to arrest this undesirable urban growth before cities reach a stage of degenerating urban environment. They should be planned for economic supremacy in the region, functional specialization for the service of the society and act as growth poles in national economy. These problems should be solved in a comprehensive and integrated way in which the cities develop along with their rural counterparts.

There has been a growing awareness of the problems associated with urban expansion, but most of the work has been done by town planners, architects and engineers. Very little work and research have been done by geographers in this field.

Patna is faced with an acute problem of uncontrolled and unplanned expansion with inequitable distribution of population. The present study is an attempt to examine the pattern of population distribution in the city of Patna and its unbridled urban sprawl. The growth of population in the city has been rapid and phenomenal in recent years on account of heavy immigration from its hinterland, thereby leading to haphazard development of the city. The author has tried to suggest means for the betterment of the society.

The study has involved collection of data and maps from different sources, data analysis and interpretation. This entire works has been possible only with the help, guidance and cooperation of my teachers, colleagues, officials of various government departments and P.R.D.A., friends and family members.

This book is based on my Ph.D. Thesis prepared under the able guidance of Dr. L. N. Ram, Ex-Head of the Department of Geography, and Pro-Vice-Chancellor, Patna University. I express my deep gratitude to him for guiding me at every stage of the work and for writing the Foreword to this book.

My efforts would have been fruitless had my father Dr. P. Dayal, Professor Emeritus, Department of Geography, Patna University and Ex-Vice-Chancellor, Magadh University, not given his valuable suggestions in the preparation of this book. He took great pains in going through the entire proof and made necessary corrections. I am extremely grateful and thankful to him.

I extend my sincerest thanks to Dr. V. N. P. Sinha, Professor of Geography, Patna University for his constant encouragement. He has helped in various ways in bringing out this book.

Lastly, I extend my thanks to Sri. M. L. Gupta, Proprietor, Rajesh Publications, New Delhi for undertaking the publication of this work and for unfailing courtesy and co-operation.

The typescript was handed over to the publishers some years ago and was also composed by the press but it could not be published earlier due to some unavoidable reason. 1991 census data published by the Census Department has been incorporated as far as possible to help comparison with the projected trends (Appendices XIX and XX).

URVIJA SHANKER

LIST OF MAPS AND DIAGRAMS

LIST OF APPENDICES

1

Introduction

'Population Pattern' and 'Urban Development' are terms inseparable and interdependent. Cities in each region have always been expressions of the culture of the region and of the people forming them. An important development in urban settlement during past several decades has been the rapid expansion of population into the unicorporated areas surrounding our large cities into their incorporated suburbs.

The emergence of a core within the city finds a strong demographic expression. The commercial core, its tall buildings swarming with workers by day when its streets are choked with vehicular traffic and its pavements tthronged by milling crowds, is at night abandoned to small maintenance staff of 'caretakers and cats'[1]. The population spreads rapidly from the centre and a stage is reached when the population of the town can only be increased by extension of its boundaries. People moving out join the immigrants to the town to colonies in rapidly growing suburbs, where buildings fill up remaining spaces extending the outer margins of the urban area.

The rapid expansion of cities in the present period and the invasion of the rural areas by urban phenomena was brought about by radical changes in the technology of transportation. As long as the power for the movement of people and goods was furnished by horse, city sizes and the areas they served outside the city limits were relatively small. Urban areas were thus compact. But with the advent of suburban service through rail-roads, surburban clusters began to appear around the rail road stations. With the passage of time the areas between these suburban nuclei filled in. This expansion was however, tied only to rail lines and the degree of accessibility dropped sharply away from these lines.

The automobile, bus, motor truck and modern paved highways enabled cities to throw off the shackles of steel rails, and an accelerated rate of urban expansion especially on the fringes of the cities took place after the 1st World War. The dormitory suburbs as well as the industrial satellite communities within metropolitan areas shared in the expansion. As the central cities grew, they absorbed many of the older nuclei in the outlying areas, which now remain areas of higher density surrounded by areas of lower density.

This process of development and expansion has been examined in a large number of studies, some by geographers and by others working in other disciplines. Much attention has been laid on to the problem of excessive urban expansion, particularly in relation to the problems of municipal planning and finance arising out of lower densities and extensive urban 'sprawl' facilitated by the motor vehicle and modern highways. The works on urban expansion have been discussed at length under 'Review of Literature'.

Conceptual Frame

Urban : According to the sociologist Nels Anderson, urban or urbanism is a way of life of man, of the condition of man, characterized by certain attitudes such as transience, superficiality and anonymity.[2]

This definition, however, is not satisfactory. It may suffice for recognition of differences in social types, but does not serve well as a working definition for geographers.

Geographers are inclined more towards a definition of 'urban' that recognizes a place of occupance instead of mode of behavior. Certainly, man in a certain environment may adopt certain behavior traits but the geographer is more concerned with the locational setting than with his life style. Most geographers are of the view that 'urban' is a locational setting[3] in which (1) the density of settlement is considerably higher than that of the general population, (2) the people in that setting are engaged mainly in non-agricultural activities, not in economic activities normally placed in the primary economic sector, and (3) the locational setting serves as cultural, administrative and economic centre for a region peripheral to the centre in question. 'Urban' as used here, refers to the activities of a human agglomeration at a specific location or place.

Urban Area, Urban Place and Town : There are various ways in which these terms have been defined in different countries. Although all are more or less the same, it is unusual to find two national definitions that are exactly the same. In the United States, for example, an urban area or an urban place or a town must have a population of 2500 or more and may be an incorporated place or an unincorporated place.[4]

To quote Mayor and Kohn[5], when, however, these activities occur in some kind of combination in permanent and compact settlement with some measure of community organization, the place assumes the character of a town.

The Census of India 1981[6] defined urban areas so as to include :

(a) All places with Municipal Corporation, Municipality, Notified Area Committee, Cantonment Board etc. and

(b) All other places which satisfy the following criteria :

(i) A minimum population of 5,000;

(ii) At least 75 percent of the male working population being engaged in non-agricultural pursuits; and

(iii) A density of population of at least 400 persons per sq. km.

Thus in India, places satisfying the above criteria are identified as census towns. By and large these criteria have been followed except in a few cases, on account of their administrative importance or their being places of tourist interest.

Suburban Areas, Urban Fringe and Rural-Urban Fringe : The rapid increase in urban population, especially during the past two decades, has been accompanied by an even more spectacular increase in the demand for urban land. Various urban land uses have also produced augmented demands for land, as deconcentration towards the suburban areas has taken place.

The concept of 'suburb' was popular as a high grade dormitory area for the population employed in the central cities. This concept was effectively changed by C.D. Harris.[7] He demonstrated that a substantial proportion of the American suburbs are types other than upper income commuting areas and that, indeed, many suburbs are predominantly of nonresidential character.

Duncan[8] used the term 'urban fringe' to denote non-suburban population of the territory in urbanized areas outside the central cities. His urbanized area had three components - central city, suburbs and urban fringe. According to him, the 'urban fringe' is limited to the corporate limit of the city and often it is found outside the limit as well. As Andrews[9] puts it, urban fringe is the active expanding sector of the compact economic activity and the 'rural - urban fringe' lies adjacent to the periphery of the urban fringe.

'Rural - Urban Fringe' is an amorphous territory created around the cities by the centrifugal forces which impel functions to migrate from the central zone of a city towards its periphery. In this zone, the salient urban and rural characteristics are found to be intermixed. As R.L. Singh puts it, "where the urban influences are essentially mingled with rural forces often without striking a proper adjustment as in the case of unplanned growth, it designates the nature of the rural - urban fringe".[10] When the characteristics of the fringe are more akin to or influenced by the urban morphology than by the rural one, the fringe is termed as 'inner fringe' and when the fringe is more akin to rural morphology than to the urban one, the fringe is termed as the 'outer fringe'. As such the inner fringe may also be called urban fringe and the outer fringe, the rural fringe. The fringe generally advances with irregular patterns of urbanity and embayments of rurality. The sprawl is haphazard, sometimes moving in one direction, skipping and exploding in another, while in some areas it may not expand.

Countryside : The area surrounding the city is linked culturally, socially and economically with the City. This surrounding area or countryside is known by various names such as Umland, City Region, Catchment Area, Urban Hinterland, Sphere of Influence, Tributary Area and Urban Field.

A city cannot be considered as an isolated unit. It is a focal area for major services. It attracts people from countryside and provides them with various services. In turn it gets raw material from its hinterland. Both are strongly dependent on each other. According to Taylor,[11] the Umland of a town is that portion of surrounding country which is linked culturally with the town as a centre.

R.L.Singh[12] is of the view that the area in which the region and the city are culturally, economically and politically interrelated, forms the Umland of the particular town or city. He also points out that Umland is the immediate rural land surrounding the town or Metropolitan Area.

The problem of delimitataion determines from where and to what degree, the people of the hinterland derive urban-produced goods and services. The assumption in western countries is that all rural areas are under the influence of some city, whether directly or indirectly through a hierarchy of satellite centres. However, in India, with a large rural population dependent mostly on primary activities and where rural -

urban differences are sharp, the hinterland may best be studied at this early stage of its development by regarding it as that area adjacent to the contiguously built up area which exhibits physical, economic and demorgraphic characteristics resembling the city more than the isolated rural areas.[13]

Urban Land Use : The people living and working in the city occupy, organize and utilize space on the surface of the earth. They have needs for space for different purposes and the space needed is devoted to different uses. Not only are there different uses made of urban space, there are different magnitudes of need for space for different uses. 'Urban space' is a broad term and includes land areas in the city, water areas in the city and the space above the surface of the city. Traditionally, urban space above the surface has not been included in the study of urban land.

All land in the urban area is considered to be either developed or vacant or water area. The term 'developed' includes all land used for purposes that are recognized as urban in character, whether public or private in nature and whether devoted to an use such as parks or playgrounds, or to the site use such as residence, industry or commerce. Vacant land is that land which is not given to any urban use even though it may be potentially available for development. Thus agricultural land is considered vacant land. Water areas represent no urban use except when embraced within a park or recreational area. Bartholomew is of the view that the land we are concerned with can be described as land now used for purposes that are characteristically urban.[14]

All urban land may be classified according to its use such as residence, commerce, industry, streets,railroads, recreation centres and public or semipublic facilities.

Urban communities have developed as part of our social and economic system. The amount of land utilized by specific activities and their spatial distribution reflect the requirements of this system. The existing land use pattern of a town is the direct outcome of its past growth and present activities. It does not necessarily represent the most efficient use but the pattern that has evolved is essentially functional. Most of the land in the city in the past as well as today is given to one or more functions or uses.

Urban Functions : The term 'urban function' refers to the services performed by a town or a city. Cities provide goods and services, both for the residents of the city as well as for the population living outside the city. These urban functions have certain characteristics that serve to differentiate them from non-urban functions. Rarely do the urban functions involve 'primary' production in the classical economic sense.[15]

Basic urban functions include the processing or trading of goods or the furnishing of goods and services for residents or establishments located outside the urban area. In turn, urban areas get goods, raw materials, food products etc. from outside. Thus, there is an exchange or interchange of commodities taking place between the city and the outside region for which the city serves as a node.

Few cities have as their most important function, the primary activities. Even though many urban centres are dependent directly upon such activities, they actually function as manufacturing or service centre, utilizing the resources produced nearby or performing essential services for the people who are directly involved in primary activities.Thus tertiary activities usually predominate in an urban centre.

Urban Development : Urban development is usually the expansion, opening out of increasing resources or unfolding gradually of a land to constructive and useful activity. But at present it is the progress in economic activity which is often understood as development. The physical development usually pertains to natural resource, agriculture, housing, transportation, industry, health facilities, educational institutions, services like electricity, water supply and sanitation and many such factors that are needed for the physical advancement or expansion of the town. This physical advancement is very closely related to the economic progress in the region. Here we are concerned only with the physical expansion of the city.

The automobile age and other technological development have accelerated the pace of centrifugal forces in Western cities, so that even a city of moderate size could decentralize some of its economic activities to its suburbs, thus developing an intense affinity with its environs. However, in India, the centrifugal forces are relatively weak and such developments are seen only in those cities where mass transportation has established such linkages over large areas.

Metropolitan Concept : The term 'metropolis', a Greek word, is made up of two words 'metro' + 'polis' meaning mother and city respectively. Historically, it had a different meaning being applied mainly to the capital city of the State. But now, it also incorporates those areas which extend beyond the boundary of a local authority,especially where they happen to include adjacent towns or suburbs largely under the influence of the main city or town.

The U.S. Bureau of Census defines 'metropolitan area' as any area containing a nuclear city of at least 50,000 population. It includes the whole country containing the city plus any contiguous country (or countries) that meets the criteria of metropolitan character and of economic and social integration with the central country. The criteria employed are population density, number of non-agricultural workers in the country and proportion of their employment in the 'Standard Metropolitan Area'.

In India, many writers have used the term 'million cities'. The absolute size of a city alone does not afford to give a city the status of being a 'metropolis'. It may be noted, however, that while all metropolises are large cities, not all large cities are necessarily metropolises.

The Census of India has discreetly avoided the use of the term and instead employed the expression 'town group' to signify a statistical unit with more than one local authority in close contiguity to a main city. There was no effort to define metropolitan cities or metropolitan regions. For this matter settlements having 1,00,000 and more population can be called as metropolitan cities and their influence regions can be delineated on the basis of some simpler criteria like density, continuity and supply of perishable goods.

Urban planning : Many towns in India are expanding at a rapid pace since the last two decades. It is, therefore, not surprising that new developments take place or spring up either in or outside the town, without amenities for community living. Houses are built here and there, trees are felled and water courses are turned into storm water drains in many such isolated developments. These developments do not render much help to the majority of the citizens in solving their civic problems, because roads and open spaces, hospitals, schools, markets and shopping facilities, amusement centre etc. fall short of requirements. The intensity of the problem has further aggravated with the phenomenal growth of urban population all over the country, and this has brought into light all kinds of evils such as housing shortage, traffic bottlenecks, lack of open spaces, inadequacy of schools and social amenities etc. As such living and working conditions are fast deteriorating in most of the towns, but strange as it may seem, such conditions are being considered inevitable and something to be put up with.

In India, unfortunately, town planning on a comprehensive scale has not yet been practised. The work done so far by the Improvement Trusts for various towns and cities has been of an indifferent nature. It has mainly pertained to the development of vacant lands on the fringe of cities, without any regard to the neighbourhood concept of planning. The layouts, too, are devoid of site planning principles and are in general aimed at producing only attractive geometrical patterns rather than ensuring a satisfactory roads plan that makes for complete traffic safety to the inhabitants.

The Master Plan or the Comprehensive Plan has been defined as the official public document adopted by a local government as a policy guide to decision about the physical development of the community.[16] It has the properties of being comprehensive because it includes all geographical areas of the community and all functional elements that bear on its development. Since it deals with the city twenty years or more in the future, it is long range and does not deal with specific location and regulations. As such it is more in the nature of a policy declaration. To be precise it serves as a basic guide for physical development of the city in years to come.

Review of Literature

The spatial expansion of cities is only a recent phenomenon. It is only in earlier part of this century that geographers have tried to investigate the evolution, the pattern and causes of expansion of urban settlements.

Burgess, Hoyt and Harris have studied the growth of American cities and put forth their views on the pattern of development of cities in the early part of this century. Burgess[17] (1925) recognized five concentric zones in the growth of the city. Hoyt[18] (1939) studied the growth of American cities and found that they developed in a sectoral fashion. Harris[19] (1943) found that suburbs either residential or industrial are characteristic of most of the larger American cities. The rise of the automobile and the improvement of certain suburban commuter rail lines in a few of the largest cities have stimulated suburbanization.

Howley[20] (1956), Schnore[21] (1958) and Pickard[22] & [23] (1959,1962) have shown that the major trends in population redistribution can be summarized as processes of concentration, structured change and decentralization, laying open the possibility of dividing the U.S.A. into a set of metropolitan regions.

Dickinson[24] (1964) has summarized the relationships between cities and their regions. He distinguished four types of regional associations - the trade area, the social area, settlement and land use areas.

Boyce[25] (1966) deals with the metropolitan expansion as a wave like phenomenon. Beyer[26] (1967) examined the urban explosion in Latin America. A similar work has been done by Arriaga[27] (1968) who dealt with the components of the city growth in some of the countries in Latin America.

Morill[28] (1968) has described urban expansion as one of the most widespread and persistent forces of spatial change and conversion of rural land to urban use.

Turner[29] (1968) found that as city industrializes, its traditional residential pattern begins to disintegrate. The elite are the first to abandon the old city core and move to the suburbs followed by the emerging middle sectors of the population. This leaves a declining down-town predominantly to the lower income groups.

Brush[30] (1968) examined the spatial distribution of population in Indian cities and found that the overall patterns were more or less the same as observed by Clark and Berry et.al.

Mayer[31] (1969) in his study of urban economic base has suggested that the development and growth of cities depends on their economic base and the basic economic support of an area is provided by its specialized functions which it performs for people and establishments outside the area.

Buchanan[32] (1969) has studied the urban development in Ireland and describes the urban structure as being weak.

Wingo[33] (1969) has discussed the urban growth problems in developing countries. Whebell[34] (1969) has outlined five stages of urban system development : initial occupance, commercial agriculture, railway transportation, motor transportation and metropolitanism. Linear elements of urban systems are introduced by Whebell in his discussions of the role of "corridors" in system evolution. Rodwin[35] (1970) directed his comments towards redistribution of population.

Gillie[36] (1971) has proposed that the future expansion of Cork City should be spread over a number of satellite towns involving at least a fifteen mile journey trip to the centre of Cork.

Sinclair, Shipton and Willis[37] (1971) together studied the urban expansion in Southwestern Macomb country in Michigan and found that the stage of urban expansion processes when looked at spatially, the overall picture is that of mounting human insecurity and increasing landscape deterioration throughout the anticipation field from the place where urbanization first is anticipated to the edge of the built up areas. In areas, where there has been a relatively even spread of suburban land use into flat, productive and relatively intensive agricultural land, an ordered sequence of the different states is apparent. In other areas where conditions are not regular and the expansion process more uneven, the sequence might not be readily discernible but the underlying order is present.

Garner[38] (1972) has studied the politics of urban development in Singapore.

The extraordinary growth of large Indian cities poses a problem that calls for scientific planning and prediction of further trends. In an effort to identify growth patterns of Indian cities since Independence, A.M.Goryacheva[39] (1977) applied the principle of component analysis.

Sinclair[40] (1978) has found that the most important aspect of the whole urban expansion process is the uncertain time period involved at all stages. Although, development sometimes takes place rapidly, normally there is a period of years and often decades between the beginning of agricultural decline and final urban development.

Todaro[41] (1980) studied urbanization in developing countries and suggested an expansion of urban and rural employment opportunities in conjunction with a number of short and medium term policies which provide a more realistic and viable pattern of urban growth than what is likely to occur, given current development strategies.

There has been a steady flow of population from the rural to urban areas after 1921 causing terrific congestion in most of the towns and cities of India. The pace of urbanization has accelerated since 1951.

The first two papers in Geography in the field of Indian urban development were contributed by C. S. Srinivasachari[42] (1927) and N. Swaminathan[43] (1928). Srinivasachari has traced the history of the city of Madras in its different stages of growth. Swaminathan discussed the problem of sewage disposal in the cities of India in general and of South India with special reference to Madras Presidency, Pointing out that many of the diseases of Indian towns could be directly traceable to the water supply and drainage.

R. Dann[44] (1931-32) has elaborated his analysis of the factors such as historical, administrative and other non-geographical factors that have dominated development and produced garden cities of the Malabar coast : Cannore, Tellichery, Calicut and Cochin, none having any definite boundary because of a continuous stretch of populated settlements along the coast.

N.Subrahmanayam[45] (1938) examined the constraints to development and indicated that the suburban development of Madras could not take place northward because of the backwaters of Ennore, nor towards west because of a lowlying basin to the west of George town and Washermenpet.

C.S. Srinivasachari[46] (1939) in his Presidential address to the Madras,Geographical Association unfolded the fascinating growth of the city of Madras in unplanned way.

G.Kuriyan[47] (1941) before describing the population distribution within Madras has briefly referred to the continuous growth of the city from 1939 to 1800 A.D. The main points emerging from his demographic study are that this city has grown from the beginning by migration of population from rural areas and that the distribution characteristics of the city has not changed since 1871, the main concentration being still found around the fort.

C.D. Deshpande[48] (1941) discussed the geographical factors favouring the evolution of towns in the former Bombay Province, on a regional basis with particular reference to the Bombay Metropolitan Region, Poona, Surat and Ahmedabad and analyzed the main trends in the urban development.

S.P. Chatterjee[49] (1949) discussed the growth of Calcutta city with the help of four sketch maps and discussed the salient features of the eight functional zones into which the city was divided.

P.P.Karan[50] (1952) in his study of two major cities of Bihar, Patna and Jamshedpur revealed that they differed considerably in urban landscape, morphology and functions, the former having a long chequerred history behind it and its original location and subsequent growth have been materially affected by its strategic location at the confluence of important rivers, while the latter being a product of the twentieth century development of iron, steel and heavy industries.

M.Guha[51] (1953) in her analysis of the morphology of Calcutta referred first to the three different stages in the functional development of the city of Calcutta within the past 250 years of its growth and divided the city into four functional zones and fourteen sub-zones.

A.B.Mukerji[52] (1953) explained how the birth and growth of Modinagar in Uttar Pradesh. a new industrial town symbolized the essential interdependence of man and nature.

A.B.Chatterjee[53] (1958) analyzed the demographic features of Howrah city with special reference to density and population movement and occupational structure. He has subsequently attempted a detailed interpretation of the physical and socio-economic background for the growth of the urban agglomeration together with thorough analysis of the urban functions, land use, social geography, transportation and supply base of Howrah in terms of the present structure, the reasons for their development and their place within the greater Calcutta complex.

S.P.Singh[54] (1959) discussed the distribution and movement of population within the city limits of Lucknow, a garden city and the present capital of Uttar Pradesh.

R.L.Singh[55] (1961) in his study of Bangalore, an example of a ridge-head town revealed a very close relationship between the physical setting and evolution of the city and its gradual extension beyond its original city wall.

U.Singh[56] (1962) summarized his finding on studies of five cities of Uttar Pradesh, namely, Kanpur, Allahabad, Varanasi, Agra and Lucknow, collectively known as 'KAVAL' towns, pointing out to more than three fold increase in population in each of the towns since 1901, the amenities of life remaining more or less the same and creating acute problems, which could only be solved if planning were undertaken with the help of geographers.

Sinha[57] (1962) has analyzed the influence of population growth on the economy of Orissa and his study revealed that the carrying capacity of the land has far outstripped its limit, still lowering the standard of living.

B. N. Ganguli[58] (1963) discussed the role of natural increase and migration in the growth of cities and the functions and sex ratio of urban centres.

T. B. Lahiri[59] (1963) described the historical evolution of the Calcutta Metropolitan District and brought out the factors influencing the linear growth of towns. He has described the characteristics of the three urban zones of the metropolitan area, that is, the core area where service and commerce are the most important occupations, the conurbation, compactly built up areas where industrial activities predominate, and the outer suburban zones where mixed economy is prevalent.

K. Bagchi and U. Sen[60] (1963) have analyzed the physical environment, historical perspective of the evolution of the urban centre and the socio - economic factors determining the growth of Giridih and the resultant land use pattern of the town.

S. S. Dhabriya[61] (1964) described the physical setting of Udaipur city, the ancient town site which was the regional centre of the 'Ahar Culture' in times of Indus civilization, the historical evolution of urban area from 16th century onwards along the lines of growing circulatory system on account of mining and industrialization.

A. Ramesh[62] (1964) presented the characteristic of location, physiography, historical evolution and demographic features of Ootacamund. The author has described functional areas as administrative, educational, residential, market and recreational.

A. N. Bhattacharya and R.Lodha[63] (1964) have discussed the impact of historical - geographical and socio - economic factors on the growth and functions of Chittorgarh.

B. N.Jha[64] (1964) has dealt with the pattern of urban growth and the general distribution of urban population in Bihar during the last sixty years.

R. L.Dwivedi[65] (1965) has traced the growth of Allahabad, the distribution pattern of population within the city, the religious composition, sex - structure, and occupational structure of population, mortality and diseases prevalent in the city and the housing problems of the city.

S. M.Alam[66] (1965) has described the historical evolution of the twin cities of Hyderabad and Secunderabad, their location and physiographic environment, the delimitation of hinterland and metropolitan region, the industrial and occupational structure, characteristics of population, urban land use and morphological classification of the twin cities.

According to U. Singh[67] (1966), the development of 'KAVAL' towns is due to the progressive development of railways, roads, cantonments, educational institutions, industrial estates and trades and commercial activities.

V.K. Srivastava[68] (1967) has analyzed the origin and evolution of urban centre of Sidhi, a district headquarter in Madhya Pradesh, its centripetal growth, the house types, the functional pattern and segregation of zones keeping in view the geographical environment.

U. Singh[69] (1968) in his study of the problems and planning of the cities of the Ganga Plain, has dealt with the general problems of space, swallowing up of the productive countryside with hapazard process of urban sprawl, slum development, lack of essential urban services and amenities, lack of job opportunities etc.. Lastly, some of the planning efforts taken up by the city corporations and governmental bodies have been outlined and a few suggestions made to accelerate the planning efforts. The author has suggested the development of new communities on the periphery of cities with adequate social , economic and communication links with the main cities for redress from reckless sprawl.

A.S. Jauhari[70] (1968) has traced the urban development in the Sutlej - Yamuna Divide. He has found that rapid urban development has taken place in the region which has been greatly assisted by the growth of transportation facilities, construction, agriculture, industry and trade. The rapid strides which Delhi has been taking during the last few decades have helped nearby towns to grow quickly.

N.B.K. Reddy[71] (1968) has dealt with the occupational structure of urban centres in Krishna and Godavari Deltas. He has given the regional features of urban centres and their intra - regional diversities and has discussed the subject matter in the light of size relationships between the population and its components, factors of location and geographic setting, features of historical antecedent and aspects of evolution and growth etc.. of the urban areas of the region.

D. Thapan[72] (1968) deals with he evolution of townscape of steel towns of Indian Steel Belt with special reference to Jamshedpur, Rourkela,

Bhilai and Durgapur. She has dealt with the pre-urban landscape and socio-economic condition of each area and has further gone into evolution of the townscape in each case.

S.P. Mathur[73] (1968) analyses the growth and functional structure of Dehradun and claims that Dehradun sets a typical example of uninuclear growth, bi-nuclear formation and multi-nuclear explosion, thus ranking three phases of distinct growth with distinct characteristics. The author has delimited the various functions in terms of morphological areas such as the core, the intermediate zone, the outer zone and the suburbs. With tremendous urbanization, the city is gradually losing its significance as a resort town.

Diskshit[74] (1970) has traced the evolution of cities in Maharashtra from 7th century B.C. to the present day. Four phases of urban development have been distinguished. The earliest phase was marked by administrative, religious and maritime trade and cave towns. During the medieval period, defence became a vital consideration and consequently many of the towns belonging to this age were 'best' towns. The advent of railways in the latter half of the 19th century gave rise to a number of new transport towns. Lastly, the phase of industrialization was associated with the growth of several manufacturing centres.

Bhattacharya and Basak[75] (1970) have investigated into the origin, land use patterns and population characteristics of Chittaranjan - a planned township.

A comparative analysis of growth and functional characteristics of towns of Ganga - Yamuna Doab has been attempted by Singh and Dabrail[76] (1970).

Devgun and Agrawal[77] (1971) have prepared a map showing levels of urban development in India by superimposing such attributes as percentage of urban population in relation to total area, average size and spacing of urban centres.

Bonifatieva[78] (1971) expressed concern over the problems of Indian cities. She has noted specific features of Indian towns and cities and traced the efforts of town planning before and after independence of the country. She has highlighted its achievements and enunciated tasks pending before it. She has favoured formulation of a national organ for dealing with the problems of urban development at different levels. She has also made out a case for evolving special plans for individual cities and regions.

D.K. Singh[79] (1972) has tried to investigate the origin, growth, functional structure and the service area of Kerakat town in Lower Gomati Valley.

Saxena[80] (1972) analyses the changing patterns of demographic structure of Dehra Dun in terms of its interactions with certain factors such as physical, economic and cultural. The density and growth direction of urban population are well reflected in the core and the periphery of the city. The grave housing problem has been accentuated by the presence of a floating tourist population.

Shastri[81] (1973) has analyzed the growth and distribution of population in Nagpur and found that the population growth in the city is because of the location and commercial and industrial importance of the city itself and the density decreases away from the centre of the city inspite of recent growth in periphery.

Bhat and Sharma[82] (1974) have examined the pattern of urban development in Karnal District, considering the temporal, spatial and functional aspects of urban structure.

Bhardwaj[83] (1974) has tried to make the common man realize his responsibility towards the improvement of his own city. The author has tried to analyse the major problems for urban development which include land acquisition, drainage, housing especially low income and industrial housing slum clearance and redevelopment, the educational, medical and health facilities etc. He has also suggested suitable solutions.

Ram Dayal Singh[84] (1975) has examined demographic and spatial relationship among the cities of Bihar and found that these cities have grown rapidly on account of general population increase and rising employment in secondary and tertiary activities. In the process of growth they have undergone changes in demographic and functional patterns.

Raza, Kundu and Nangia[85] (1975) have found that urban growth or urban accretion has only served to weaken the agrarian base as it is not accompanied by industrial growth. They have come to the conclusion that Delhi has but a restricted and weak interelationship with its hinterland.

Bonani Ghosh[86] (1976) studied the growth of population in Calcutta from 1901 - 71 in terms of spatial distribution of population and pattern of population concentration with special reference to the spatial distribution of the congested wards of the city. On the basis of the study which points towards rising congestion in the city followed by the declining growth rate of population in the core city, the author feels that the city has reached its optimum stage of growth. She thus suggests that the decentralizing trend which has already set in should be properly guided to achieve balanced regional development.

Tripathy and Sinha[87] (1976) have attempted to find out the capacity of an urban centre to grow through increase in work opportunities or employment.

Dhabriya[88] (1976-77) brings out the role of centrifugal and centripetal forces in the expansion of cities. Generally an increase in urban population and the variety of urban functions together with the diffusion of transport network accelerate the process of city expansion. The paper deals with factors causing the activation of these pull and push forces,in the peripheral zone. Finally various types of urban expansions have been described.

C.R. Pathak[89] (1980) has tried to explain the process of urban growth in spatial context to India and the resulting pattern of regional imbalance. The author has suggested certain strategies and policies developing a symboitic relationship between the rural and urban growth and to formulate strategies for synthesizing the social, economic and physical factors for decentralizing urban growth in the rural hinterland.

Singhal[90] (1980) has found that the spatial expansion of Gaya city has much influenced the fringe rural settlements, in terms of high percentage of rural household density, population density, land occupancy and settlements pattern.

M. Irshad Hussain[91] (1980) attempts to emphasize one of the demerits of haphazard urbanization, i.e. urban encroachment on rural lands. For this purpose Muzaffarnagar in U.P. has been selected. He is of the opinion that urban expansion undoubtedly cannot be checked but it can be so planned that good quality agricultural land is not acquired for non-agricultural purposes without accounting for the social cost involved.

Sinha[92] (1980) has studied the impact of urbanization on land use in the rural - urban fringe of Patna and found remarkable changes in its land use pattern, occupational structure and density of population.

Vasantha Vishawanth[93] (1981) deals with the growth and distribution of urban settlements in Tamil Nadu in the present century. Based on trends in urbanization during past eighty years, what strikes most is the evolution of axial development of zones of urban agglomeration along transportation lines which also attract multifarious activities such as industries, trade and commerce.

Apart from studies done by several geographers, both within the country and abroad, there are quite a number of works done by different agencies and offices of the government of which a few are mentioned here. The Master Plan for Delhi[94] was the first comprehensive urban development plan with metropolitan and regional perspectives. This work was undertaken by Delhi Development Authority in 1962. The focus of this study was mainly on land development, housing and community facilities, solutions to all urban problems with sound and consistent planning according to priorities and stages of development in the light of available resources.

The Master Plan for Patna[95] (1962) also provides a comprehensive analysis of all the problems in development of the city and suggests ways to tackle them.

The Calcutta Basic Development Plan[96] (1966) was drawn up by the Calcutta Metropolitan Planning Organization and taken up for implementation by the Calcutta Metropolitan Development Authority. Here the perspectives were somewhat different. Conditioned by the immense backlog of deficit in all aspects of urban living, the planners viewed their immediate tasks so as to find ways to arrest the deterioration in urban services and facilities of Calcutta and to discover positive growth forces that can be accelerated to the point at which they become regenerative and self sustaining.

Besides, several plans in different parts of the country have been prepared by the state, Town and country Planning Organization with a view to improving deteriorating conditions of the cities and expenditing means to arrest them.

Problem Under Study

The present study is designed to examine the pattern of population in and around the city of Patna in order to establish the trend of change in its growth and distribution, its functional character and its relationship with the land use and city functions. The shortcoming in the development of the city and the trend of its expansion will be studied to suggest guidelines for a better distribution and organization of the population within the city on the basis of established planning standards.

More specifically, the following questions are to be investigated and answered in the course of this study :

1. Has the growth of population in Patna (particularly intra city pattern) been influenced in any way by its physical environment ?

2. Does the present population pattern bear a close relationship with the functional pattern of land use in the city ?

3. Can any pattern be distinguished in the development of the city in the past ?

4. What are the possibilities of planned development of population and land use in Patna ?

Methodology

Sources of Data : The data for the study have been mainly compiled from various documentary (published or unpublished) sources. For the study of population, data were collected from the Patna District Census Handbooks of 1951, 1961 and 1971 and for 1981, it was collected from the census office in unpublished form. These have been largely helpful in Chapters III and VI in analyzing population growth, population changes, distribution, density, age and occupational structure.

The unpublished data were collected from different sources namely, the Census Office and various government departments, viz. Patna Regional Development Authority, Patna Municipal Corporation, Patna Water Board, General Post Office and Patna Electric Supply Undertaking. Data from above sources have been generally utilized for the second part of the study - the Urban Development

Data Analysis : Before suggesting a scheme for better population distribution and organized urban development to a desired extent it is necessary to know the population structure and the distribution and extent of civic services, land use and functions within the city. Regarding this, data for four decadal years i.e. 1951, 1961, 1971 and 1981 were collected and suitably computed.

Patna has been expanding since its birth. This posed a lot of problems to the author as the data regarding population of 1951 were not comparable with those of 1981. In 1951, Patna had 32 wards and now it has 37 wards. The city has engulfed several villages since 1951 owing to frequent changes in the urban limits under Government order. Hence the difference in area. The entire study has, therefore, been done on the basis of 1981 Census and 1981 ward level and zone level data available through different sources have been utilized. The inter decadal comparisons have been made wherever it was practicable by adjusting the earlier data to conform to the present boundary.

Calculations concerning density of population, intercensal growth of population of the city as whole, growth of population (ward level) , age-sex structure, literacy, occupational structure, accommodation and density of households have been attempted in the present work. Since the categorization of occupational structure has changed in 1981 census, data for occupational structure have been based on 1971 and isopleth maps prepared and discussions made accordingly.

As regards the data for age - sex structure, sample data was collected from the P.R.D.A. Office which had conducted a field survey in 1983. On the basis of this data a map has been prepared.

Choropleth maps have been prepared to show ward level density of various indices. Population for the city as well as the zones for 2001 has been projected through geometric progression.

Functional zones of Patna have been demarcated on the basis of Land Use Map of Patna.

The map regarding urban development of Patna was prepared on the basis of the four density maps of Patna (1951 to 1981) and the map showing successive growth of Patna during the last century.

The Metropolitan Region of Patna has been demarcated on the basis of the distance travelled in one hour irrespective of the distance. Time factor and accessibility have been taken as important indicators of demarcation. The map for Patna Metropolitan Region has been prepared accordingly

For the preparation of maps, the help of following maps has also been taken.

1. Topographical Sheet No. 72 G/2 one inch map.
2. Topographical Sheet No. 72 G/N.W. half inch map.

3. Topographical Sheet No. 72 G, quarter inch map.
4. Patna Municipal Corporation Map (1951) 4" = 1 mile.
5. Patna Municipal Corporation Map (1961) 2" = 1 mile.
6. Patna Municipal Corporation Map (1971) 2" = 1 mile.
7. Patna Municipal Corporation Map (1981) 2" = 1 mile.
8. Patna Regional Development Authority Map 2" = 1 mile.
9. Maps in the Master Plan for Patna, 1962.

The technique used for cartographic representation comprise isopleth and choropleth maps, bar and line graphs, and symbolic representation. All maps are based on data processed by appropriate statistical techniques.

Planning Standards : Apart from the general nature of population distribution and nature of urban expansion of the city, this study is also designed to propose for further distribution of population and expansion of the city in a proper and congenial way. For this, various planning standards have been adopted[97]. However, these standards differ from place to place and country to country. for example, the Delhi Development Authority and Calcutta Metropolitan Planning Organization have standards which are quite different from each other.

In the present study, the Planning Standard[98] as approved by the Government of Bihar for cities having more than 1,00,000 population, has been considered. The discussions of these have been made in Chapter VI.

***References* :**

1. Smailes, A. E. (1967) : A Geography of Towns, London, p. 91.
2. Anderson, N. (1959) : The Urban Community : A World Perspective, Henry Holt and Co., New York.
3. Northam, R. M. (1975) : Urban Geography, John Wiley and Sons, Inc., U.S.A. pp. 6-7.
4. Ibid : p. 8.
5. Mayer, H. M. and Kohn, C. F. (1967) : Reading in Urban Geography, Central Book Depot, Allahabad, pp. 7-9.
6. Census of India (1981) : Bihar Series 4, Paper I of 1982, p. 6 and 7.
7. Harris, C. D. (1943) : "Suburbs", American Journal of Sociology, No. 49, pp. 1-13.

8. Duncan, O. D. & Reiss, A. J. Jr. (1956) : Social Characteristics of Urban and Rural Communities, John Wiley, p. 372.

9. Andrews, R. B. (1942) : "Elements in the Urban Fringe Pattern", Journal of Land and Public Utility Economics, Vol. 18, pp. 169- 83.

10. Singh, R. L. (1955) : Banaras : A Study in Urban Geography, Nandkishore and Bros., Banaras, p. 61.

11. Taylor, G. (1951) : Urban Geography, New York, p. 216.

12. Singh, R. L. : op. cit.

13. Ellefsen, R. A. (1962) : "City - Hinterland Relationships in India" in Roy Turner (Ed.), India's Urban Future, Oxford University Press, Bombay, p. 96.

14. Bartholomew, H. (1955) : Land Uses in American Cities, Harvard University Press, Cambridge, p. 14.

15. Mayer, H. M. (1967) : "A Survey of Urban Geography", in P. M. Hauser and L. F. Schnore (eds.) : The Study of Urbanization, John Wiley and Sons, Inc., New York, London, Sydney, p. 83.

16. Northam, R. M. : op. cit., p. 396.

17. Burges, E. W. (1925) : "The Growth of the City", in the City, (eds.), Robert, E. Park, E. W. Burgess & R.D. Mackenize, University of Chicago Press, Chicago : pp. 47-62.

18. Hoyt, H. (1939) : "City Growth and Mortage Risk", Insured Mortage Portfolio, Vol. I, Nos. 6 - 10 (Dec. 1936 - April, 1937), passim; & idem (U. S. Federal Housing Administration), The Structure and Growth of Residential Neighbourhoods in American Cities (Washington : Government. Printing Office, 1939), passim.

19. Harris, C. D. (1943) : "Suburbs", American Journal of Sociology, Vol. XLIX, p. 6.

20. Hawley, A. M. (1956) : The Changing Shape of Metropolitan America, Gencoe, Illinois, The Free Press, p. 177.

21. Schnore, L. F. and Peterson, G. B. (1958) : "Urban and Metropolitan Development in U. S. and Canada", Annals of the American Academy of Political and Social Science, 316, p. 60-68.

22. Pickard, J. P. (1959) : "Metropolitanization of U. S.", Urban Land

Institute, Research Monograph 2, p. 95.

23. Pickard, J. P. (1959) : "Urban Regions of the U. S.", Urban Land, Vol. 21, No. 4, pp. 3-10.

24. Dickinson, R. E. (1964) : City and Region : A Geographical Interpretation London, Routledge & Kegan Paul, p. 533.

25. Boyce, R. R. (1966) : "The Edge of the Metropolis : The Wave Theory Analog Approach", British Columbia Geographical Series, No. 7, pp. 31-40.

26. Beyer, G. M. (ed.) (1967) : The Urban Explosion in Latin America, Ithaca Cornell University Press, p. 360.

27. Arriaga, E. E. (1968) : Component of the City Growth in Selected Latin American Countries, Milkbak Memorial Fund Quarterly 46, Part 1, pp. 237-52.

28. Morill, R. (1968) : "Expansion of Urban Fringe : A Stimulation Experiment", Papers of Regional Science Association, No. 15, pp. 185-202.

29. Turner, J. F. C. (1968) : "Housing Priorities, Settlement Pattern and Urban Development in Modernizing Countries", Journal of the American Institute of Planners, No. 34, pp. 354-63.

30. Brush, J. E. (1968) : "Spatial Pattern of Population in Indian Cities", Geographical Review, Vol. 58, pp. 362.

31. Mayer, H. M. (1969) : "Making a Living in Cities : The Urban Economic Base", Journal of Geography, Vol. LXVIII, 2, pp. 70-87.

32. Buchanan, C. & Patterns (1969) : Regional Studies in Ireland. An Foras Forbatha, Dublin.

33. Wingo, L. Jr. (1969) : Latin American Urbanization - Plan or Process in Frieden B. J. & Nash, W. (Eds.), Shaping an Urban Future, Cambridge, Mass MTT Press, pp. 115-46.

34. Whebell, C. F. J. (1969) : "Corridords : A Theory of Urban Systems", Annals of the Association of American Geographers, No. 59, pp. 1-26.

35. Rodwin, L. (1970) : Nations and Cities : A Comparison and Strategies for Urban Growth, Boston Houghton Mifflin, p. 395.

36. Gillie, F. (1971) : The Cork Sub - Regional Planning Study, A Foras Forbartha, p. 82.

37. Sinclair, R.Shiptton, R. Willis, H. (1971) : A Case Study of Urban Expansion in South Western Macomb Country, Michigan, Michigan Academician, Vol. 4, No. 2.

38. Garner, R. E. (1972) : The Politics of Urban Development in Singapore, Ithaca : Cornell University Press, p. 263.

39. Goryacheva, A. M. (1977) : "Factor Analysis of the Differentiation of Economic Functions", Soviet Geography, Vol. XVIII, No. 6., pp. 384-395.

40. Sinclair, R. (1978) : "Spatial Change & the Urban Landscape" Geographia Polonica, Vol. 80, pp. 33-46.

41. Todaro, M. P. (1980) : "Urbanization in Developing Nations : Trends, Prospects and Policies", Journal of Geography, Vol. 79, No. 5, Sept./ October.

42. Srinivaschari, C. S. (1927) : "Growth of City of Madras", Journal of Madras Geographical Association, Vol. 2., No. 3.

43. Swaminathan, N. (1928) : "Sewage and City Geography"Jaurnal Madras of Geographical Associations, Vol. 2, No. 4.

44. Dann, R. (1931-32) : "A Note on the Urban Geography of Malabar" Journal of Madras Geographical Association, Vol. 2, No. 3.

45. Subramanayam, N. (1938) : "Some Aspects of the Growth of Greater Madras", Journal of Madras Geographical Association, Vol. 13, No. 1.

46. Srinivasachari, G. S. (1930) : "Growth of Madras City", Journal of Madras Geographical Association, Vol. 14, No. 2.

47. Kuriyan. G. (1941) : "Distribution of Population in the City of Madras", Indian Geographical Journal, Vol. 16, No.1.

48. Deshpande, C. D. (1941) : "Cities and Towns of Bombay Province : Aspects of Urban Geography", Journal of Madras Geographical Association, Vol. 16, No. 3.

49. Chatterjee, S. P. (1949) : 24 Parganas and Calcutta (Bengali Edition) Calcutta City Book Co.

50. Karan, P. P. (1952) : "Patna and Jameshedpur", Geographical Review of India, Vol. 14, No. 2.

51. Guha, M. (1963) : "Morphology of Calcutta", Geographical Review of India, Vol, 15, No. 3.

52. Mukerji, A. B. (1953) : "Modinagar : A Study in Urban Geography", Geographical Review of India, Vol. 20.

53. Chatterjee, A. B. (1958) : "Demorgraphic Features of Howrah City", Geographical Review of India, Vol. 20.

54. Singh, S. P. (1959) : "Demorgraphic Features of Lucknow", National Geographical Journal of India, Vol. 5, No. 3.

55. Singh, R. L. (1961) : "Evolution of Bangalore City", National Geographical Journal of India, Vol. 5, No. 4.

56. Singh. U. (1962) : " Role of Geographers in Town Plan with special ref. to KAVAL towns Proc. S. S. G.

57. Sinha B. N. (1962) : "The Bearing of Population Growth on the Economy of Orissa" The Deccan Geographer Vol. 1, No. 2.

58. Ganguli B. N. (1963) : Some Characteristics of Population of Cities Town group and towns with population of 50,000 and (over A.U.J.R,.) Vol. 11, No. 2.

59. Lahiri T. B. (1963) : Calcutta Metropolitan District Proceedings of the Indian Science Congress.

60. Bagchi K. and Sen U. (1963) : "Giridih" In Growth & Land Use Geographical Review of India Vol. 25, No. 4.

61. Dhabriya S. S. (1964) : "Evolution of Cultural Landscape in Udaipur City" National Geographical Journal of India Vol. 10, No. 2.

62. Ramesh A. (1964) : "Evolution of Ootacamund" National Geographical Journal of India Vol. 10, No. 1.

63. Bhattacharya A. N. and Lodha R. (1964) : Evolution of Chittorgarh" University of Udaipur Research Studies, Vol. 2.

64. Jha B. N. (1964) : "Recent Trends of Urbanization in Bihar" Journal of Ranchi University, Vol. 2 & 4.

65. Dwivdi, R. L. (1965) : "Demorgraphic Features of Allahabad City",

Geographical Review of India, Vol. 27, No. 4.

66. Alam, S. M. (1965) : Hyderabad - Secunderbad Cities - A Study in Urban Geography, Bombay.

67. Singh, U. (1966) : "Changes in the built up area of Kaval Towns in the Ganga Plain", National Geographer of India, Vol. 12, No. 4.

68. Srivastava, V. K. (1967) : "Sidhi District headquarters in Transition" Geographical Thought, Vol. 13, No. 1.

69. Singh, U. (1968) : "Cities of the Ganga Plain - Their Problems and Planning", in Singh, L. (ed.) Urban Geography in Developing Countries, Proceedings of I.G.U. Symposium, No. 15, Varanasi, pp. 343-50.

70. Jauhari, A. (1968) : "Urban Development in Sutlej - Yamuna Divide", in Singh, R. L.(ed.) Urban Geography in Developing Countries, Proceedings of I.G.U. Symposium No. 15, Varanasi, pp. 65-71.

71. Reddy, N. B. K. (1968) : "Occupational Structure of the Urban Centre in Krishna and Godavari Delta", in Singh, R. L. (ed.) Urban Geography in Developing Countries, Proceedings of the I.G.U. Symposium, No. 15, Varanasi, pp. 119-136.

72. Thapan, D. (1968) : Evolution of Steel Towns, in Singh, R. L. (ed.) Urban Geography in Developing Countries, Proceedings of I.G.U. Symposium No. 15, Varanasi, pp. 158-66.

73. Mathur, S. P. (1968) : "The Growth of Functional Structure of Dehradun : A Case Study of an Indian Resort Town", in Singh, R. L., (ed.) Urban Geography in Developing Countries, Proceedings of I.G.U. Symposium, No. 15, Varanasi, pp. 234-243.

74. Dikshit, K. R. (1970) : "Evolution of Cities in Maharashtra : An Analysis of the Phases of Urbanization", Indian Geographical Journal, Vol. XLV, pp. 53-64.

75. Bhattacharya, S. and Basak, T. (1970) : "The Morphology of Chittaranjan Township", Geographical Review of India, Vol. XXXII, pp. 262-68.

76. Singh, R. P. and Dabrail, M. P. (1970) : "A Comparative Analysis of Growth and Functional Characteristics of the Towns of Ganga - Yamuna Doab", The Indian Geographical Journal, Vol. XLV. Nos. 1 & 2, pp. 40-45.

77. Devgun, S. K. and Agrawal, S. K. (1971) : Levels of Urbanization in India", The Geographical View Point, Oct., pp. 15-22.

78. Bonifatieva, Lidia, I. (1971) : "Problems of Urban Planning in India", in Economic and Socio - Cultural Dimensions of Regionalization, Office of Registrar General of India, pp. 343-63.

79. Singh, D. K. (1972) : "Kerakat : A Rurban Service Centre ; Lower Gomati Valley", National Geographical Journal of India, Vol. XVIII, pp. 28-41.

80. Saxena, P. B. (1972) : "The Changing Pattern of Demographic Structure of Dehradun City", The Deccan Geographer, Vol. X., No. 2, pp. 51-71.

81. Shastri, P. (1973) : "Growth and Distribution of Population in Nagpur City", National Geographer, Vol. VIII, pp. 63-70.

82. Bhat, D. R. and Sharma, A. N. (1974) : "The Pattern of Urban Development in Karnal District", Geographical View Point, Vol. V, Nos. 1 and 2.

83. Bhardwaj, R. K. (1974) : Urban Development in India, National Publishing House, Delhi.

84. Singh, R. D. (1975) : " Demorgraphic and Spatial Relationship among the Cities in Bihar", Indian Geographical Studies, No. 5, pp. 56-63.

85. Raza, M., Kundu, A. and Nangia, S. (1975) : "Urban Rural Continum in India", Indian and Foreign Review, Vol. XII, Nos. 15, 16, pp. 13-14 and 19.

86. Ghosh, B. (1976) : "Trend and Pattern of Population Growth of Calcutta City", Geographical Review of India, Vol. XXXVIII, No. 1. pp. 85-90.

87. Tripathy, S. N. and Sinha, B. N. (1976) : An Investigation into Urban Growth : Through Applications of Employment and Location Quotients : Bhubaneshwar - A Case Study", Research Bulletin Eastern Geographical Society, No. 2.

88. Dhabriya, S. S. (1976 - 77) : "Centrifugal and Centripetal Forces and City Expansion", Indian Journal of Geography, Vol. XI - XII, No. 1, pp. 68-78.

89. Pathak, C. R. (1980) : "Urban Problem and Policies in India", Indian Journal of Regional Science, Vol. 12, No. 1, pp. 71-90.

90, Singhal, G. D. (1980) : "Spatial Growth of Gaya and its impact on Fringe Settlements", Indian Geographical Studies, Patna, Research Bulletin, No. 14, pp. 24-28.

91. Hussain, M. I. (1980) : "Urban Expansion or Encroachment", Geographical Review of India, Vol. 42, No. 2, pp. 131-139.

92. Sinha, M. M. P. (1980) : The Impact of Urbanization on Land Use in the Rural - Urban Fringe : A Case Study of Patna, Concept Publishing, New Delhi.

93. Vishwanath, V. (1981) : "Growth and Development of Towns in Tamil Nadu, 1901 - 1981", The Indian Geographical Journal, Vol. 56, Nos. 1 & 2, pp. 43-53.

94. Master Plan for Delhi, Work Studies, Vol. I Delhi Development Authority, Delhi, 1962.

95. Master Plan for Patna, Vol. I, Text and Photographs, Patna Improvement Trust, Patna, 1962.

96. Basic Development Plan for the Calcutta Metropolitan District 1966 - 86, CMPO, Government of West Bengal, 1966.

97. Gowda, K. S. R. (1972) : Urban and Regional Planning, Principles and Case Studies, Prasaranga, University of Mysore, pp. 75-91.

98. Planning Standards and Building Bye - Laws for Cities with population more than 1,00,000 of Bihar 1976, prepared by Bihar Government Building Bye - Laws Committee, Patna, 1976.

2

Geographical Setting and Historical Evolution

The site of a town invariably influences its development throughout its history. It is in the initial stages that advantages of site are most stimulating to urban growth and disadvantages most inhibiting. As time passes, a momentum is acquired that makes continued growth less dependent upon site conditions although the form it takes is always affected by them. No matter how favourable the site may have been for the initial establishment of the earliest nucleus, there must come a time when further extension meets site features that are handicaps. Physical handicaps, long felt or newly apparent are overcome only at a cost, which represents the operation of a law of diminishing returns. The past weighs heavily upon the present[1].

Location

Patna, the capital city of the Bihar is geographically located between 25° 35' and 25° 38' north latitudes and between 85° 5' and 85° 16' east longitudes and has a mean elevation of 173 feet above the sea level. The city is bounded by the mighty river Ganga on the north, the flood plain of river Sone on the west, the flood plain of river Punpun on the south and the confluence of the rivers Punpun and the Ganga near Fatwa on the east. It is one of the most important historic cities of India and is situated along the natural levee of the river Ganga in the Middle Ganga Plain.

Patna with an area of 24097.9 acres or 79.42 sq. kms. gives shelter to a population of 7,76,371 persons (1981 census) in its 37 municiple wards. The average density of population is 32.23 persons per acre. The city is long and linear, shaped like a sword with the handle in the west and the point to the east. It runs for about 12 miles in length and one to 3 miles in width.

Since Patna is the capital of Bihar, it enjoys its own regional significance. It is administrative headquarters of the District, the Division and the State. It houses local administration, Judiciary and Legislature and is marked by educational, health, commercial and several other professional services.

Patna has a close relationship with the surrounding countryside in respect of social, economic, cultural and political contacts. It acts as an important centre for trade and commerce not only for its countryside but for the State as well.

The city is well connected with the other parts of the region by a network of railways and roads as well as by air (Fig.1). The main broad gauge railway line of the Eastern Railway which connects Howrah with Delhi runs parallel to the Ganga along southern and central parts of the city. The Patna - Gaya line connects Patna with the Grand Chord line of the Eastern Railway and through the South Eastern Railway to the industrially rich region of the Chota Nagpur Plateau. There is another parallel metre gauge railway line of the North Eastern Railway to the north of Patna across the Ganga. It connects Lucknow and Gauhati and is linked with Patna through a road bridge over the Ganga.

Patna has four railway stations on the main line namely (1) Patna Junction, (2) Gulzarbagh, (3) Patna Sahib, and (4) Rajendra Nagar. There are 2 branch lines in the city. One is in the Western zone connecting Patna Junction railway station with Digha Ghat and the other in the Eastern Zone connecting Patna Sahib railway station with Patna Ghat.

There is a proposal to construct a railway line parallel to the new bye-pass road about 400 yards to the south of it. It will branch out from Patna-Gaya railway line in the west and run towards east, turning north near Mahatma Gandhi Setu to cross the Ganga and connect Hajipur with Patna.

There are other private ferry services for passengers from Bans Ghat and Mahendru Ghat to Pahleza Ghat and Raghopur. Thousands of country boats sail on the river from the numerous ghats along the river bank of the city.

The National Highway No. 30 passes through Patna and connects it with all important cities in Bihar as well as with other parts of the country. It meets N.H. 2 in the West and N.H. 33 at Bakhtiarpur in the east.

A newly constructed road bridge known as Mahatma Gandhi Setu has been built across the Ganga near Gulzarbagh in Patna. This has

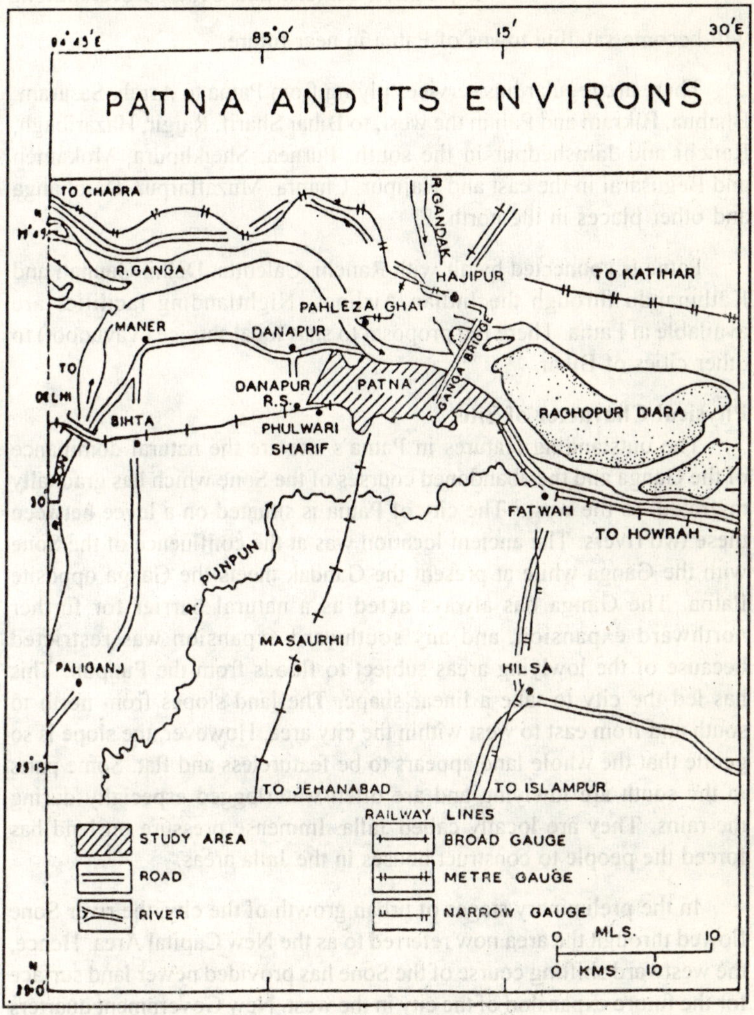

Fig. 1

eliminated ferry services at Mahendru Ghat and L.C.T. Ghat and has led to an enormous increase in traffic movement within the city and an increased rate of immigration is also visible. Commercial activities between the parts of North Bihar and Patna have increased tremendously well beyond expectation.Moreover, since the expansion of Patna is impeded because of physical constraints, the city is likely to grow northward across the Ganga and it is probable that Hajipur and Sonepur will become satellite towns of Patna in near future.

There are regular bus services plying from Patna to Arrah, Sasaram, Bhabua, Bikram and Pali in the west, to Bihar Sharif, Rajgir, Hazaribagh, Ranchi and Jamshedpur in the south, Purnea, Sheikhpura, Mokameh and Begusarai in the east and Hajipur, Chapra, Muzaffarpur, Darbhanga and other places in the north.

Patna is connected by air with Ranchi, Calcutta, Delhi, Gauhati and Kathmandu through the Indian Airlines. Nightlanding facilities are available at Patna. There is a proposal to start local service (Vayudoot) to other cities of Bihar.

Physical Character of Site

The outstanding features in Patna's site are the natural dominance of the Ganga and the abandoned courses of the Sone which has gradually migrated to the west.[2] The city of Patna is situated on a levee between these two rivers. The ancient location was at the confluence of the Sone with the Ganga while at present the Gandak meets the Ganga opposite Patna. The Ganga has always acted as a natural barrier for further northward expansion, and any southward expansion was restricted because of the lowlying areas subject to floods from the Punpun. This has led the city to take a linear shape. The land slopes from north to south and from east to west within the city area. However, the slope is so gentle that the whole land appears to be featureless and flat. Some parts in the south are lowlying and are often waterlogged especially during the rains. They are locally called Jalla. Immense pressure on land has forced the people to construct houses in the Jalla areas.

In the preliminary stages of urban growth of the city, the river Sone flowed through the area now referred to as the New Capital Area, Hence, the westward shifting course of the Sone has provided newer land surface for the future expansion of the city in the west. New Government quarters and several residential housing colonies are coming up in this area.

The stability of the site of Patna through centuries suggests the presence of some kankar reef in the alluvium of the southern bank of the river Ganga. The convexity of the bank east of Bakarganj nala to the easternmost limit of the city combined with the pushtas (brick walls) is sufficient safeguard for this part of Patna against erosion.[3] Moreover, the river bank is also lined with bricks to avoid erosion.

The stable southern bank has provided a permanent site for

development and expansion of Patna. The whole area south of river Ganga bears imprint of shifting courses of rivers - the Sone and the Punpun. Because of the high southern bank of the river Ganga in the north, the Punpun flows parallel to the main river for a few miles before joining it from the south. When both the Ganga and the Punpun are flooded, the high Ganga water restricts the Punpun water to flow into it and as such the flow of natural drainage is reversed. Consequently, the area in the south - east gets inundated for a few months during the monsoon.

To the west of Patna - Gaya railway line, conditions are slightly different. The river Sone flows in a north - easterly direction and joins the Ganga near Bhawani Tola, about 35 kilometeres west of Patna. The land slopes towards the north and is completely flat. The Serpentine channel in Western Patna is said to have formed the old bed of the river Sone.[4] The rive Ganga received a side channel from the Sone in the west which passed through Maner and Sherpur and met the Ganga at Nasriganj near Danapur. Now the Sone meets the Ganga just beyond Bihta towards west.

The river Ganga is very wide near Patna. It is characterised by meandering courses, sand banks and sand bars, diara lands and abandoned channels. The highest flood level of the Ganga is higher than the general level of the city hence a protective wall has been built to protect the city from floods from the north. Floods in the south are similarly checked by the Punpun embankment and also by the newly constructed new bye - pass road further south of the old bye - pass road. The old courses of the Sone also control drainage of Patna to a certain extent. Moreover, the construction of Patna Canal Embankment in the west restricts the flood waters of the Sone from entering into Patna.

In early times river banks acted as a promoting factor for the ideal location of towns. In the case of Patna, this was true in its early stages of growth. Now it is an inhibiting factor because of the restrictions it imposes on the future expansion of the city.

Physical Constraints to Development : The following are the physical constraints to the development of the City.

1. The development of the City is linear because of the levee of the Ganga. The road arteries run parallel to the levee creating traffic problem.

2. The natural slope of the city is towards the south but urban drainage is oriented towards the north. This results in reverse flow of the drains

when the River Ganga is in spate.

3. Western, Central and Southern parts of the city are lowlying which has resulted in late development of the City in these directions.

4. Climate has an adverse effect on the development in two ways.

(a) Rainfall is heavy and more than 60 per cent of the rain falls in three monsoon months. As the level of the Ganga is generally higher than that of the drains in these months, almost all parts of the city are waterlogged.

(b) The winds are on the whole westerly. Thus the airport runway runs east - west in conformity with the wind direction. However, this has led to a limitation on the construction of high rise buildings in the approach path of planes which is over the linear city.

Evolution of the City

Ancient Period : Patna (the then Pataliputra) is one of the most ancient cities of the world, and its known history dates back to 600 B.C. Several stories exist regarding the origin of the name of Patna. The most popular is Patali or 'trumpet flower' which ascribes it to Prince Putraka who created it with a stroke of his magic staff and named it in honour of his wife, the Princess Patali. This story is found in Katha Sarit Sagar and in Hiuen Tsiang's Travels.[5] Ajatsatru constructed a fort here around which the city grew and later became the capital of Magadh.[6] Magadh which embraced the present districts of Patna, Nalanda, Nawada, Aurangabad and Gaya, was earlier a powerful kingdom. Bimbisara, a notable king of the Magadhan dynasty built a city named 'Rajgriha' at the foot - hills north of Giriraja. Since it was situated inland, it became difficult for the king to protect the northern borders of the Kingdom. So, Ajatsatru, son of Bimbisara, fortified the village of Pataligram situated at the confluence of the Ganga and the Sone, with a view to check the growing might of the northern tribes especially the Lichchhivis of Vaishali. Later, king Udayan, grandson of Ajatsatru, built a town within the fortress and shifted his capital there from Rajgriha. The town so founded is believed to have been built according to a plan and remained the chief city of India for about a thousand years. This town has been known by various names - Kusumpur, Pushpapur meaning the 'City of flowers' and later as Pataliputra. The present city of Patna has grown contiguous to this old town of Pataliputra, drifting continuously westwards and southwards owing to the pressure on land.[7] Patliputra remained the seat of Government during the regimes of the Mauryas and the Guptas. It was then not only the capital of Magadh, but in fact, of the whole of northern India, as its writ ran far and wide. It received the Greek Ambassador. Megasthenes at the Court of Chandragupta Maurya. Megasthenes called the city by the name 'Palibhotra'. Chandragupta Maurya became the king of Magadh after defeating the Nandas and expelling Greek garrisons left by Alexander. Then, Pataliputra had a population of 4,00,000. It was 9.2 miles long and 1.7 miles broad and was surrounded by a moat 600 ft. broad and 30 cubits deep. It had 570 towers and 64 gates.[8] Sugangey Palace was situated in the central part of the city and is believed to have been more spectacular and beautiful than the Persian palaces of Susa and Ekbatana.

In 272 B.C. Ashoka the grandson of Chandragupta acceded to the throne and in 279 B.C. he become the emperor. Ashoka the Great completely changed the appearance of the city. Earlier during the period 500 B.C. to 320 B.C. the architecture of Pataliputra was mainly wooden. However, during the Muryan period (322 B.C. to 185 B.C.) a change took place, when monuments made of stone appeared in the city. This is evident from the accounts of Fa - Hiean, a Chinese traveller who visited the city in 500 A.D. The monolithic Ashokan columns prove the craftsmanship of the people in those days. The columns were made of beautiful Chunar stones. The contemporary sculpture was appreciated by many and attained a high mark of perfection. Of these, the Didarganj Yakshi, a life size female figure standing with a Chauri (fly whisky) in her right hand is a rare piece lying in Patna Museum.

Colonel Waddell in 1896. when excavations were being carried out in Bulandibagh and Kumhrar in south Patna, discovered a quasionic capital and broken fragments of colossal stone pillars. After several inspections he has tried to show the location of the ancient village of Pataligram, the Mauryan Palace and several other important monuments[9].

The cultural conquest of contemporary world by Ashoka through the tenets of Buddhism is of universal significance. The death of Ashoka followed by the fall of Maurya Empire led to the decay of Pataliputra and for a while its history went into oblivion.

However, because of its rich fertile land and being at the threshold of major transport routs, Pataliputra once again gained prominence as a capital during the reign of Samudragupta (335 A.D. to 375 A.D.). During the Gupta period, the city's urban morphology underwent a secular change. According to Toynbee, "an imperial capital many retain its prestige long after it has ceased to perform that function.[10] The fostering of arts and science under Samudragupta, along with his conquests is no less remarkable. The glory of Pataliputra was reduced to ashes by the Huns in 500 A.D. They completely destroyed and ransacked the city. This was reported by Chinese piligrim Hiuen Tsang who visited the imperial city in 637 A.D. and found the city desolate and deserted.

Pataliputra remained unaccounted for after the fall of Hindu dynasties and immediately before the instrusion of Muslim invaders. Its administrative ability was lost and it was reduced to an insignificant town. However, in the 16th century it again came into prominence. Though it has seen rise and fall of several empires, it has shown a remarkable capacity for survival and regrowth, mainly because of its favourable location and setting.[11]

Medieval period : In 1541, the Afghan chief Sher Shah Suri established his capital at Pataliputra and once again the city became an important centre for trade and commerce. He built magnificent fortress on the bank of the Ganga in eastern Patna of which the "Paschim Darwaza" and the "Purab Darwaza" are the two significant remnants of the fortress even to this day. A large market settlement grew around Purab Darwaza which later developed into an important market centre and the area around Marufganj grew into prominence as a wholesale trading centre for various commodities such as opium, cloth, sugar, grains etc.[12]

It was also a principal river port. Soon Sher Shah was ousted by the Moghuls. In 1580 Portuguese settlements developed along the river but could not survive long because the Dutch established their control over some parts of Bankipore (central Patna) in 1610.

The city reached the zenith of its splendour during the reign of Azim - us -Shah, the grandson of Aurangzeb. In 1704 A.D. he named the city as 'Azimabad' after himself. Azimabad encouraged poetry, music and other fine arts. As Francis Buchanan says, at that time music in respect to quantity was on a very thriving footing.[13]

The city extended well beyond the fortified walls and suburban developments spread along the bank of the river as far as Bankipore. It also regained its status as a commercial centre.[14] Muradpur Market developed in Central Patna near Dutch establishments. The accounts of

Manucci, Taverniers and Bowney clearly depict the commercial character of Patna in the middle of 17th century. Its character as a centre of inter - provincial trade changed into international character and it was one of the largest towns in India, being not less than 4 miles in length[15] (Fig.2)

Modern Period : In 1757, when East India Company acquired the Company Bagh, a new chapter was created in the history of territorial growth of Patna under the British. During the entire British period, Patna served as a secondary capital. Patna became a provincial capital of the newly created province of Bihar and Orissa in 1911-12 and the new capital city was laid down to the west of Patna - Gaya Road (now known as Budha Marg). The establishment of Patna University in 1917 provided cultural importance to the city. This attracted a large number of people from outside. Several new buildings were constructed in the west, namely the Raj Bhawan, the Secretariat, the High Court, the Council Chamber, residences of Ministers, Judges and other public and private sector buildings. Growing population attracted many small and consumer oriented industries which developed mainly in the eastern and southern parts of Patna. These gave employment to several thousand labourers. The commercial belts started to expand westwards from Patna City (Eastern Patna), mainly concentrated along the Ashok Raj Path upto Gandhi Maidan.

Post Independence Period : Patna continued to be the capital of Bihar. During this period governmental activities have increased manifold. The implementation of Five Year Plans and government's welfare programmes have promoted building activities in the city especially in the western side. With the influx of people, commercial activities have also increased and several planned commercial complexes have come up in various parts of the city.

The Present : Today, Patna is a linear city - 12 miles long and one to 3 miles broad. It has mainly developed along the Ashok Raj Path, the main thoroughfare of the city. It runs east - west parallel to the river Ganga. Although northward expansion of the city is restricted because of the presence of the river Ganga, the city is growing fast in its southern part despite the area being low - lying and subject to water - logging (Fig.3.). The historic character of Patna is clearly discernible in its various forms of development. Patna displays a marked contrast in its functional and physical characteristics on the basis of which it can be divided into four separate zones - Eastern, Central, Western and Southern. All of these are contiguous to each other. (Fig. 4).

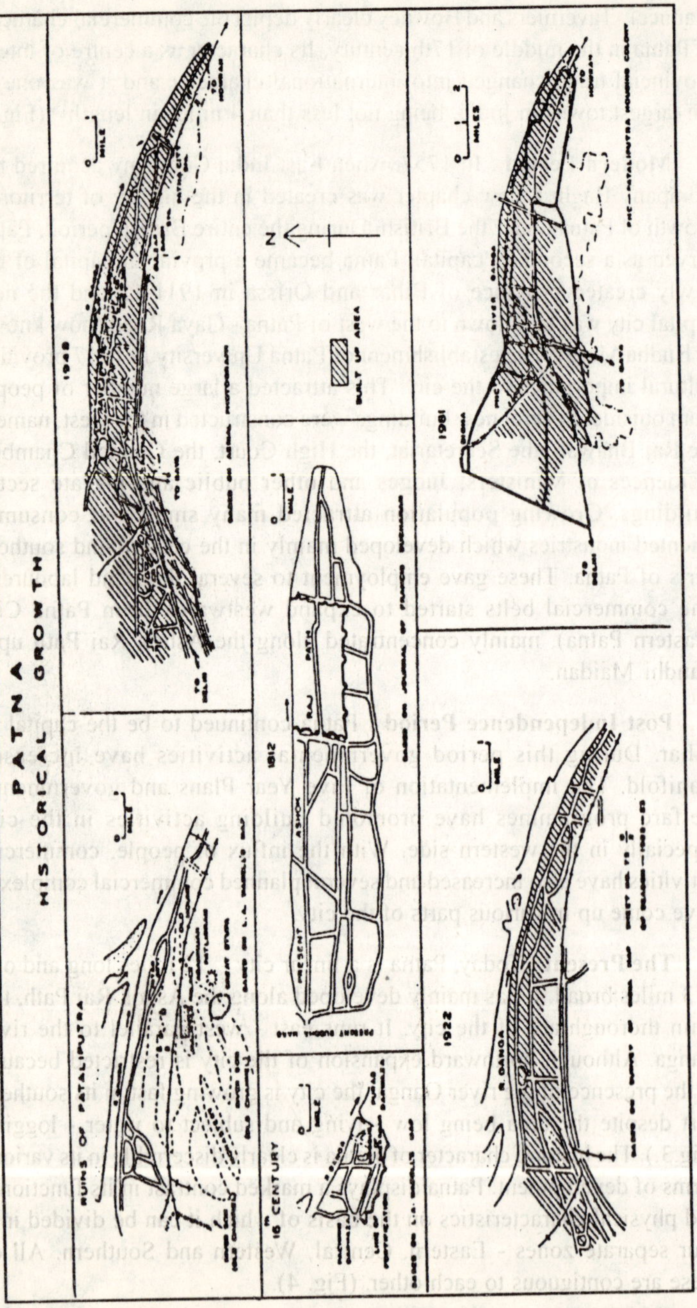
HISTORICAL PATNA GROWTH
16 CENTURY
1912
1922
1948
1981
BUILT UP AREA
N
MILE
MILES

Fig. 2

The Eastern zone which covers the Old City and the ancient capital is highly congested. It is full of derelict buildings lined along narrow lanes and bye - lanes where insanitary conditions prevail. It shows signs of decay. Biggest centres of wholesale trade - Maroofganj and Mansurganj lie in this zone. It also contains the Harmandir, the most sacred place for the Sikhs, which is the birth place of Guru Govind Singh. This zone has 13 wards within its limit viz. ward numbers 25 to 37.

The Central Zone lies to the west of the Eastern Zone covering the area roughly between Paschim Darwaza in the East and Budha Marg in the west lying to the north of main railway line. It is the commercial core of the city and contains several institutional, cultural and district administration buildings. It is the most crowded zone of the city. The zone presents a striking contrast within itself - a group of fine buildings around Gandhi Maidan on one hand and extremely congested and densely populated area of Mahendru, Lalbagh, Darzi Tola, Langartoli, Sabzibagh and Bakerganj on the other. These can be termed as slums as they are full of obsolete and insanitary dwellings. This zone comprises ward numbers 5, 9, 10, 12, 13, 15, 17, 19, 20, 22 and 23. It also includes parts of ward nos. 11, 18, 21 and 24.

The Western Zone lies to the west of the Central Zone which forms the new capital area. It has quite a different appearance. It has monumental buildings and well planned ring and radial road pattern with planned underground sewerage system. Important government buildings in this zone are the Raj Bhawan, the Secretariat, the High Court and the residences of State VIPs. Besides, a fair amount of private developments has taken place in this zone and several new colonies have sprung up. To name a few, they are Pataliputra, Kidwaipuri, Yarpur, Punaichak, Srikrishnapuri,Mithapur, Patel Nagar, Shrikrishna Nagar, Electricity Board Colony, Rajvanshi Nagar etc.. Although many of these Colonies have modern facilities, their development has taken place in a haphazard manner. Several colleges and schools have also come up and shopping complexes have been constructed. The Western Zone includes ward numbers 1, 2, 4, 6 and 7.

The Southern Zone lies to the south of railway line and stretches up to the southern Municipal limit of the city going beyond the new bye - pass road. It houses one of the biggest residentialy colonies in India, the Kankarbagh. Although the colony is developing very fast with modern residential houses, the development is rather haphazard and unplanned. It is actually an admixture of old and new developments juxtaposed on

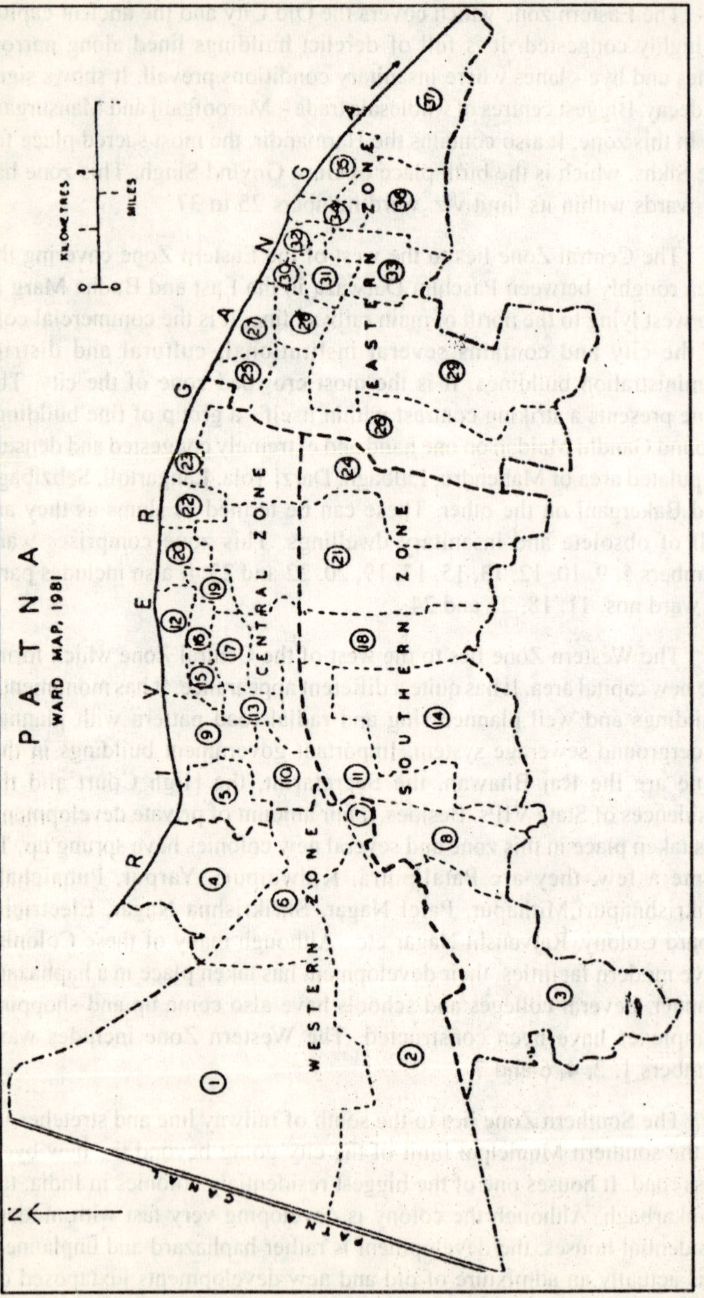
PATNA
WARD MAP, 1981
RIVER GANGA
KILOMETRES
MILES
WESTERN ZONE
CENTRAL ZONE
SOUTHERN ZONE
EASTERN ZONE
PATNA CANAL
N

Fig. 3

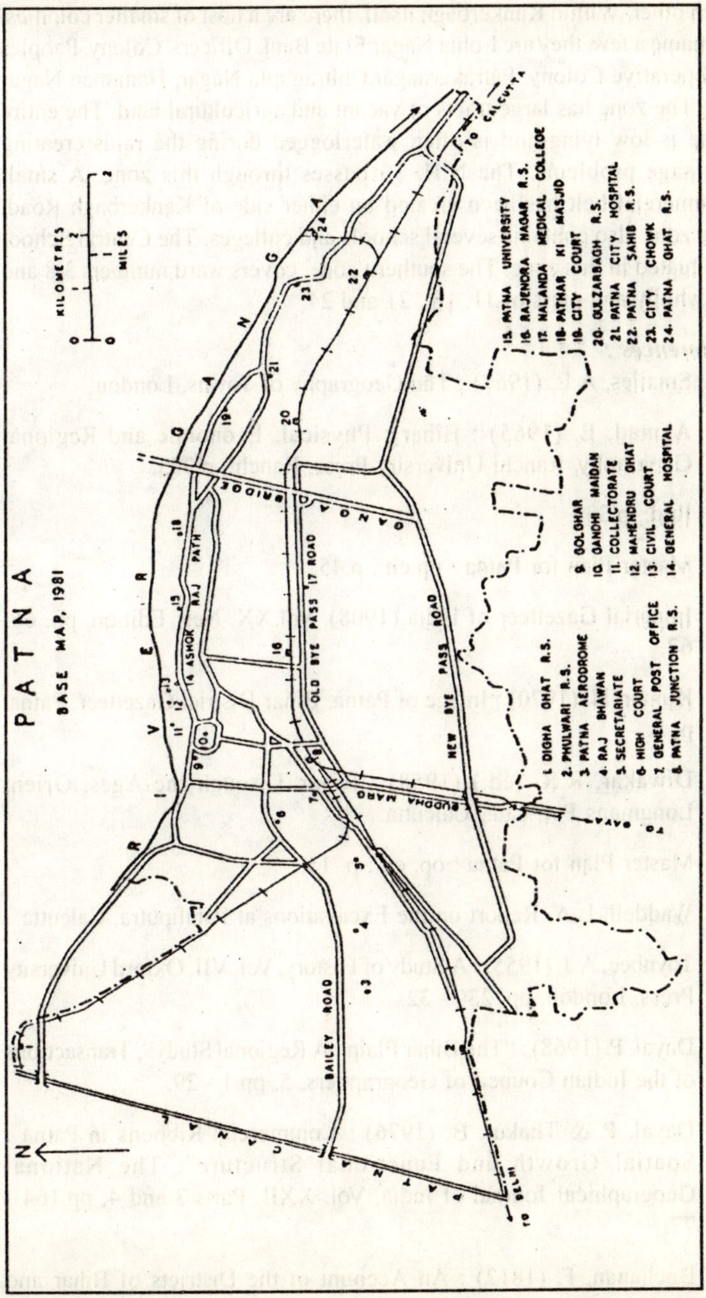
PATNA
BASE MAP, 1981
RIVER GANGA
KILOMETRES
MILES
N
ASHOK RAJ PATH
OLD BYE PASS ROAD
NEW BYE PASS ROAD
BAILEY ROAD
BUDDHA MARG
GANGA BRIDGE
TO CALCUTTA
TO DELHI
TO GAYA
1. DIGHA GHAT R.S.
2. PHULWARI R.S.
3. PATNA AERODROME
4. RAJ BHAWAN
5. SECRETARIATE
6. HIGH COURT
7. GENERAL POST OFFICE
8. PATNA JUNCTION R.S.
9. GOLGHAR
10. GANDHI MAIDAN
11. COLLECTORATE
12. MAHENDRU GHAT
13. CIVIL COURT
14. GENERAL HOSPITAL
15. PATNA UNIVERSITY
16. RAJENDRA NAGAR R.S.
17. NALANDA MEDICAL COLLEGE
18. PATHAR KI MASJID
19. CITY COURT
20. GULZARBAGH R.S.
21. PATNA CITY HOSPITAL
22. PATNA SAHIB R.S.
23. CITY CHOWK
24. PATNA GHAT R.S.

Fig. 4

each other. Within Kankerbagh itself, there are a host of smaller colonies. To name a few, they are Lohia Nagar,State Bank Officers Colony, Peoples Cooperative Colony, Patrakarnagar,Chitragupta Nagar, Hanuman Nagar etc. The zone has large tracts of vacant and agricultural land. The entire zone is low lying and is often waterlogged during the rains creating drainage problems. The N.H. 30 passes through this zone. A small commercial belt has been created on either side of Kankerbagh Road. The zone also contains several schools and colleges. The Central School is situated in this zone. The southern zone covers ward numbers 3,8 and 14 wholly and parts of 11, 18 , 21 and 24.

References :

1. Smailes, A.E. (1967) : The Geography of Towns, London.
2. Ahmad, E. (1965) : Bihar : Physical, Economic and Regional Geography, Ranchi University Press, Ranchi, p.335.
3. Ibid., p.335
4. Master Plan for Patna : op.cit., p.45.
5. Imperial Gazetteer of India (1908), Vol.XX, New Edition, pp. 66-67.
6. Kumar, N. (1970) : Image of Patna, Bihar District Gazetteer, Patna, p. ix.
7. Diwakar, R.R. (ed.) (1958) : Bihar Through the Ages, Orient Longmans Pvt. Ltd., Calcutta.
8. Master Plan for Patna : op. cit., p. 15.
9. Waddell, L.A. Report on the Excavations at Pataliputra, Calcutta.
10. Toynbee, A.J. (1955) : A Study of History, Vol. VII, Oxford University Press, London, pp. 230 - 32.
11. Dayal, P. (1968) : "The Bihar Plain : A Regional Study", Transactions of the Indian Council of Geographers, 5, pp.1 - 29.
12. Dayal, P. & Thakur, B. (1976) : Commercial Ribbons in Patna : Spatial Growth and Functional Structure", The National Geographical Journal of India, Vol. XXII, Parts 3 and 4, pp.164 - 77.
13. Buchanan, F. (1812) : An Account of the Districts of Bihar and

Patna in 1811 - 12, published by B.O.R.S., pp. 612-13.

14. Sinha, M.M.P. (1980) : The Impact of Urbanization on Land Use in the Rural Urban Fringe, Concept Publishing Company, New Delhi. p.35.

15. Dayal, P. & Thakur, B. : op.cit., p.168.

3

Population

Evolution of the City

Patna is an ancient city. It population in the earlier period is not known. However, during the reign of Chandragupta Maurya (322-185 B.C.), Megasthenes, a Greek envoy visited the city and mentioned in his chronicles that the city had a population of 4,00,000. This figure seems quite exaggerated. Pataliputra was completely destroyed by the Huns in 500 A.D. This was confirmed by the Chinese traveller Hiuen Tsinag. He visited the city in the seventh century, found it deserted and estimated its population to be 5,000 approximately. The city remained in the dark for quite some time. However, in the 16th century it again came in the limelight.

The population of Pataliputra in 1518 is estimated to have been around 30,000. With the capture of the city by the various Moghul chieftains one after the other as well as the city's gaining importance as a trading centre was further enhanced in the 17th century when the Dutch established their control in some parts of Bankipore (Western Patna). Patna gradually became one of the larger towns in India and its trade took international character.

In the middle of the 18th century the city came under the rule of the British. This was followed by territorial expansion of the city which led to the growth of its population as well. According to Buchanan[1], the population of the city was 3,12,000 approximately. The figure is rather misleading because the population was taken for an area of 20sq. miles around Patna, while the city actually covered an area of only one and a half sq. miles. In 1857, William Taylor estimated Patna's population to be 4,00,000. This figure also seems quiet exaggerated.

The distributional pattern of the population of Patna was not uniform throughout the city. There were two main pockets of population concentration: one in Eastern Patna around the Purab Darwaza and the other in Central Patna around Bankipore. Moreover. the stretch along the river bank was more densely populated as the land was higher and the river bank was used for trade.

Intercensal Growth

The study of population of a city in terms of space and time forms an important part of urban analysis, because a city attains its form and function from the people who live and work in that city. Information on the socio-economic composition of the population and the age- sex structure are important for assessing the amenities that are needed in different parts of the city. Chapin is of the view that population studies not only provide a means of scaling the total space needs for selected needs for the selected land use categories of the different periods of time in future, but also give an indication as to how the total space needs should be allocated to different parts of an urban area at any particular time.[2]

Table 1
Decennial Growth of Population (1872 - 1981)

Year	Total Population	Variation	Percentage
1872	158900	-	-
1881	170654	+11754	07.39
1891	165192	-5492	-3.2
1901	134785	-30407	-18.41
1911	136153	+1368	+1.01
1921	119976	-16177	-11.88
1931	159690	+39714	+33.10
1941	196415	+36725	+23.00
1951	250285	+53870	+27.43
1961	363700	+113415	+45.31
1971	473001	+109301	+30.05
1981	776371	+303370	+64.14
1991	1058000	+281619	+36.29
2001	1442000	+384000	+36.29

Source : Census of India.

The first Census took place in the year 1872 when the population of Patna was found to be 1,58,900. However. the method used for counting people was very unscientific and crude. Hence. the reliability of data was low. A complete and correct Census took place in 1881 when a more scientific method was adopted for counting. Since then, population is counted at regular intervals of ten years which is known as Censal year.

A glance of the Table I reveals[3] that the population of Patna declined from 1881 to 1921. It dropped from 170,654 to 119,976 persons i.e., a decrease of 50,678 persons which amounts to a negative growth of 29.70 per cent. This decrease may be ascribed to outbreaks of epidemics, droughts, floods etc. as well as the falling economic status of the city. In the beginning of the 19th century Patna was an important entrepot of trade between Upper India and Bengal. With the construction of the railways in the latter part of the 19th century, the river borne traffic was badly affected. The traffic from up-country which originally passed along the Ganga to Calcutta was now attracted by the railroads and hence the commercial aspect of the city, which was largely dependent on the river, began to decline. Moreover, abandonment of the opium trade added to the setback. The population between 1818 and the 1901 decreased by 21.02 per cent. During the time of the census in 1901 plague had spread all over the city taking innumerable lives. Moreover, the fear of its attack `forced the people to move to countryside and at the same time also prevented people from moving from the countryside into the city. The position was slightly better in 1911. The population increased by 1.01 per cent. But again between 1911-21, the population decreased by 11.88 per cent. The variation in population was largely affected by floods, droughts and frequent outbreak of epidemics. Thus the period between 1881 - 1921 may be termed as a period of negative growth.

The decadal year 1921 - 31 has its own significance. It marks the turning point in the census history of Patna. During this period, the population grew by 33.10 per cent as no untoward natural disaster took place. Between 1931 - 41, the rate of growth (23%) was lower as compared to the earlier decade. It improved slightly in the decennial year 1941 - 51 (27.43%). The period between 1921 and 1941 may be referred to as a period of slow or marginal growth.

The population figures after 1941 show an accelerated rate of growth which jumped from 27.43 per cent in 1941 - 51 to 45.31 per cent in 1951 - 61. With the partition of India and creation of Pakistan, many refugees from West Punjab and East Bengal migrated to Patna in search of employment.

In between 1961 - 71 the rate of growth was 30.05 per cent. It was slightly less than in the previous decade. But the growth rate was remarkable in between 1961 - 71. Thus the population grew rather rapidly after 1941 or in other words it can be said that the growth was phenomenal during this period.

This may be attributed to a number of factors. First, with the advancement in the medical field, death rate was checked to a greater extent. Secondly, manifold increase in commercial activities attracted people from neighbouring villages. Thirdly, owing to the spurt of small - scale and cottage industries, a large number of people moved into the city from the city's hinterland. Besides, there are several other factors which helped people to settle within the city, such as growing educational, medical and other civic amenities. New avenues in various fields of education and technology opened for employment which also attracted the population to settle in the city. However, after independence much emphasis was laid on the upliftment of rural economy, decentralization of administrative machinery, encouragement to small scale and cottage industries, reforms in agrarian and social orders etc. All these to some extent, have tended to restrict the emigration of rural population to the city. The maximum growth (64.14%) during 1971 - 81,however, has surpassed all plan estimates. Consequently, various problems such as housing shortage, lack of civic amenities etc. are being faced by the residents of Patna.

The problem of population forecast is comparatively simpler for areas which in the past have shown marked stability in population and where no great political, social - economic changes are anticipated for the future. On the other hand, however, in areas where there have been irregular or sporadic fluctuations in the rate of growth of population, the problem of projection becomes complex and less reliable.

It is estimated through geometric progression that in the year 1991, Patna's population[4] will be 10,58,000 and in 2001 it will be 14,42,000. This shows an increase of 36.27 per cent in 1981 - 91 and 36.29 per cent in 1991 - 2001 (Fig. 5). It is likely, therefore, that in future such an increase will result in more severe civic problems which will later become hazardous for the growth of Patna. This is a serious matter which requires immediate attention. The problems and their proper solutions have been discussed later in the chapter on urban development.

Distribution and Trends of Growth

As stated earlier, Patna has always been a centre of trade and

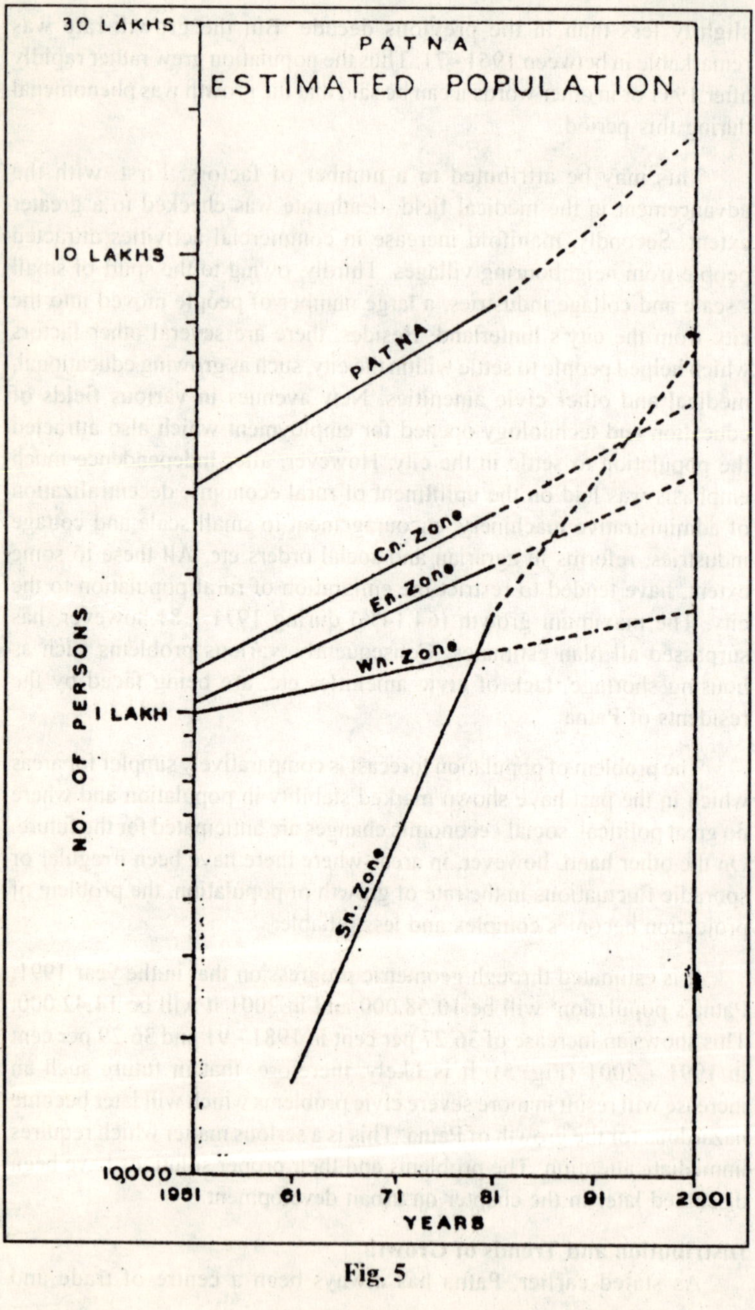
PATNA
ESTIMATED POPULATION
30 LAKHS
10 LAKHS
1 LAKH
10,000
NO. OF PERSONS
PATNA
Cn. Zone
En. Zone
Wn. Zone
Sn. Zone
1951
61
71
81
91
2001
YEARS

Fig. 5

commerce, but unfortunately has not yet been able to promote any important industry. It has nurtured great institutions of learning and has been the seat of administration from 1541 onwards. Thus, trade, commerce, administration and cultural activities have been the main functions of the city since long. The city's population has mainly grown in the past because of the expansion of these functions. Moreover, the population in the pre - independence days was concentrated in the areas pronounced in such activities. The general tendency of people then, was to settle near the place of work. As such population was denser around the Chowk in the walled city (Eastern Patna).

With the expansion and development of trade and commerce, especially in opium and cotton cloth, Patna started expanding in size both in terms of population and area. In 1741, it extended beyond the walls of Paschim Darwaza. The rich people had their garden houses in the suburbs and along the river bank as far as Bankipore, where the East India Company had a garden (Company Bagh, which is now occupied by Magadh Mahila College) along the Ganga. The shifting of the factory of this area and the growth of the bazar which served the need of the Brigade at Bankipore (Bakerganj Market) resulted in considerable development of the western suburbs. This process of westward expansion continued after the Brigade was moved to Dinapur (7 miles west of Patna).[5]

In 1786, the Gola (Golghar) was built by John Ganstin. It was used as a grain silo. The old cantonment area was built in 1765 (east of Bankipore Club). All these and the residential areas of Bankipore (mainly east of Gandhi Maidan) were served by two important markets of Muradpur and Bakerganj. Muharrampur and Muradpur were westward extensions of Patna during the eighteenth century.[6] With the passage of time during the nineteenth century a belt of dense population was created along the Ashok Raj Path, then called Main Road which constituted the main thoroughfare of the city. Area of dense population included Golakpur, Musallahpur, Muradpur and Salimpur.

In the 20th century, the separation of Bihar and Orissa from Bengal in 1911 brought an overall change in the internal structure of the city. Patna started moving west i.e., west of Patna - Gaya Road (Budha Marg). A planned township known as the New Capital was built by the British in Western Patna to house their offices and employees. Various government buildings, Government House, Secretariat,Council Chambers, Museum and the High Court came into existence during this period. Establishment of Patna University (1917), new colleges. schools. hospitals and technical centres attracted a large number of people to avail of the facilities provided by the city. This added to the total population of the growing city. Several small and consumer oriented industries were also established. Again these gave employment to a large number of labourers both within and outside the city. Consequently, pockets of residential areas started coming up in Central Patna and Western Patna. The area between Malsalami and Gandhi Maidan became full of shops intermingled with residential and educational pockets. People settled in and around Bakerganj, Sabzibagh, Lodipur, Patna Junction and Mithapur - all being small market centres of retail activity.

In 1936, Bihar was separated from Orissa to form an independent Province. Its headquarters continued to be at Patna. This provided tremendous opportunity to the city to develop further. People from different areas started pouring in and settling in the various areas of the city. After 1947, Machchuatoli, Langertoli, Kadam Kuan, Nayatola, Lalji tola, Pirmohani and Salempur Ahra, all in Central Patna became more densely inhabited.

In the middle of the 20th century a new planned residential colony namely Rajendra Nagar was developed to the east of Arya Kumar Road and to the north of railway line in the south.

A few residential pockets also grew to the south of the railway line and the old bye- pass road. The entire area to the south of the railway line and in between Budha Marg in the west and the bend of the old bye - pass road in the east is known as Kankerbagh, In the south, population was concentrated around Channari, Kumhrar and Choti Pahari.

To the west of Budha Marg, people settled along the railway line both to the north and to the south and as far as Khagaul road in south. In the north the population spread along Bailey road and also to the north of it along Boring road and Boring Canal road.

In the later part of the 20th Century various job opportunities in the fields of trade, commerce, administration and education attracted people from the countryside and other parts of India as well. Eastern and Central Patna had become very densely settled and congested and vacant space was available only in the southern and western parts of the city. Subsequently, various new colonies such as Patrakarnagar, Lohianagar, Chitraguptanagar, Hanumannagar, etc. were built in Southern Patna. In Western Patna Nageshwar colony, Shastrinagar, Rajbansinagar, Shrikrishnagar, Shrikrishnapuri, Patel Nagar, Electricity Board Colony and Gardanibagh, to name a few were developed to accommodate the people. Several new colonies given to various private Housing Cooperative Societies are coming up fast in western Patna near Raja Bazar on Bailey Road, in Sheikhpura, Khajepura and also in Kankerbagh in South Patna.

A review of the distribution and trends of population growth in various parts of Patna shows that in the pre - independence period the population was mainly concentrated in Eastern Patna, the chief centre for wholesale trade in the city. Later, people moved west, slightly away but still near to their place of work giving rise to twin city character to the urban landscape.[7] Lately, the trend has been to settle far from the city's congestion and pollution in the west and the south.

Thus, at present, the tendency of urban growth is being noticed in the following three directions :

(a) One main thrust of urbanization is taking place along the Patna-Danapur road westward along the Ganga.

(b) Another important thrust is along the Bailey Road and Gardanibagh Road towards Phulwari and Khagaul, and

(c) A general spill - over is apparent in areas between the railway line and the new bye - pass road in South Patna, where already the density of population has become quite high.

Decennial Variation by Wards

It has become difficult to compare data of various decadal years viz., 1951, 1961, 1971 and 1981 owing to frequently changing ward boundaries as well as enormous changes that have been brought about in the Municipal area of the city. The ward numbers have been changed (Fig. 6) and hence they are no longer compatible. For instance, in 1951 there were only 32 wards. In 1961, the municipal area of the city was extended and the number of wards increased to 37. In 1971 although the number of the wards remained the same as that of 1961, their numbers were changed and the boundaries were readjusted so that the previous ward numbers were no longer applicable. Even the municipal area of the city was extended. Again in 1981 Patna's Municipal boundary was extended right upto Patna Canal in the west and in the south as far as and even beyond the new bye - pass road. To be more explicit, examples of a few wards are given as under.

(a) The area of old ward no. 34 in west Patna was increased from 112.4 acres in 1961 to 828.4 acres in 1971 and renumbered as ward no.1. It was further increased to 3398.4 acres in 1981 by extending it to

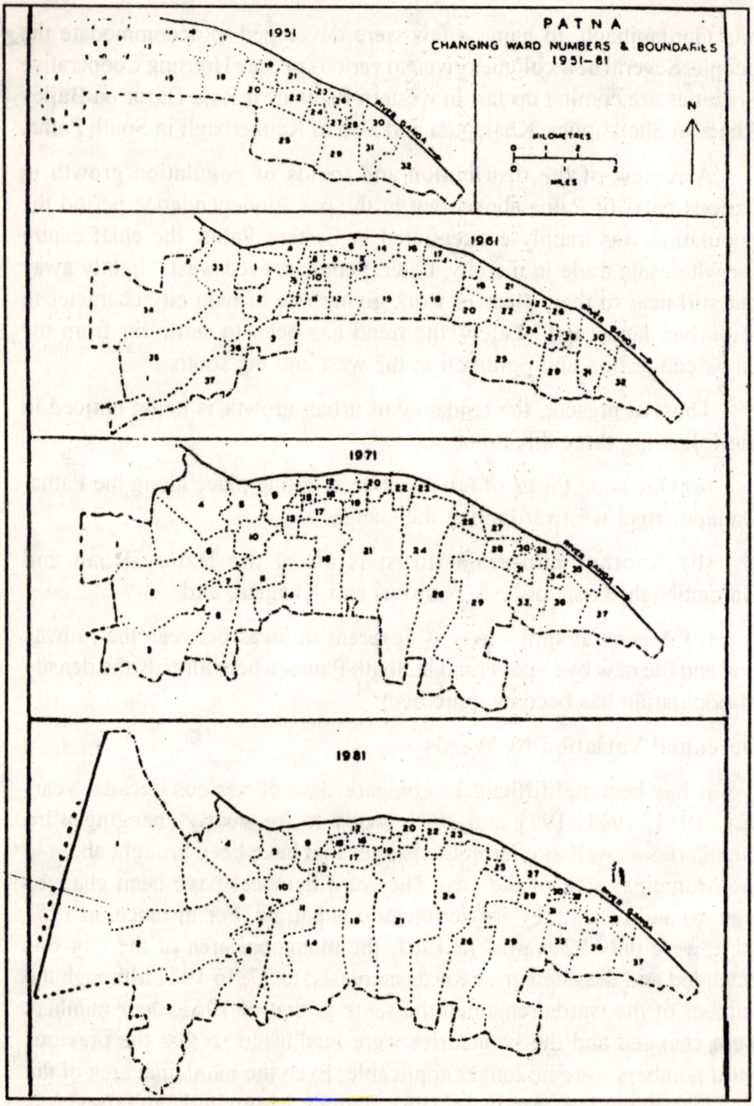

Fig. 6

Patna Canal.

(b) Old Ward no. 12 accommodating Machchuatoli and Rajendra Nagar has now been divided in new ward nos. 16,17,18 and 19 and additional area has been incorporated by including vacant agricultural land to the south. In this way, Rajendranagar which was a part of ward no.12 now falls in ward no.18, which extends far to the south of the railway line upto village Jaganpura (beyond Hanuman Nagar).

(c) Similarly, new ward nos. 21 and 24 extend on either side of the railway line comprising parts of old wards and incorporating large new and unbuilt rural areas to the south as well.

(d) Several other wards have been subdivided and boundaries readjusted, such as old ward numbers 1 and 4 have been divided in new wards 5 and 9 with readjustments.

As such ward level population data of the earlier decades cannot be strictly compared with the ward level figures of today. This is also not possible because the break up of ward level data by mohallas is not available. So, in order to make the data of at least one decade (1971 - 81) comparable, the population of 1971 by wards has been calculated on the basis of the area of the wards in 1981. In 1981 ward numbers 1, 2, 3, 14, 18 and 21 have registered large change in their areas and hence there is a corresponding change in their respective population. Obviously, these calculated ward level figures for 1971 will not at all tally with the census figures of 1971.

It is evident from Fig. 7 and that the maximum growth of population has taken place in ward no.6 (331.71%) which falls in Western Patna. This immense growth has been possible because of the occupance of vacant spaces for construction of several planned residential colonies. Ward no. 11 which falls both in Central Patna and Southern Patna has also grown tremendously in terms of population. This may be ascribed to an increase in commercial activities which encouraged people to settle near their place of work thus giving way to the construction of houses. Another area of high growth being 179.59. The map clearly shows that the growth has mainly taken place around the boundaries of Central - Western zones and Southern - Western zones ranging between 100 and 350 per cent. The growth has been a little less i.e. less then 100 per cent in Eastern Patna which is already saturated. Parts of Central, Western and Southern Patna have also registered small growths. Since Eastern and Central Patna have very high density of population with a corresponding lack of building space, the people are now moving south or west. It is, therefore, expected that in the next few decades,, the rest of Patna will also experience a high rate of population growth and will become densely populated. The way developmental activities are taking place in the urban life of Patna, this feature of population explosion will

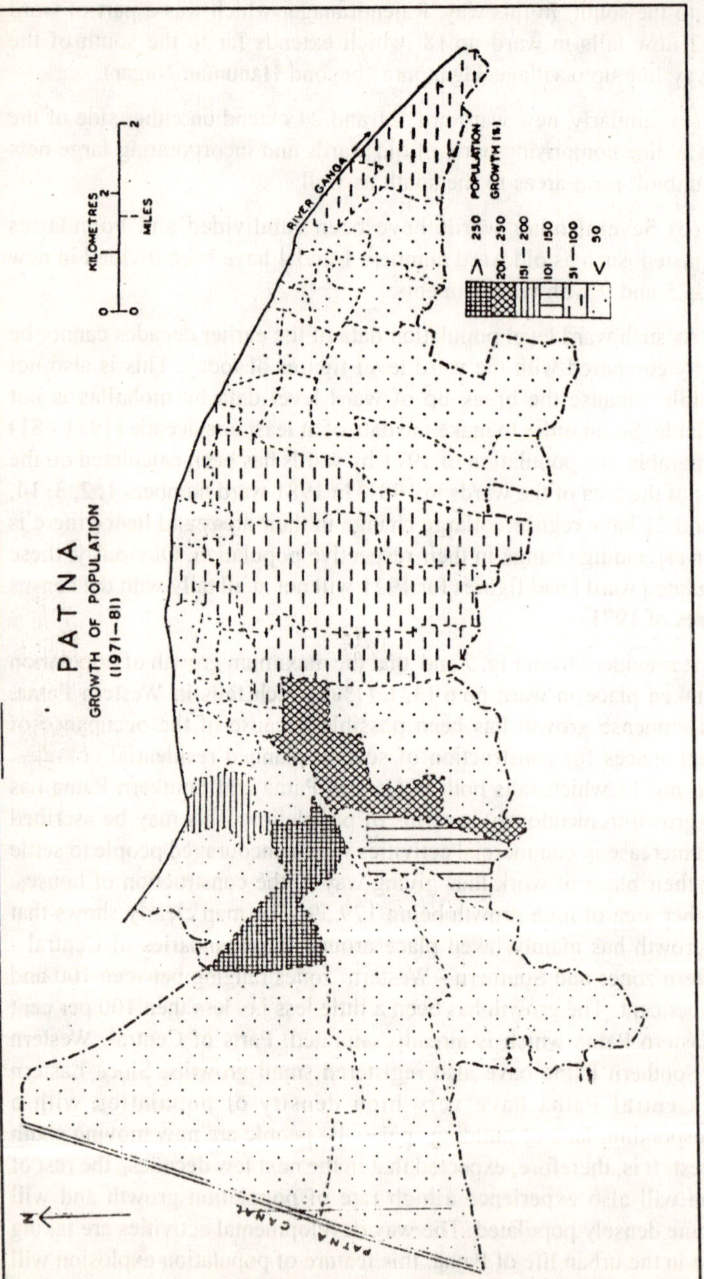
PATNA
GROWTH OF POPULATION
(1971–81)
KILOMETRES
0 1 2
0 1 2
MILES
POPULATION GROWTH (%)
> 250
201 — 250
151 — 200
101 — 150
51 — 100
< 50
RIVER GANGA
PATNA CANAL
N

Fig. 7

not come as a surprise.

Density of Population

The distribution pattern of Patna's population and the functional character of the city's land are very much related to each other. The people settled earlier along the southern levee of the river Ganga on either side of the Ashok Raj Path running east - west parallel to the river. According to 1981 Census, the average density of population of the city is 32.338 persons per acre. In 1951,1961 and 1971 the corresponding figures were 35.19, 32.40 and 26.94 respectively,. The apparent gradual decrease in the density in these decennial years has been mainly due to the absorption of vacant and agricultural land nearby, thus increasing the municipal limit of the city in each decennial year. In 1981 too, Patna's Municipal limit was extended further south and west but at the same time the population also increased by more than 60 per cent and hence there has been an increase in population density over the 1971 figure.

When maps and the associated Appendices II, III, IV and V of different decennial years viz., 1951,1961,1971 and 1981 are visualized, it is found that right from 1951, density has been highest in central parts of the city ranging between 150 and 350 persons per acre. It is followed by Eastern Patna with 50 to 150 persons per acre. The density gradually decreases towards the south and the west coming down to less than 50 persons per acre. (Fig. 8/9/10/11).

There is marked contrast in the intra - city distribution of population of 1981 ranging between 255.33 persons per acre in ward no.15 (Central Patna) to as low as 8.39 per acre in ward no.1 (Western Patna) .

It is evident from Fig. 11 that the density is very high in the central and northern parts of Central Patna ranging between 100 and more than 250 persons per acre. This zone contains ward no.15 which has the highest density among all other wards. The commercial hub of the city, the Muradpur complex lies in this ward. In Western Patna, ward no.7 is the only ward which has density of 208.93 persons per acre. Densely populated area of Mithapur with another commercial centre lies in this ward. The rest of Western Patna has a density below 20 persons per acre. Similar is the case with some parts of Southern Patna. This is because of the presence of large tracts of agricultural and vacant lands in these zones. The size of wards in these two parts is larger compared to those of Central and Eastern Patna while the population is comparatively low. In Eastern Patna, especially in its northern parts, the density is high being between 100 and 250 persons per acre. This is the oldest part of the city.

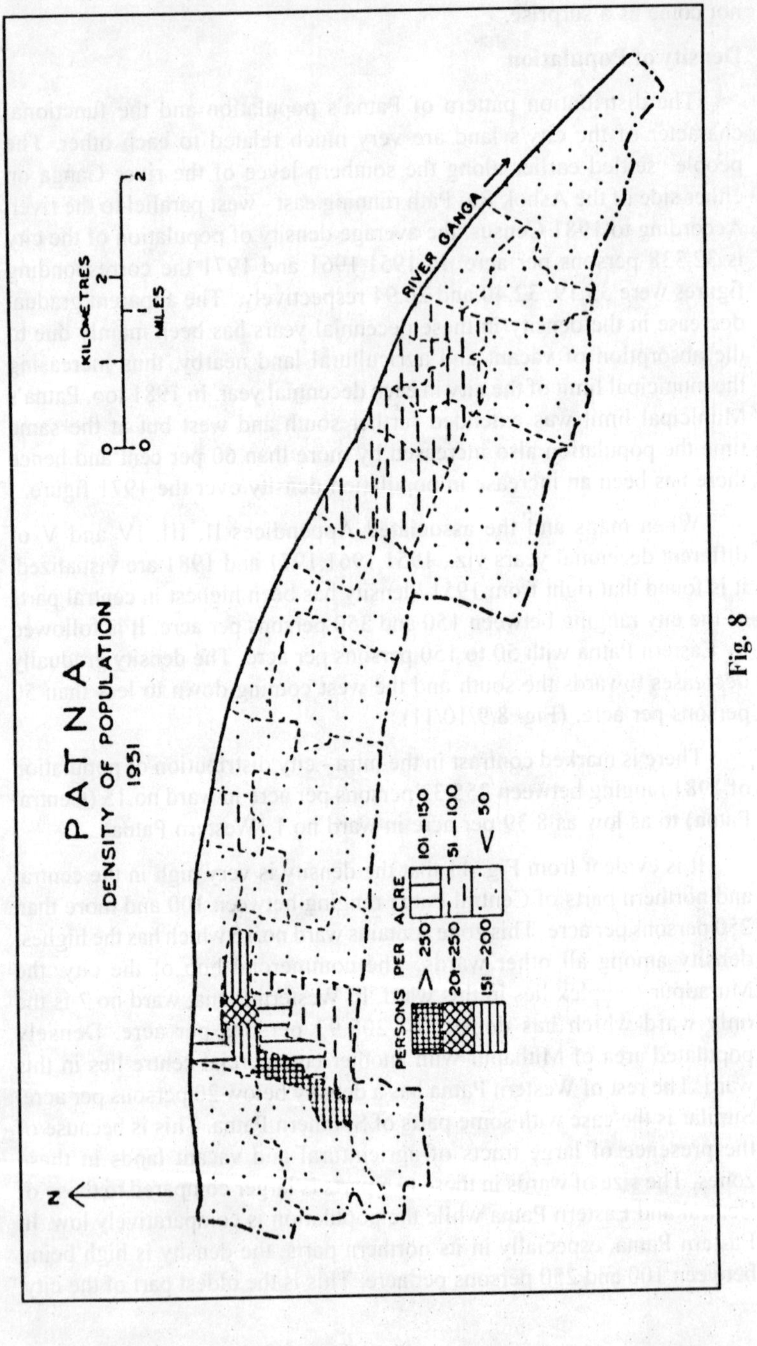
PATNA
DENSITY OF POPULATION
1951
PERSONS PER ACRE
> 250
201-250
151-200
101-150
51-100
< 50
KILOMETRES
0 1 2
MILES
0 1
RIVER GANGA
N

Fig. 8

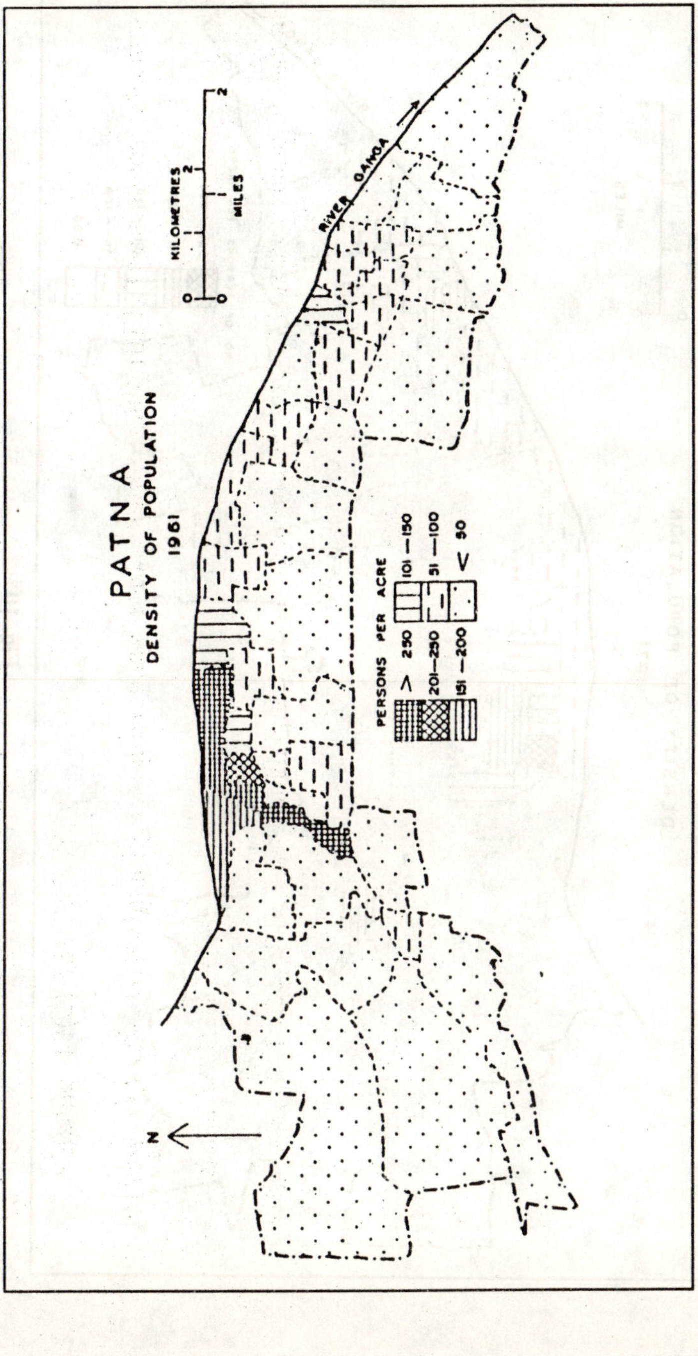
PATNA
DENSITY OF POPULATION
1961
PERSONS PER ACRE
> 250
201—250
151—200
101—150
51—100
< 50
KILOMETRES
0 1 2
MILES
0 1 2
RIVER GANGA
N

Fig. 9

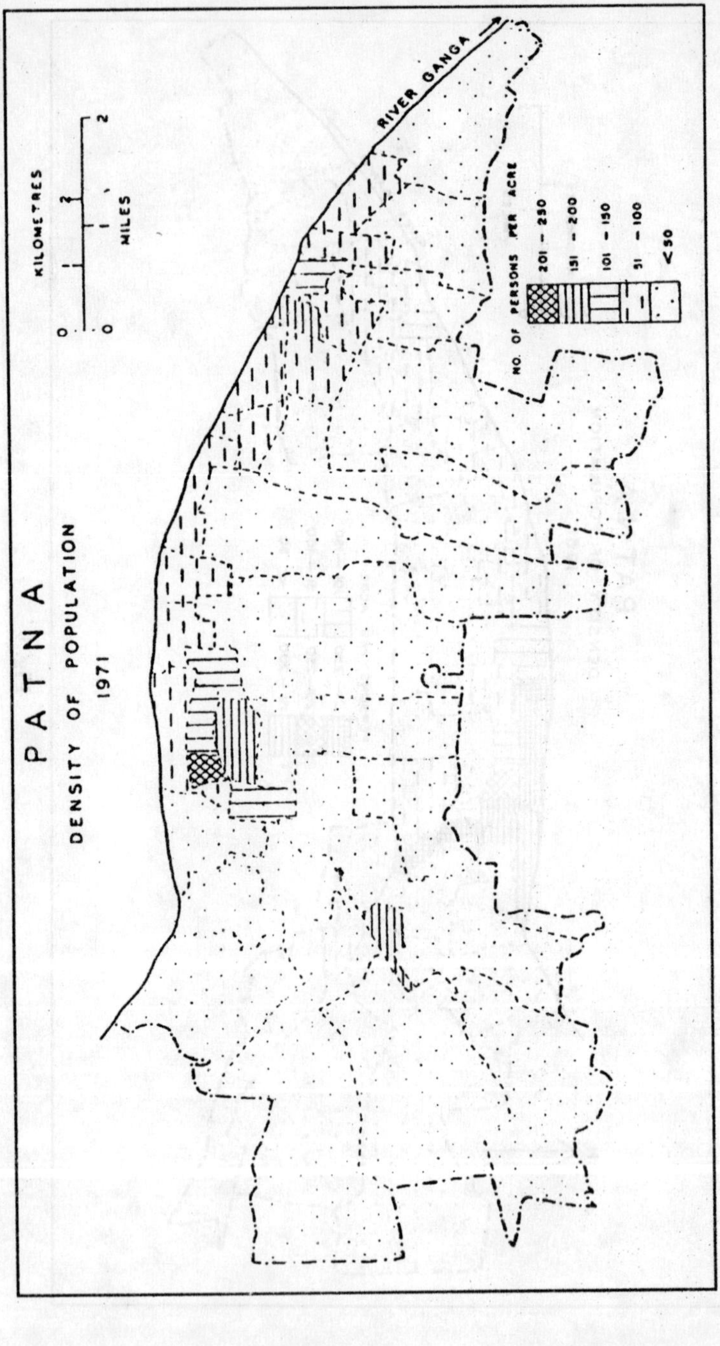
PATNA
DENSITY OF POPULATION
1971
KILOMETRES
0 1 2
MILES
0 1 2
RIVER GANGA
NO. OF PERSONS PER ACRE
201 – 250
151 – 200
101 – 150
51 – 100
<50

Fig. 10

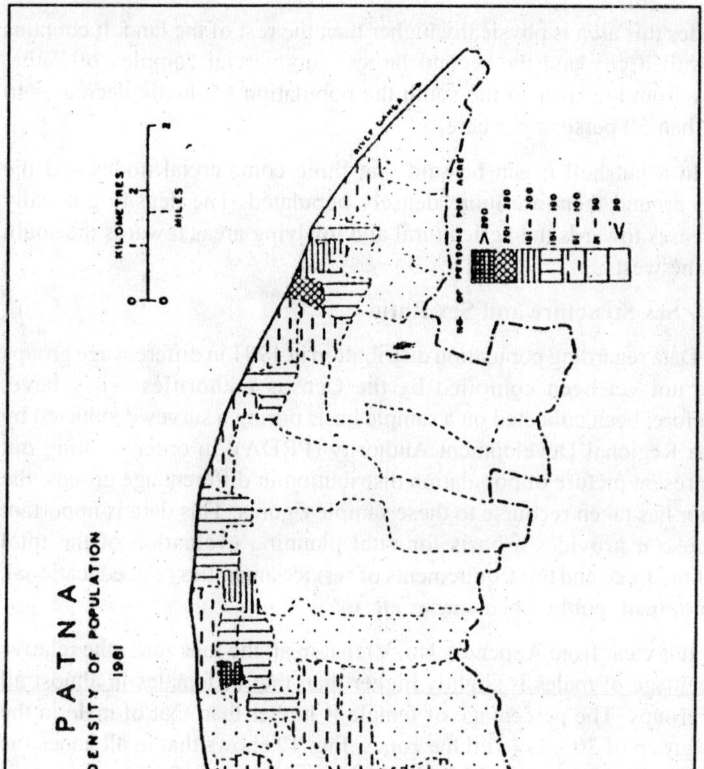
PATNA
DENSITY OF POPULATION
1981
KILOMETRES
MILES
NO. OF PERSONS PER ACRE
RIVER GANGA
PATNA CANAL
N

Fig. 11

Besides this area is physically higher than the rest of the land. It contains the walled city and the second largest commercial complex of Patna. Away from the river to the south the population gradually decreases to less than 50 persons per acre.

In a nutshell it can be said that three commercial nodes and the areas around them are more densely populated. The density gradually decreases towards the agricultural and lowlying areas towards the south and the west.

Age - Sex Structure and Sex Ratio

Data regarding population distribution in 1981 in different age groups have not yet been compiled by the Census authorities. They have, therefore, been collected on a sample basis during a survey conducted by Patna Regional Development Authority (PRDA). In order to bring out the present picture of population distribution in different age groups, the author has taken recourse to these sample figures. This data is important because it provides a basis for vital planning evaluation of the total working force and the requirements of service amenities (e.g. educational, institutional, public open spaces etc.)

It is clear from Appendix No. VI that in all the four zones the relative percentage of males is slightly higher than that of females in almost all age groups. The percentage of female is higher than that of male in the age group of 30 - 34 in all the zones. Fig. 12 shows that in all zones the number of both males and females in the age group of 10 - 14 is high. This may be ascribed to a high number of students living in Patna. The number of males and females in the age group of 25 to 54 is also high being more or less the same in the Eastern and the Central zones while it is slightly less in the western and the southern zones. The main reason behind this distribution is more job opportunities in the Eastern and Central zones which contain most of the industries and commercial houses/shops in Patna.

Sex Ratio

According to 1981 Census, Patna had a population of 776,371 of which 428,951 are males and 374,420 are females. Thus males constitute 55.25 per cent of the total population of the city and the females 44.75. In 1971, the respective percentages were 55.78 and 44.22. This shows a slight decrease in the percentage of male population leading to slightly better sex ratio. This may be attributed to increased female migrants from the neighbouring area. An analysis of the data regarding sex - ratio

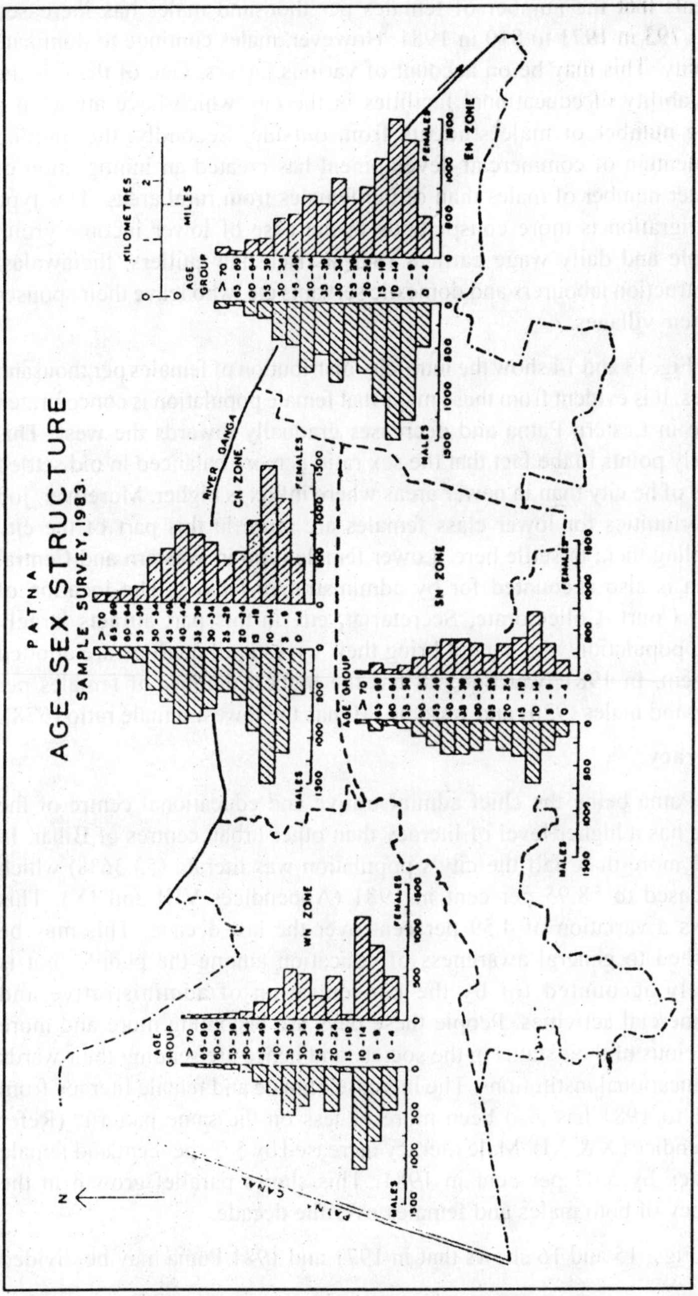
PATNA
AGE-SEX STRUCTURE
SAMPLE SURVEY, 1983.
KILOMETRES
MILES
RIVER GANGA
CANAL
EN ZONE
CN ZONE
WN ZONE
SN ZONE
AGE GROUP
MALES
FEMALES

Fig. 12

reveals that the number of females per thousand males has increased from 793 in 1971 to 810 in 1981. However. males continue to dominate the city. This may be on account of various factors. One of them is the availability of educational facilities in the city which have attracted a large number of male students from outside. Secondly, the gaining momentum of commercial development has created an immigration of greater number of males than of the females from rural areas. This type of migration is more conspicuous in the case of lower income group people and daily wage earners such as rickshaw pullers, thelawalas, construction labourers and domestic servants etc. who leave their spouses in their villages.

Fig. 13 and 14 show the intra-city distribution of females per thousand males. It is evident from these maps that female population is concentrated more in Eastern Patna and decreases gradually towards the west. This clearly points to the fact that the sex ratio is more balanced in old settled parts of he city than in newer areas where influx is higher. Moreover, job opportunities for lower class females are more in this part of the city enabling them to settle here. Lower female ratio in Western and Central Patna is also accounted for by administrative factors. The location of High Court, Collectorate, Secretariat, etc. in this part attracts largely male population who cannot bring their wives until quarters are allotted to them. In 1981, ward no. 28 has the highest number of females per thousand males (920) and ward no. 10 has the lowest female ratio (678).

Literacy

Patna being the chief administrative and educational centre of the State has a higher level of literacy than other urban centres of Bihar. In 1971 more than half the city's population was literate (53.36%) which increased to 58.95 per cent in 1981 (Appendices VIII and IX). This shows a variation of 4.59 per cent over the last decade. This may be ascribed to general awareness of education among the people, but is largely accounted for by the concentration of administrative and commercial activities. People these days are becoming more and more conscious of their status in the society and hence are sending their wards to educational institutions. The increase of male and female literacy from 1971 to 1981 has also been more or less on the same pattern (Refer Appendices X & XI). Male literacy increased by 5.09 per cent and female literacy by 5.07 per cent in 1981. This shows parallel growth in the literacy of both males and females over the decade.

Figs. 15 and 16 shows that in 1971 and 1981 Patna may be divided

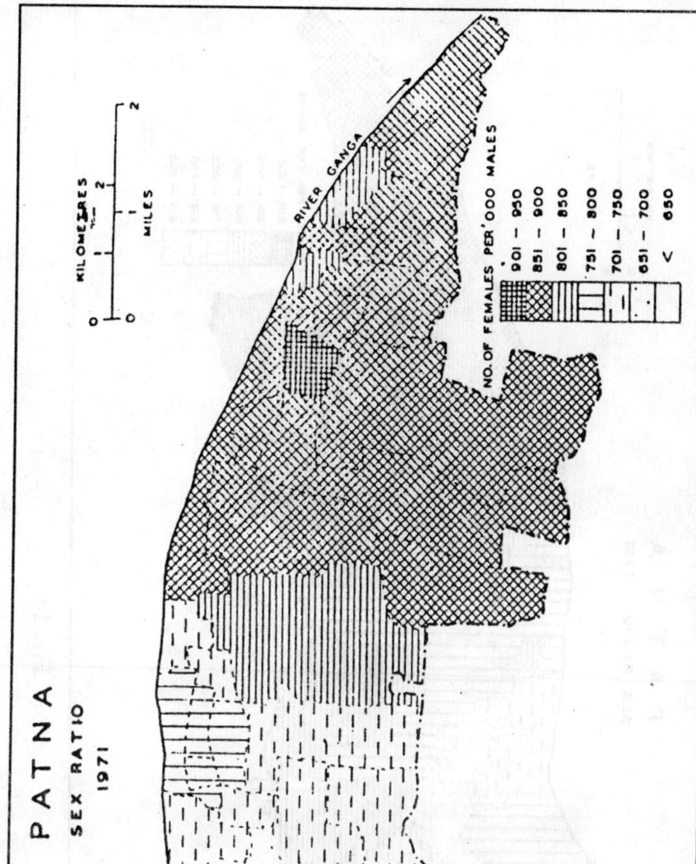

PATNA
SEX RATIO
1971
KILOMETRES
0 1 2
MILES
0 1 2
N
RIVER GANGA
NO. OF FEMALES PER '000 MALES
901 – 950
851 – 900
801 – 850
751 – 800
701 – 750
651 – 700
< 650

Fig. 13

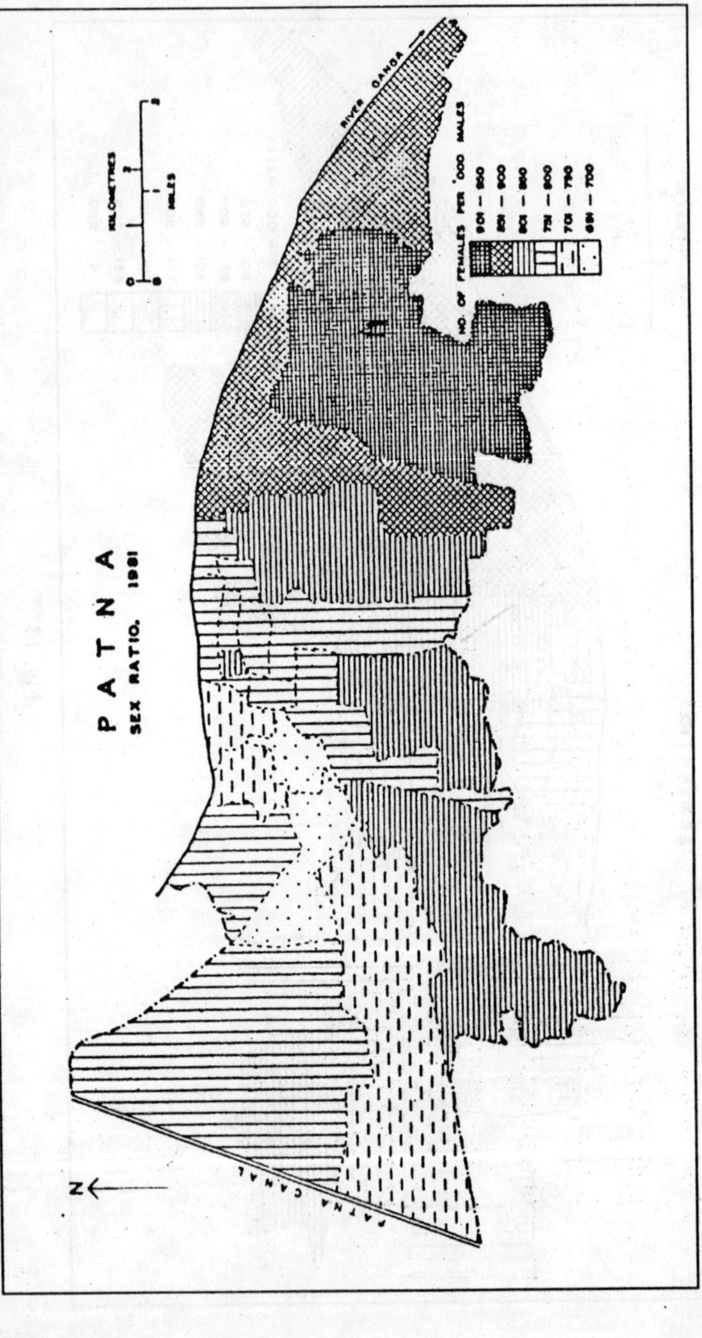
P A T N A
SEX RATIO. 1981
KILOMETRES
MILES
RIVER GANGA
NO. OF FEMALES PER '000 MALES
901 — 950
851 — 900
801 — 850
751 — 800
701 — 750
651 — 700
N
PATNA CANAL

Fig. 14

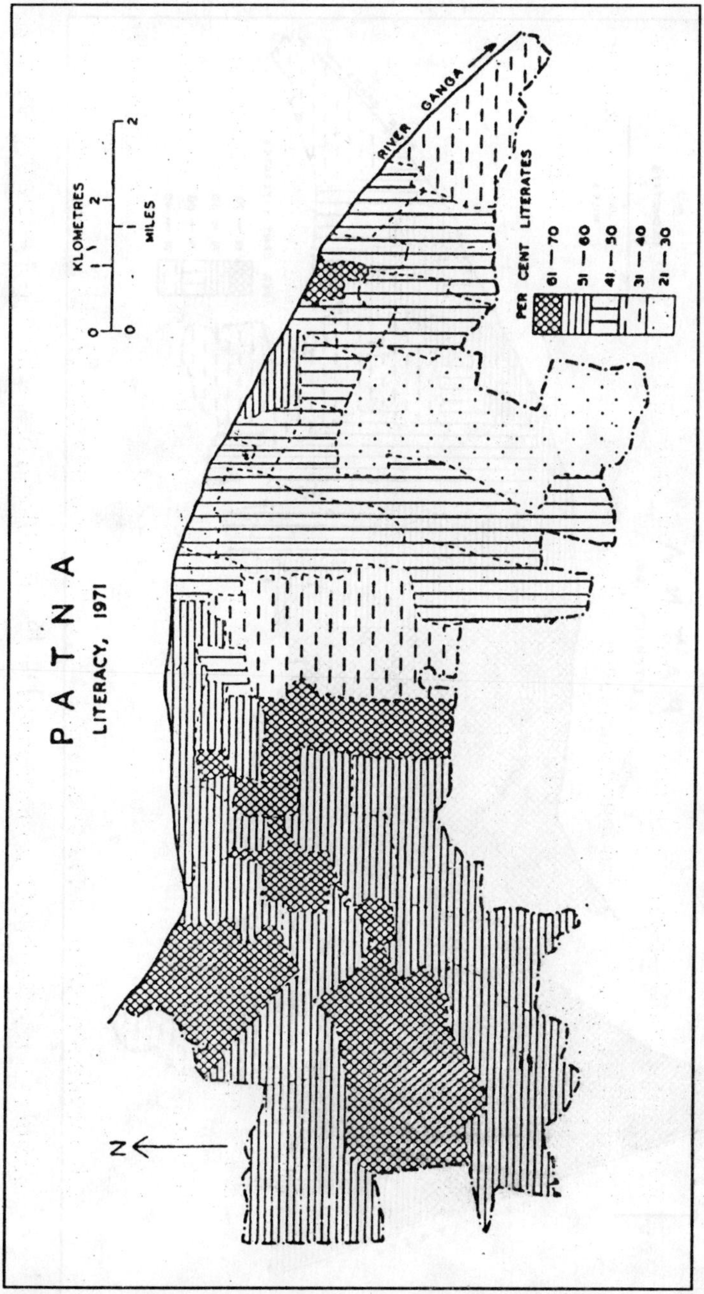
PATNA
LITERACY, 1971
KLOMETRES
0 1 2
MILES
0 1 2
RIVER GANGA
N
PER CENT LITERATES
61 — 70
51 — 60
41 — 50
31 — 40
21 — 30

Fig. 15

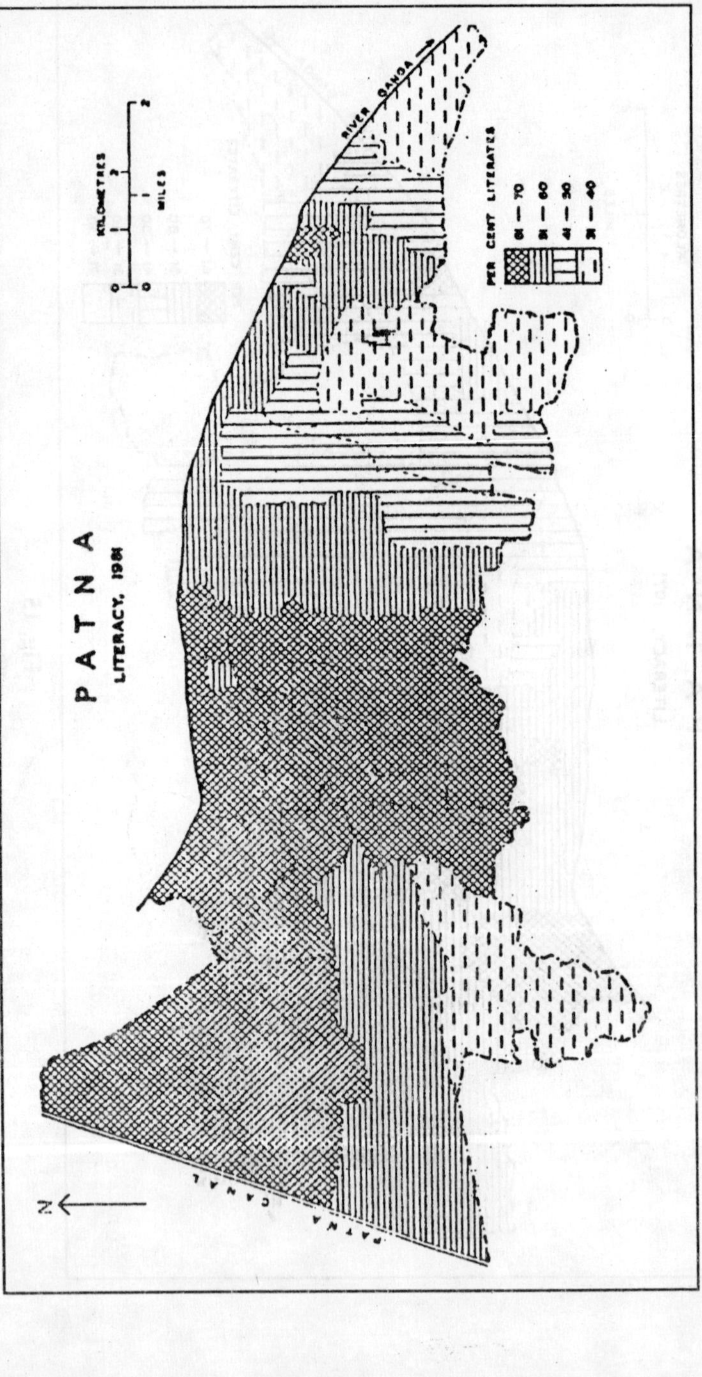
PATNA
LITERACY, 1981
KILOMETRES
MILES
RIVER GANGA
PER CENT LITERATES
61 — 70
51 — 60
41 — 50
31 — 40
PATNA CANAL
N

Fig. 16

into two halves. To the west of the boundaries of the ward Nos. 19,20 and 21, the whole area right up to the western limit of the city has a high literacy ranging between 60 and 70 per cent. However, in 1981 Ward No.3 has low literacy because this is basically a rural area and has been included within the municipal limit of the city only in 1981. In the other half i.e.up to the eastern limit to the city the percentage of literacy is comparatively low being 50 per cent. Here the literacy is lower than the average literacy of the city. Only ward nos. 32 and 22 have a high literacy figure. Ward No. 29 has the lowest literacy because it is an agricultural area. Highest literacy is found in Ward No. 18 in Central Patna.

So far as literacy among males and females is concerned it also presents some spatial variation. Figs. 17 and 18 shows that in 1971 there was only ward no. 18 which had both high male as well as high female literacy. Entire Western Patna and parts of Central had high male and moderate female literacy. The rest of the city had low male literacy and very low female literacy. In 1981, the conditions improved. It is interesting to see that almost two - thirds of Patna has male - female literacy in the ratio of 3.2. In some areas it is 1.1 but no where do females exceed males in terms of literacy. Ward No. 13 in Central Patna has both high male and female literacy. High male literacy in the west may be ascribed to concentration of upper class people and low females literacy may be the result of presence of uneducated migrants females from the rural areas. In Eastern and Central Patna female literacy is low because Eastern Patna has a bulk of Muslim population who do not allow free movement of women. They are confined to their houses, and hence lose the opportunity of going to school. Besides this area has a higher percentage of economically poor people who cannot afford to send their wards to school.

Future Pattern of Population Character

The growth of Patna's population over decades has been conditoned by many complex social, political, physical and economic factors. These factors are likely to play increasingly dominant roles in the future population pattern of the city. Upliftment of rural economy through government planning, establishment of Community Development Blocks and National extension services and increasing public participation in these nation building works, have generated new factors in the control and stabilization of population in the countryside. It is expected that migration of rural population to urban areas may, in course of time, become restricted and more organised.

There may be other factors (e.g. establishment of big industry) which

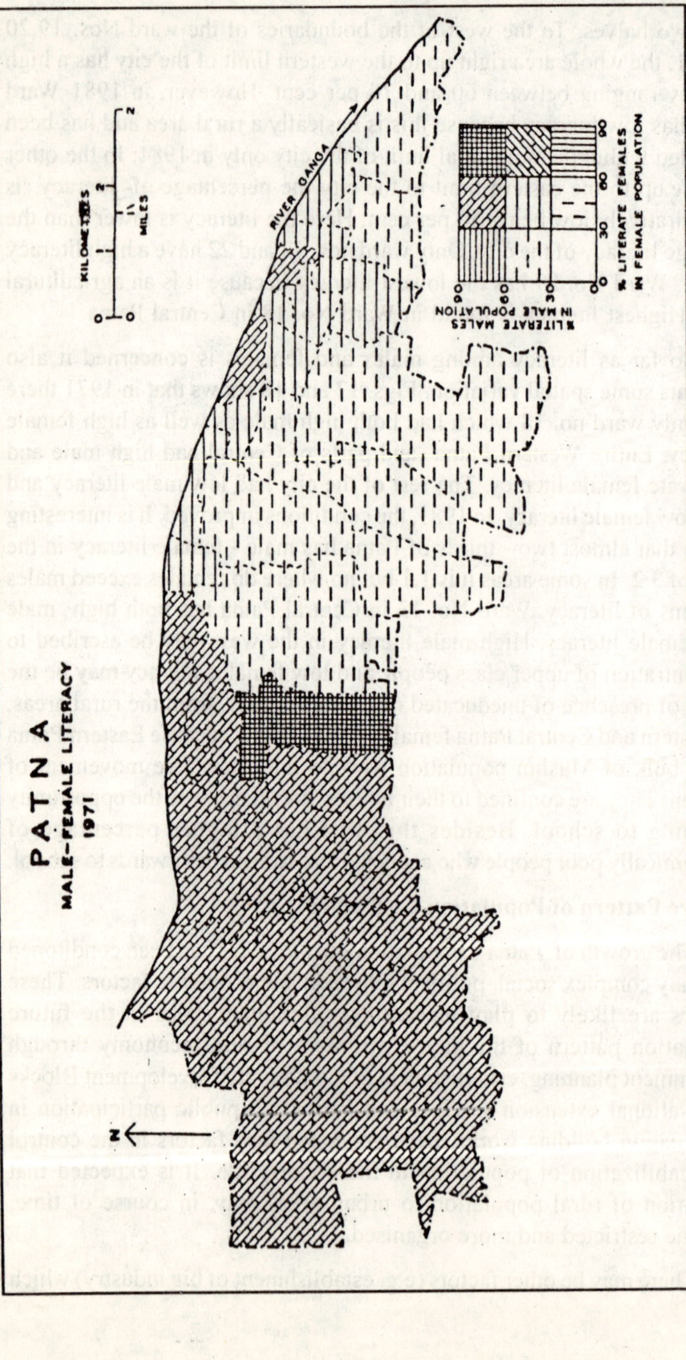
PATNA
MALE-FEMALE LITERACY
1971
RIVER GANGA
KILOMETRES
MILES
% LITERATE FEMALES IN FEMALE POPULATION
% LITERATE MALES IN MALE POPULATION
0
30
60
90
2
N

Fig. 17

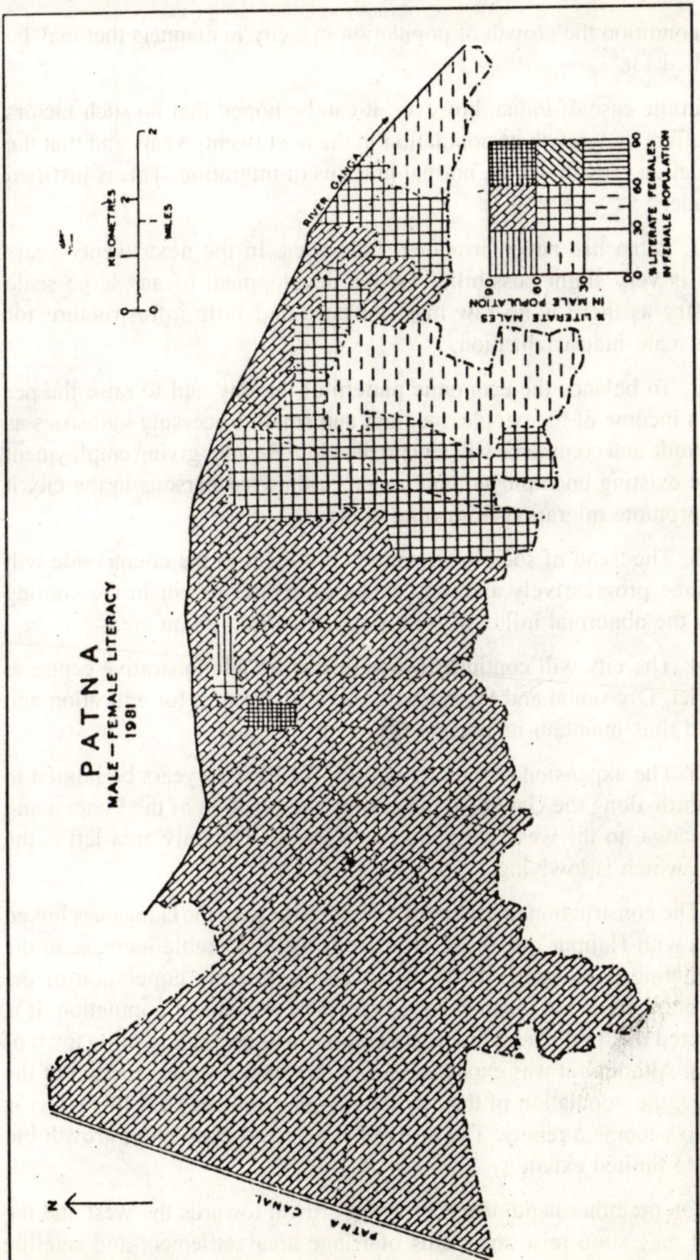
PATNA
MALE – FEMALE LITERACY
1981
RIVER GANGA
PATNA CANAL
N
0 1 2 KILOMETRES
0 1 MILES
% LITERATE MALES IN MALE POPULATION
% LITERATE FEMALES IN FEMALE POPULATION
0 30 60 90

Fig. 18

may condition the growth of population in a city in manners that may be uncalled for.

In the case of Patna, however, it can be hoped that no such factors will affect the growth of population in the next twenty years and that the population growth will be normal in terms of migration. This is justified as under :

1. Patna has never promoted industries. In the next twenty years there is very slight possibility for the development of any large scale industry as there is no raw material base and little infrastructure for large scale industrialization.

2. To balance the economic pattern of the city and to raise the per capita income of the people, medium and small processing industries as well trade and commerce will tend to develop. Besides giving employment to the existing unemployed and under - employed persons in the city it will promote migration from rural areas.

3. The trend of socio - economic upliftment in the countryside will continue progressively and may check to greater extent in the coming years the abnormal influx of rural population into urban areas.

4. The city will continue to function as an administrative centre at District, Divisional and State levels and also a centre for education and would thus maintain its present character.

5. The expansion of the city will for the next 20 years be limited in the north along the Ganga, to the east by the junction of the Punpun and the Ganga, to the west along the Patna Canal. The only area left is the south which is lowlying.

The construction of Mahatma Gandhi Setu over the Ganga has linked Patna with Hajipur due to which there is a considerable increase in the commuting population. It has increased the floating population of the city, but there is not much change in level of permanent population. It is expected that in the next few years Hajipur will become satellite town of Patna. Although it was expected earlier that with the construction of the bridge, the population of the city would get a sudden push this effect is still to become a reality. The bridge has affected population growth but only to limited extent.

On the other hand, the population growth towards the west and the south may soon raise the status of fringe area settlement and satellite towns such as Digha - Mainpura, Danapur, Khagaul and Phulwari and make them merge into the parent city. Already buildings stretch along the roads leading to Danapur, Khagaul and Parsa bazar and there is continuous urban belt linking these nuclei with Patna. By 2001 a greater Patna Metropolis may emerge whose population will easily exceed 2 millions. This includes the population of 1.44 million for the parent city as predicted in earlier pages of this chapter.

References :

1. Buchanan, F. (1811-12) : An Account of District of Bihar and Patna, Calcutta : Bihar and Orissa Research Society, pp. 59-61.
2. Chapin, F.S. (1957) : Urban Land Use Planning, Harper and Brothers, New York.
3. Changing Municipal area in different years has not been considered while calculating these percentages.
4. The population for 1991 and 2001 has been calculated on geometric progression on the basis of 1961-81 population figures. When zonewise figures are projected for 1991 and 2001 and when they are totalled for Patna as a whole, the projected population of Patna in 1991 comes to 10, 70, 768 and in 2001 it comes to 15, 37, 623. The zonewise figures will be discussed later. This has been mentioned here only to avoid confusion.
5. Sami. A. (1980) : Intra Urban Market Geography : A Case Study of Patna, Concept Publishing Company, New Delhi, p. 57.
6. O'Malley, L. S. S. (1934) : Bihar and Orissa District Gazetteer, Patna, p.179.
7. Prasad, A. (1958) : "Double Towns of India"[4] : A Problem in Urban Morphology, "Geographical Outlook, Vol. 2, No. 1."[4]
8. The total area of Patna as given in the District Census Handbook is 24097.9 acres, but when the areas of all the wards are added up the total area comes to 24013.4 acres. The difference is of 84.5 acres. The leads to a difference in density. In the former case the density will be 32.22 and in the latter 32.33 persons per acre. The author has used the figure 24097.9 acres and its relative density while discussing the area of Patna as a whole. However, the figure 24013.4 acres and its relative density have been used everywhere else so as to compare wardwise figures as they are.

4

Functional Character

Urban Land Use

Land use may be described as nature and extent of land put to any kind of use by man. Cities are the focal points in the occupation and utilization of the earth by man. Both a product of and an influence on surrounding regions, they develop in definite patterns in response to economic and social needs. These growing needs associated with ever increasing human skill and know - how have resulted in a continuous field of tension between land resourses and human efforts. This human intervention calls for a cautious and careful handling of the land so as to make the best use of its potentialities without affecting its inherent capabilities.

Urban Land Use is a term commonly used to refer to the spatial distribution of functions in an urban area.[1] Urban Land Use may be broadly divided into two parts : (a) built up land and (b) open space. These may be further subdivided into (1) residential, (2) commercial, (3) industrial, (4) administrative, (5) institutional comprising of educational, medical, religious and other cultural institutions, (6) transportational, (7) recreational, comprising of parks, playgrounds, cinemas, theatres, etc. and (8) open space including agricultural land, orchards, water - bodies and wasteland.

The study of land use is very important because only the functional character of a particular settlement determines whether it is to be recognised as a town. The functional activities determine the level of growth of an urban centre. These are mainly residential, commercial, administrative, industrial, recreational, educational, transportational and medical etc. A characteristic feature of urban land use is its transitional character. There is no finality or strict binding of 'use' to which a particular land is put today and this will remain so for all times to come. Changes do and always take place but their frequency and extent are conditioned by factors that control land use patterns. The land use pattern of an urban centre is closely associated with the natural surroundings and gives a vivid account of physical evolution, morphology and functional character of a town and together with demographic structure, it provides a key to its sustenance, growth and status.

Patna with its long history of evolution and development has areas given mainly to mixed land uses. However, three major land uses are distinctive in the city (Fig.19).

Major Land Uses

1. **Residential Land Use :** The residential areas in Patna cover most of the developed area and have 45.49 per cent of the total land of the city. Developed area includes only the built - up areas and roads whereas it excludes vacant and agricultural land. Total land includes vacant land. Although residential areas spread throughout the city, there are three areas of dense concentration. One is around Kankerbagh Colony in South Patna. It houses middle class income - group people. The second is a small area in the central part of the town near the bank of River Ganga and the third area is around Paschim Darwaza running from north to south. These are poor residential areas having a high density of population. Due to the difference in the pressure of population on residential areas, the newly built colonies in Western and Southern Patna have more area given to residential use but do not have an equally high density of population. In Bankipore, on the other hand, the density of population is higher in comparison with the area under residential use. [2]

2. **Commercial Land Use :** The commercial area in Patna runs in close vicinity of River Ganga from the City Chowk in the east to Muradpur in the central part of the city. From here it takes a south - westward turn covering Kadamkuan, Rajendra Path, Exhibition Road, Dak Bungalow Road and Station Road and goes to New Market located around Mithapur. In Patna 7.24 per cent of the developed land is given to commerce. The City Chowk has the highest concentration of commercial land use. This area specialises in wholesale trade. The Muradpur area, the second and larger centre of trade is basically a retail centre and is spread out along all the radial routes. In fact, the Ashok Raj Path forms the backbone of trade and commerce east of Gandhi Maidan. The third commercial complex is around the Railway Junction, stretching into Mithapur. The region between Muradpur complex and Mithapur is being filled in with commercial houses and soon the two are likely to coalesce forming a much larger zone. A few patches of trade and commerce have also developed in Southern and Western Patna along the Bye - Pass Road and

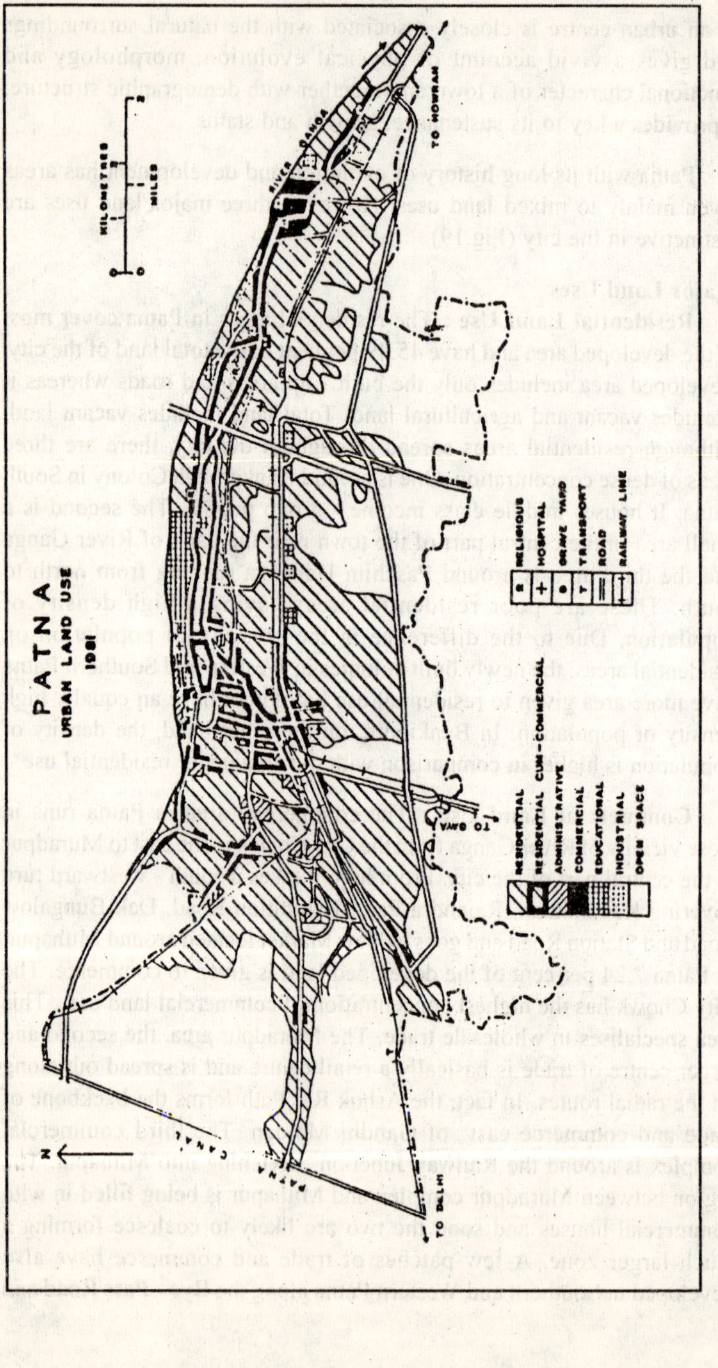
PATNA
URBAN LAND USE
1981
RESIDENTIAL
RESIDENTIAL CUM-COMMERCIAL
ADMINISTRATIVE
COMMERCIAL
EDUCATIONAL
INDUSTRIAL
OPEN SPACE
RELIGIOUS
HOSPITAL
GRAVE YARD
TRANSPORT
ROAD
RAILWAY LINE
KILOMETRES
MILES
N
RIVER GANGA
TO HOWRAH
TO GAYA
TO DELHI
PATNA CANAL

Fig. 19

Boring Road. However, their share of land is negligible.

3. Administrative - cum - Institutional Land Use : It covers 10.62 per cent of the developed land of the city. Patna has two distinct zones of administration and institutions. The administrative sector falls in the western part of the city covering Raj Bhawan, Old and New Secretariats, Circuit House, High Court, G.P.O. etc. while the institutional sector is confined more to the central part of the city. In fact, it forms a compact administrative-cum - institutional zone. It covers Divisional Offices, Collectorate, District Court, Patna Medical college and Hospital, M.M. College, B.N. College, Oriental College, Engineering College, Patna College, Science College and Law College together with their hostels and residential quarters. This zone stretches from Gandhi Maidan to Ranighat, north of Ashoka Raj Path, the centre of which is the Patna University, its office, Colleges and Post-graduate Departments.

Apart from these major uses, there are various other uses such as industrial, recreational and transportational. The extent of land occupied by them is small and they are distributed all over the city without forming any compact zone. The vacant lands are situated mainly in the west and the south in the peripheral parts of the city. As such Patna may be said to be an administrative, institutional and commercial city.

Effect of Land Use on Population Characteristics

The effect of land use can be determined by the occupational structure of the city because both are closely associated. However, the percentage of workers engaged in certain activity is not equal to that of the respective land use. This is because certain functions such as commerce require more people and less land and certain others, such as agriculture require more land and less people.

Since the data of occupational structure is not available in detail with the Census of India for 1981,, the discussion here has been based on 1971 data and maps have also been prepared accordingly.

In 1971, total workers in city formed 27.23 per cent of the total population but their percentage went down slightly in 1981 to 25.70. This probably reflects the growing unemployment. While the population has been growing rapidly as a result of immigration as well as natural increase, the rate of growth of employment opportunities has not kept pace in the absence of significant industrial expansion in the city.

It appears from Figures 20 and 21 that the highest concentration of

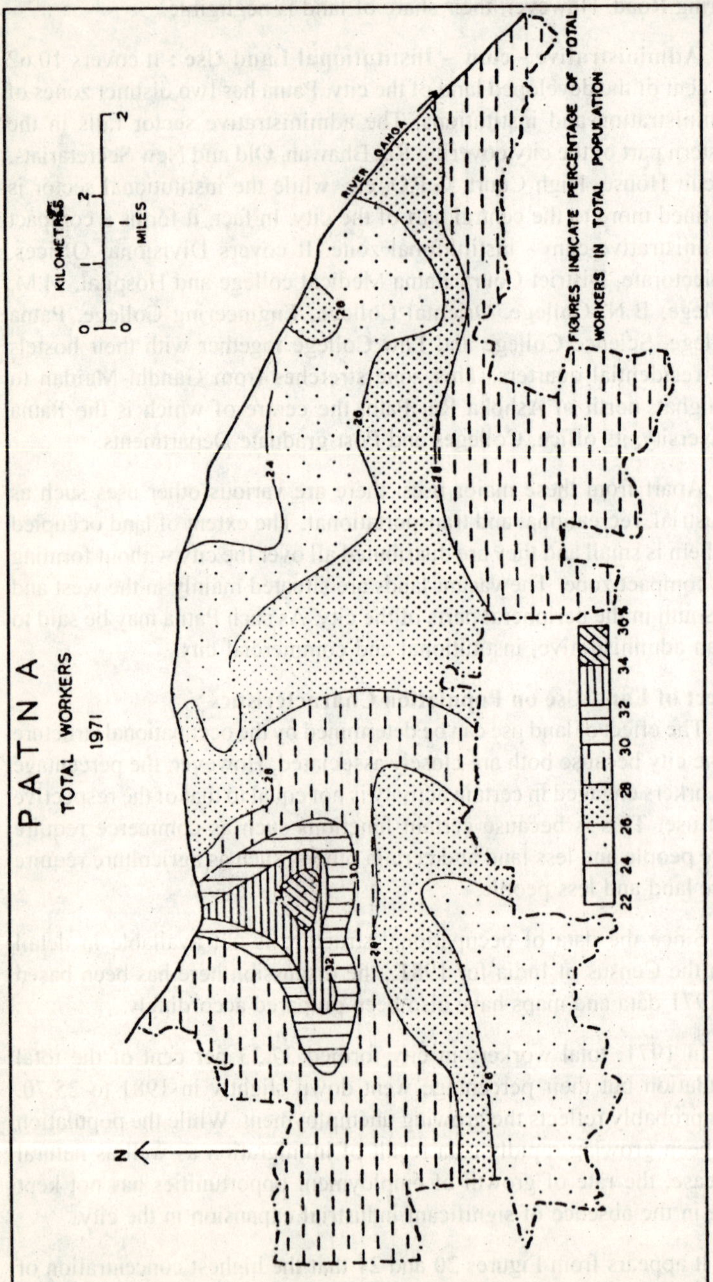
PATNA
TOTAL WORKERS
1971
KILOMETRES
MILES
RIVER GANGA
FIGURES INDICATE PERCENTAGE OF TOTAL
WORKERS IN TOTAL POPULATION
22 24 26 28 30 32 34 36%
N

Fig. 20

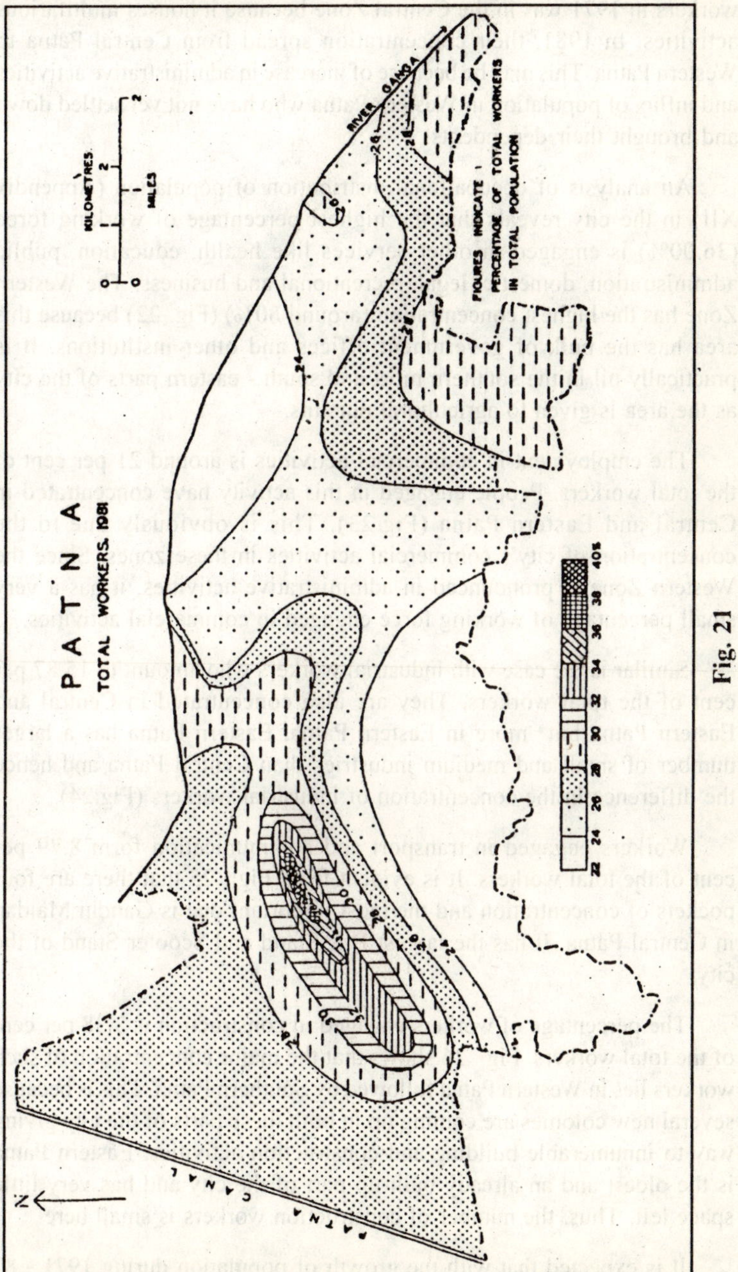
PATNA
TOTAL WORKERS 1981
KILOMETRES
0 1 2
0 1 2
MILES
FIGURES INDICATE PERCENTAGE OF TOTAL WORKERS IN TOTAL POPULATION
RIVER GANGA
CANAL
N
22 24 26 28 30 32 34 36 38 40%

FIG. 21

workers in 1971 was in the Central Zone because it houses multifarious activities. In 1981, their concentration spread from Central Patna to Western Patna. This may be because of increase in administrative activities and influx of population in Western Patna who have not yet settled down and brought their dependents.

An analysis of occupational distribution of population (Appendix XII) in the city reveals that the highest percentage of working force (36.00%) is engaged in other services like health, education, public administration, domestic, legal, recreational and business. The Western Zone has the highest concentration (around 80%) (Fig. 22) because this area has the bulk of government offices and other institutions. It is practically nil in the southern most and south - eastern parts of the city as the area is given to agricultural pursuits.

The employment in commercial activities is around 21 per cent of the total workers. People engaged in this activity have concentrated in Central and Eastern Patna (Fig.23). This is obviously due to the concentration of city's commercial activities in these zones. Since the Western Zone is pronounced in administrative activities, it has a very small percentage of working force engaged in commercial activities.

Similar is the case with industrial workers who amount to 15.87 per cent of the total workers. They are also concentrated in Central and Eastern Patna but more in Eastern Patna. Eastern Patna has a larger number of small and medium industries than Central Patna and hence the difference in the concentration of industrial workers (Fig.24).

Workers engaged in transport and communication form 8.79 per cent of the total workers. It is evident from Fig. 25 that there are four pockets of concentration and the most important one is Gandhi Maidan in Central Patna. It has the largest Bus Stand and Scooter Stand of the city.

The percentage of workers engaged in construction is 3.38 per cent of the total workers. Fig. 26 shows that the major concentration of such workers lies in Western Patna followed by Southern Patna. This is because several new colonies are coming up in both these parts of the city giving way to innumerable building and construction activities. Eastern Patna is the oldest and an already built-up part of the city and has very little space left. Thus, the number of construction workers is small here.

It is expected that with the growth of population during 1971 - 81

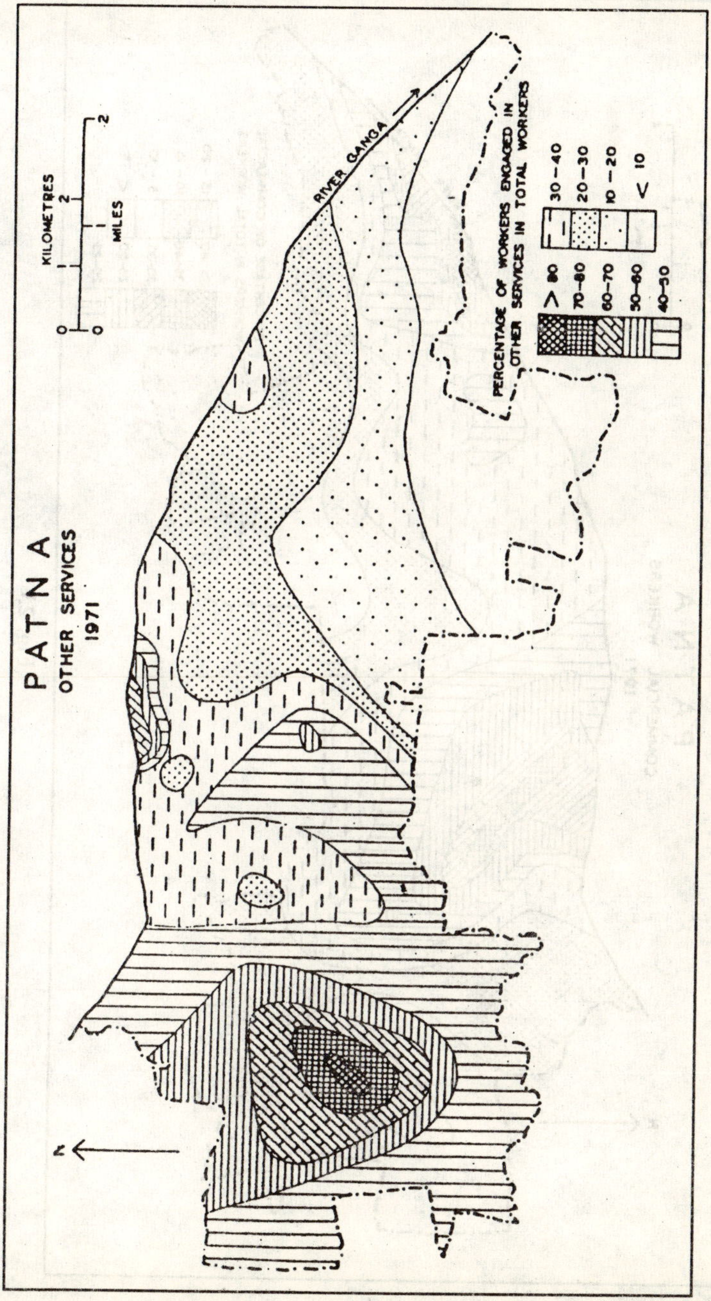
PATNA
OTHER SERVICES
1971
KILOMETRES
0 1 2
0 1 2
MILES
N
RIVER GANGA
PERCENTAGE OF WORKERS ENGAGED IN
OTHER SERVICES IN TOTAL WORKERS
> 80
70–80
60–70
50–60
40–50
30–40
20–30
10–20
< 10

Fig. 22

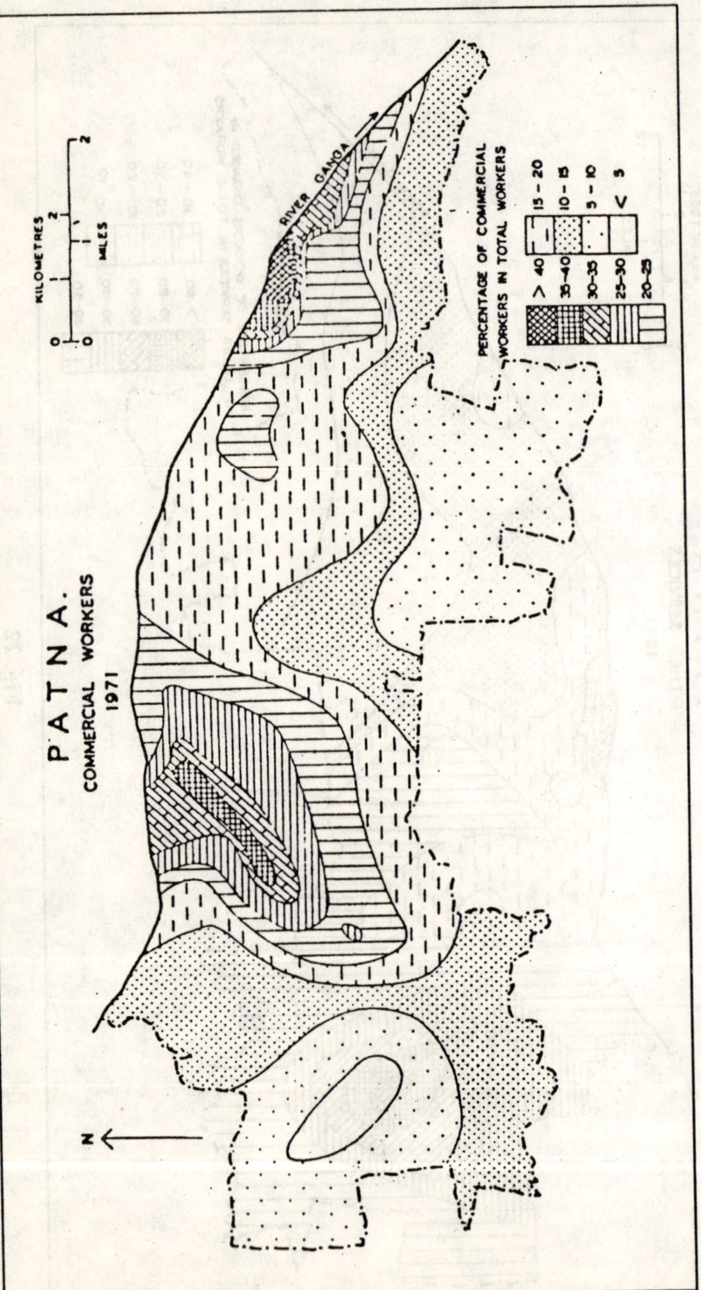
PATNA.
COMMERCIAL WORKERS
1971
KILOMETRES
0 1 2
0 1 2
MILES
RIVER GANGA
PERCENTAGE OF COMMERCIAL WORKERS IN TOTAL WORKERS
> 40
35–40
30–35
25–30
20–25
15 – 20
10 – 15
5 – 10
< 5
N

Fig. 23

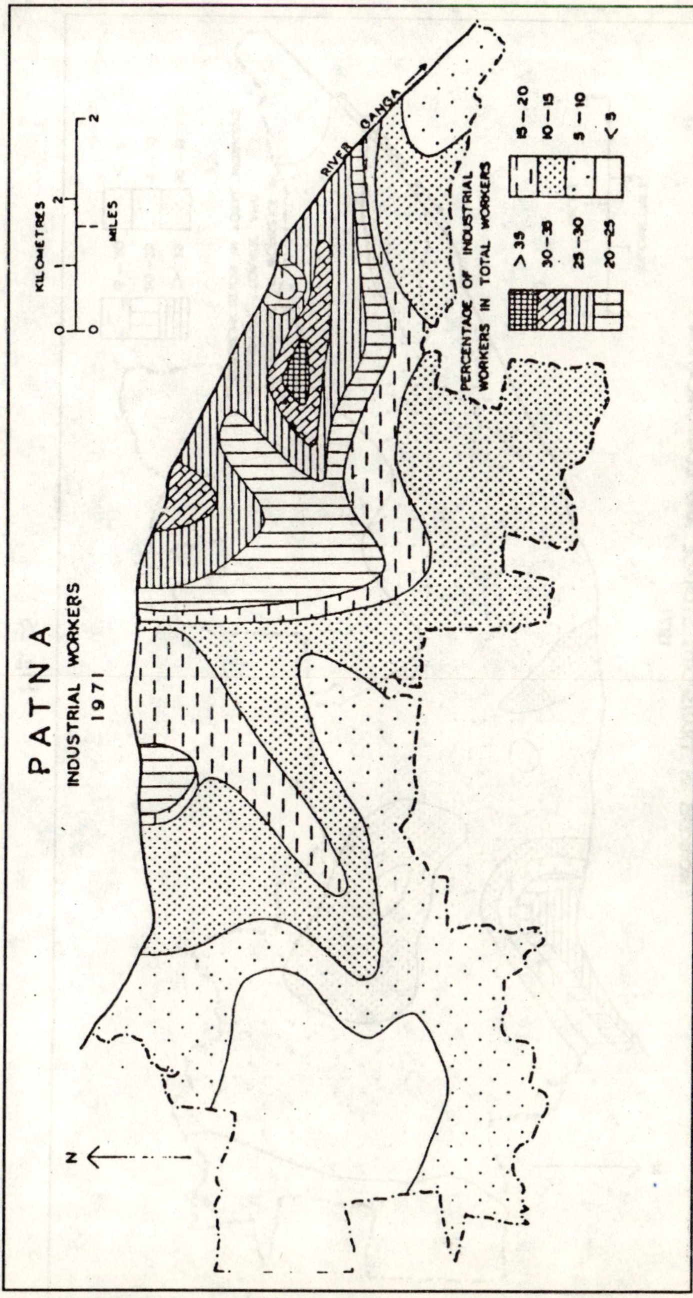
PATNA
INDUSTRIAL WORKERS
1971
KILOMETRES
0 1 2
MILES
0 1 2
N
RIVER GANGA
PERCENTAGE OF INDUSTRIAL WORKERS IN TOTAL WORKERS
> 35
30–35
25–30
20–25
15–20
10–15
5–10
< 5

Fig. 24

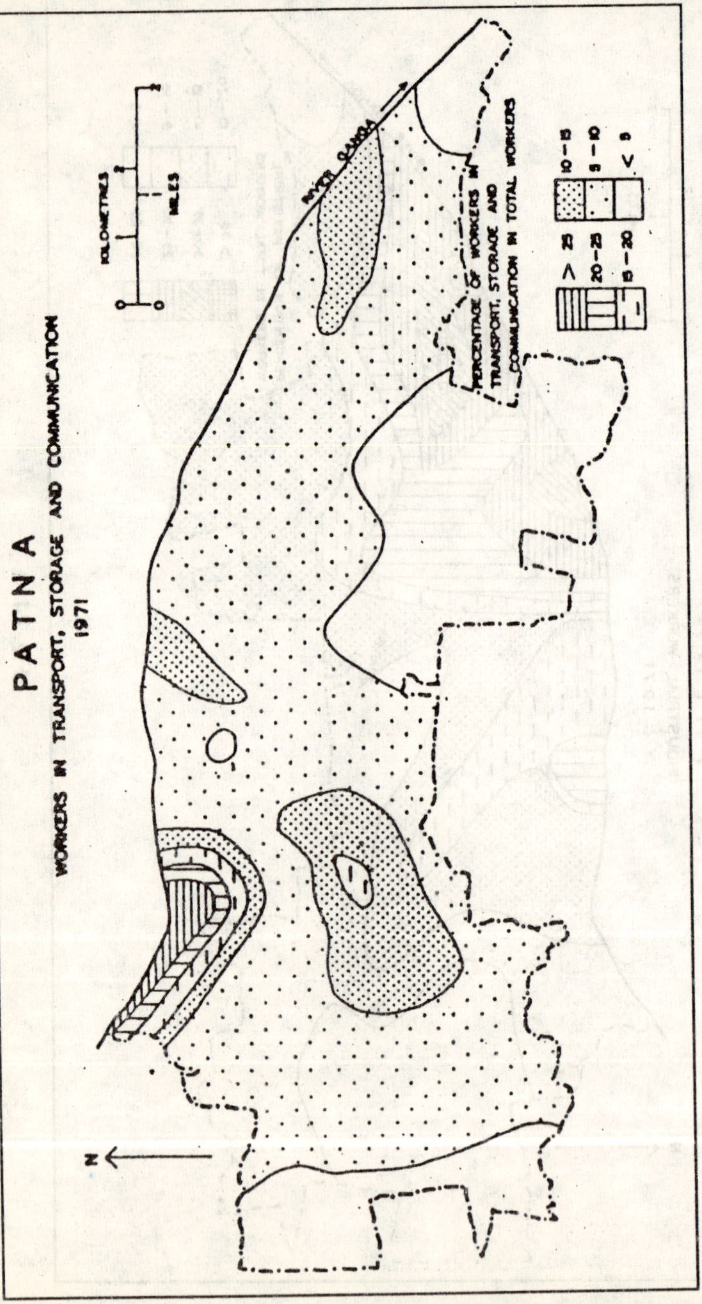
P A T N A
WORKERS IN TRANSPORT, STORAGE AND COMMUNICATION
1971
KILOMETRES
MILES
RIVER GANGA
N
PERCENTAGE OF WORKERS IN TRANSPORT, STORAGE AND COMMUNICATION IN TOTAL WORKERS
> 25
20 – 25
15 – 20
10 – 15
5 – 10
< 5

Fig. 25

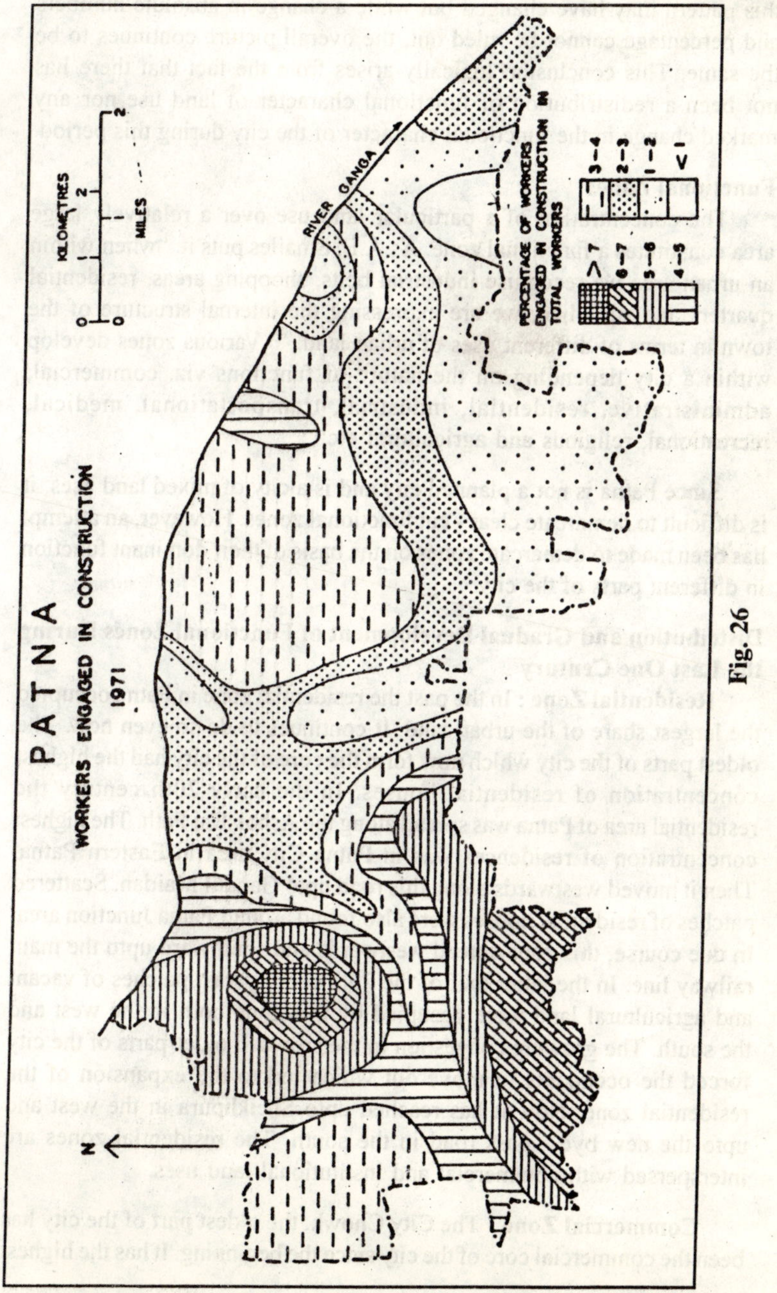
PATNA
WORKERS ENGAGED IN CONSTRUCTION
1971
KILOMETRES
0
2
MILES
0
2
RIVER GANGA
PERCENTAGE OF WORKERS ENGAGED IN CONSTRUCTION TO TOTAL WORKERS
>7
6–7
5–6
4–5
3–4
2–3
1–2
<1
N

Fig. 26

this pattern may have changed but while a change in absolute numbers and percentage cannot be ruled out, the overall picture continues to be the same. This conclusion logically arises from the fact that there has not been a redistribution of functional character of land use nor any marked change in the functional character of the city during this period.

Functional Zones

The concentration of a particular land use over a relatively large area constitutes a functional zone. As A.E. Smailes puts it, "when within an urban area we recognise industrial belts, shopping areas, residential quarters and such like, we are expressing the internal structure of the town in terms of different uses of urban land. "[3] Various zones develop within a city depending on the nature of functions viz. commercial, administrative, residential, industrial, transportational, medical, recreational, religious and agricultural etc.

Since Patna is not a planned city and is a city of mixed land uses, it is difficult to demarcate clear - cut functional zones. However, an attempt has been made to demarcate zones on the basis of their dominant function in different parts of the city.

Distribution and Gradual Development of Functional Zones During the Last One Century

Residential Zone : In the past the residential zone in Patna occupied the largest share of the urban land. It continues to do so even now. The oldest parts of the city which now form the core of the city had the highest concentration of residential houses. In the early 20th century the residential area of Patna was spread along the Ashok Raj Path. The highest concentration of residences was in Patna City area in Eastern Patna. Then it moved westwards along this road upto Gandhi Maidan. Scattered patches of residential houses were also found around Patna Junction area. In due course, this zone spread westwards and southward upto the main railway line. In the latter half of the 20th century vast patches of vacant and agricultural land were occupied by this zone both in the west and the south. The growing congestion in the crowded older parts of the city forced the occupants to move out which led to the expansion of the residential zone. Now it has reached upto Sheikhpura in the west and upto the new bye - pass road in the south. The residential zones are interspersed with commercial and institutional land uses.

Commercial Zone : The City Chowk, the oldest part of the city has been the commercial core of the city since the beginning. It has the highest concentration of trade and commerce. From here, the commercial activities spread along the main road, Ashok Raj Path right upto Gandhi Maidan. In Central Patna the shops are aligned along the southern flank of the main road, and spread along adjoining roads such as Bari Road. The entire commercial zone appears like a narrow ribbon. This has been possible only because the shops have followed all the major routes within the city. Gradually the commercial activities extended right upto Mithapur covering Fraser Road, Dak Bungalow Road, Station Road etc. This feature is largely a post - independence development. At present, patches of commercial activities are seen around the cross roads of Boring Road and Boring Canal Road, and also around Raja bazar on Bailey road in western Patna, along old Bye - Pass Road in Southern Patna and in various other small areas of Patna.

Administrative Zone : Patna is an ancient city and throughout its life it has housed different types of administrative centres. When the new Province of Bihar and Orissa was formed in 1911 - 12, Patna became the Provincial Capital. Henceforth, a new Capital City was laid out in the west towards the west of Patna Gaya Road (Budha Marg) to house the Raj Bhavan, the Secretariat, the Council Chambers, the High Court and the residences of Ministers, Judges and other officials. This part was then outside the Municipal limit of the city. It can be seen in Fig. 27. As time passed, the Municipal limit was extended westwards and took within its boundaries all administrative functions. So the administrative zone is centred in Western Patna. During the post - independence period, governmental activities have increased rapidly and so have its administrative machineries. Now, the administrative zone extends upto Gandhi Maidan where the Collectorate, Civil Court etc. are located.

Institutional : The establishment of Patna University in 1917 created a cultural focus in the city. It is located in the central part of the city. It is the oldest and the most important academic and research institution in the State. It has a beautiful site being located to the north of the Ashok Raj Path along the Ganga. This zone extends from Ranighat in the east to the Bankipore Club in the west. This zone also has Patna's largest hospital, Patna Medical College Hospital and the Tuberculosis Centre near Sabzibagh. A few other institutions lie scattered in other parts of the city away from this zone.

These are the major functional zones of the city. The city does have other functions as well but they do not form compact zones. Fig. 27 shows the major functional zones in 1951 and 1981.

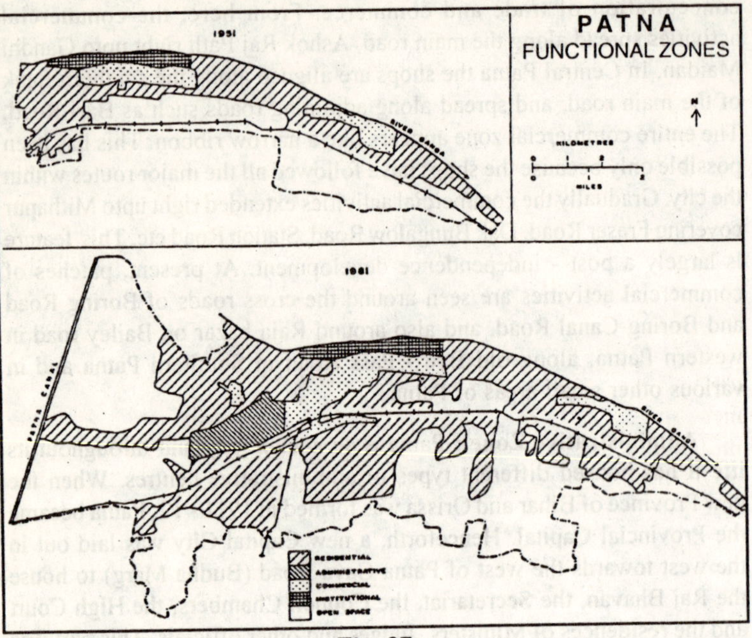

Fig. 27

Present Distributional Pattern of Functional Zones

1. Residential Zone : To quote Bartholomew, "More land of the urban area in general, is devoted to residential use than to any other use".[4] And it is, in fact, the most significant land use in Patna. The share of residential area in total area is 35.52 per cent in Patna. The higher percentage of residential use indicates the age of the city, i.e. the higher the percentage of residential use the older is the city.

The influence of urban activities on the social and economic structure of the city has led to the development of different types of residential areas indicating different levels of development with time. This is true of all the cities because the development of residential areas is not sudden, rather it is historic. The residential areas of Patna may be classified into 3 major categories based on their character, differences in land values, density of houses, types of houses and the amount of urban facilities available.

(a) Lower Class Residential Areas : The lower class residential areas surround the three commercial nuclei of the city. They are mohallas of Yarpur, Jakkanpur, Mithapur and Dujra in Western Patna and a vast stretch of area between Musallahpur Hat and 'Purab Darwaza' in Eastern Patna. All these areas have poor living conditions. The houses are brick built and are congested and cramped having no way for sunshine and ventilation especially on the ground floors.Most of them are damp, dark and unsuitable for human living. Tremendous increase in population and increasing demand for land in these areas have led to the vertical expansion of the buildings leading to multi storeyed houses. These buildings beaded along the roads and streets of the city are not completely residential, as the ground floor and sometimes even the first floor are given to shops and commercial activities and offices. Purely residential areas lies just behind commercial- cum - residential areas. There is a dearth of adequate parks, playgrounds and open spaces. Rapid urbanization, tremendous growth of population and unhealthy and uncontrolled construction activity have converted most of these areas into slums. The houses are old and dilapidated and density of population in these areas is very high. All these are very much indicative of the fact that these areas belong to Older Patna.[5]

(b) Upper Class Residential Areas : The upper class residential areas have mainly sprung up in the Western Patna after 1911. They house the industrialists and businessmen as well as as doctors, government officers, lawyers and educationists. Apart from British built quarters several new posh colonies have developed and are coming up in Western Patna. A few like Rajbanshi Nagar, Srikrishnapuri, Patel Nagar, Shashtri Nagar etc. may be mentioned. The Pataliputra Housing Colony also is of this category but lies just outside the municipal borders. In Central and Southern Patna too, there are colonies of upper class people such as Rajendra Nagar and in some parts of Kankerbagh in South Patna, e.g. Doctors' Colony.

These have developed away from the congested parts of the city. The houses are well planned, having enough space for proper sunshine and ventialation. They are mostly single or double storied and are built quite apart from each other with large green lawns or gardens in front. These areas are devoid of congestion and insanitary conditions. The density of population is low as compared to lower class residential areas.

(c) Middle Class Residential Areas : There is no demarcation line for these areas because they are found throughout the city. However, most of such areas are located in Central and Southern Patna. Kadamkuan and Pirmohani in Central Patna have living conditions similar to those of lower class residential areas. However, colonies in Southern Patna namely Patrakarnagar, Lohianagar, Hanuman Nagar and Chitragupta Nagar etc. have living conditions similar to the upper class residential areas though not upto that standard. The density of population is moderate in the localities of Southern Patna but is very dense in parts of Central Patna.

The population of the city is growing and spreading out towards the outskirts both to the west and to the south and so are the residential areas. However, ample space still exists for future expansion in these two directions.

2. Commercial Zone : The Commercial Zone of the city has been divided into four categories on the basis of land value, location, nature of business centres and their concentration etc. The land under commercial use of the city is 5.43 per cent.

(a) Chief Market Cores : Patna has three most important market nuclei namely, City Chowk in Eastern Patna, Muradpur in Central Patna and Mithapur plus New Market Area in Western Patna. The City Chowk excels in wholesale and extends upto Maroofganj wholesale grain market in the east. The other two are retail trade centres. Of these, Muradpur area forms the present CBD of Patna. It is extending towards South - west now. All these areas are characterized by relatively high buildings, high land values and maximum concentration of day time population and traffic. The shops are small so as to bring maximum return from the land. They deal both in consumer as well as shopping goods.[6]

(b) Local Retail Business Areas : The important and busiest retail shopping areas in Patna are aligned along the Ashok Raj Path in Central and Eastern Patna right from Simli Bazar in the east to Gandhi Maidan in the west with, of course, intermittent breaks. Thus commercial centres can be seen along all major road junctions of the city.

(c) Wholesale and Specialized Business Areas : These are located in Eastern as well as in Western Patna. Maroofganj and Mansoorganj are reputed for wholesale grain markets; Musallahpur Hat and Gulzarbagh-Kushwah Hat for wholesale and retail vegetable markets; Bazar Samiti for wholesale fruits, fish and vegetable market; the areas to the south of Ashok Raj Path, opposite Patna University for book stalls; areas opposite Patna Medical College Hospital for medical stores; Exhibition road for hardware stores; Nala road for furniture and Kankerbagh Road for motor parts.

(d) Shopping Ribbons : The development of shops along the chief transport lines form shopping ribbons. Patna being a linear city, presents a very good example of this kind of development. Almost along every road, street, lane and bye - lane of Patna retail business is carried on, forming ribbons. They include Gandhi Maidan Road, Exhibition Road, Dak Bungalow Road, Frazer Road and Station Road etc. These commercial areas have developed adjacent to residential areas in order to fulfill the basic requirements of the residents.

Apart from the above categories there are various small business establishments such as restaurants, betel shops, tea stalls, fruit shops, snack bars etc. which have developed along some of the busy streets and lanes which cater to the needs of floating population.[7]

3. Administrative Zone : This zone occupies 1.16 per cent of the total land of Patna. Patna as a capital city and headquarters of divisional and district administration houses many government offices. The Old and New Secretariats, Raj Bhawan, High Court and Assembly form the hub of the state Government offices located in Western Patna. Many of the Government Offices are scattered over several other places in private rented buildings in the Western as well as other zones of the city.

The second major concentration of government offices is in the Central Zone where the Divisional Offices, the Collectorate and the District Courts are located west and north of Gandhi Maidan. The District Courts are situated on the bank of River Ganga, to the west of General Hospital.

The third concentration is formed by subdivisional courts and jail in East Patna at Gulzarbagh. Various other government offices are scattered all over the city viz. the Municipal Corporation offices in Eastern, Western and Central Patna, Gulzarbagh Press in Eastern Patna and the Bankipore Central Jail near Patna Railway Junction in Western Patna.

The growing requirements of these buildings completely rule out the feasibility of their further expansion because of their being located in densely built - up areas. Hence, in order to facilitate smooth functioning of the civic administration as well as to establish co - ordination between local administration and the government organization it is essential that a new location preferably in Central or Southern Patna should be specifically developed for this purpose.

4. Institutional Zone : About 3.26 per cent of the total land is given to institutional purposes. This zone comprises education and medical activities. It would be better if each of these is studied separately.

(a) Educational Zone : Recognized schools though few in number are located in all the four zones of the city in densely populated areas. However, this shortage has led to a mushroom growth of hundreds of private schools practically on all roads throughout the city especially in residential areas.

Patna University, the oldest in Bihar, is located in Central Zone to the north of Ashok Raj Path along the Ganga, Although having a favourable location, the congestion around it breaks the calm and pleasant atmosphere of the campus. Out of he total ten constituent colleges of the University, six namely, Patna College, Science College, Engineering College, Law College, Medical College and B.N. College are located in one compact educational campus. Only Patna Women's College lies in the Western Zone. Magadha Mahila and Womens's Training College form another group to the north of Gandhi Maidan.

In addition to these Colleges, there are a number of colleges either belonging to or affiliated to Magadh University or are Government colleges. To name a few, Bihar Veterinary College and A.N. College in Western Patna; Commerce College and Nalanda Medical College in Southern Patna; Tibia College and Ayurvedic College and Madarsa Shamshal Hoda in Central Patna; and Oriental College and G.S. College in Eastern Patna may be mentioned. Not only there is a need for more schools and colleges to cope with the ever increasing number of student population but also there is need for basic requirements regarding play - grounds, game facilities and building accommodation.

There are four good public libraries in Patna namely Sinha Library in Western Patna, British Council and Khuda Baksh Library in Central Patna and Bihar Hitaishi Pustakalaya in Eastern Patna.

Besides there are a few technical institutions such as Industrial Training Institute and a few research institutes such as A.N. Sinha Institute, Indira Gandhi Institute of Medical Science and L.N. Mishra Institute for Socio - Economic Development located in various parts of the city. None of these forms any compact functional zone.

(b) Medical Zone : There are four general hospitals in the city located in the four different zones. They are Patna City General Hospital in Eastern Patna, Nalanda Medical College Hospital in Southern Patna, Patna Medical College Hospital in Central Patna and Kurjee Holy Family

Hospital in Western Patna. The T.B. Centre is also located to the west of Patna Medical College Hospital. Patna Medical College Hospital is located in the most densely populated part of the city and covers a vast area. Its northern flank has a very good view of the Ganga but its southern flank being right on the Ashok Raj Path the business route in the city, is always in midst of city's noise and bustle, thus losing the tranquil atmosphere which is very essential for any hospital's location. Just opposite of this Main Hospital, various arterial roads running north-south and joining Bari Road with Ashok Raj Path are full of medical shops.

Apart from these, there are three major hospitals namely Tripolia Hospital, Rajendra Nagar Hospital and Gardanibagh Hospital. Besides, there are a host of dispensaries, private nursing homes and clinics spread all over the city but their biggest concentration is in the Central Zone.

Apart from educational and medical zones the institutional zone also includes religious and cultural activities. Patna does have a host of religious and cultural organizations but one of them forms a distinct zone. Among these Patna's Harmandir, Bari Pattan Devi, Pathar Ki Masjid and Patna Museum are worth mentioning.

5. Transport Zone : Patna has two well developed transport nodes. One is around Gandhi Maidan where both bus and scooter stands are located and a large number of roads converge. The second is around Patna Railway Junction where a bus stand is also located. Several smaller nodes also exist in the city, such as around Paschim Darwaza and at Agam Kaun and a newly constructed bus stand near Hardinge Park in Western Patna.

The area given to transportational purposes is around 12.5 per cent of the total area. It has been observed that the older parts of the city have narrow, zig - zag and winding streets whereas the newer parts have well laid out wide roads.

6. Recreational Zone : In any urban centre open space is essential for recreational purposes as well as for a better living. Its dearth leads to the vertical expansion of the city creating many problems. Although Patna has large areas in its western and southern parts given to agriculture yet there is a general shortage of parks and playgrounds in the city. The area covered by open space is 40.83 per cent of the total land. There are four large open spaces for public use covering about 115 acres of land. The Gandhi Maidan in Central Patna is the largest and is mainly used for public meetings and games and sports. The second is the Moinul Haque

Stadium at Rajendra Nagar used for organised games. The next is Saheed Park in Western Patna situated near the General Post Office. The fourth one is the Mangles Tank Park in Eastern Patna. The newer residential colonies do have parks within them but they are actually used for animal grazing and for the people defecating in them. They exhibit most unhealthy and unhygenic conditions and can be better termed as waste lands.

There are a few other recreational centres such as cinema halls and clubs. There are thirteen cinema halls and two clubs at Patna. The most important recreational centre is in Western Patna - the Sanjay Gandhi Jaivik Udyan. It has both botanical and zoological gardens. The other important centre is Kumhrar in Southern Patna.

There are a number of other recreational centres namely, Ravindra Bhawan, Bhartiya Nritya Kala Mandir, Sri Krishna Memorial Hall and Indian Medical Association Hall where dramas in various languages and musical programmes are organized, Shrikrishna Vigyana Kendra - small centre for science education; Bankipore club and new Patna Club for public use and Lala Lajpat Rai Hall for public functions are notable centres. None of these forms any zone.

7. Industrial Zone : Patna does not have any large scale industry. However some medium and small engineering workshops are located in the Industrial Estate[8] and along Exhibition Road, Bari Path, Frazer Road and Budh Marg. Other important factories are Shree Madho Bihari Grain Mills at Maroofganj, Pradeep Lamp Works at Begumpur (both in Eastern Patna) and Bhanamla Iron Works at Mithapur in Western Patna. Brick manufacturing is carried on towards the east and the west of the city along the Ganga.

After analysing all functional zones of the city, it becomes apparent that although the residential zone occupies a major part of the total land which is true of all the cities, the most important function of Patna is administration followed by trade and commerce. So, Patna may be termed as an administrative - cum - commercial city.

A map has been prepared (Fig. 28) to show the locations of important functional centres, the list of which can be seen in Appendix no. XIII.

Interzonal Relationships

The spatial pattern of population distribution in a city is necessary for land use planning. The information regarding this would help in providing community facilities and amenities in different localities and facilitate the allocation of land to different uses.

Patna is an administrative - cum - commercial city. Hence the pattern and growth of population is well reflected in administrative and commercial zones of the city. The whole city has experienced growth and expansion of its population. However, population has mainly grown in parts of Western Patna north of Bailey road and in Southern Patna at Kankerbagh. This growth may be ascribed to the increased building activities in these areas which are the outcome of the ever increasing administrative activities (Western Patna) and commercial activities along Kankarbagh Road.

The commercial - cum - residential zone of the city spread mainly over Central and Eastern Patna is the most congested part of the city. Eastern Patna in particular which is the oldest settled part is over - saturated with people. Not a single inch of land is left vacant in this zone. Lack of space has forced the people to construct double or triple storeyed houses. The houses are so closely built that they do not provide room for proper ventialation and sunshine. City's worst slums have developed in Eastern Patna. The over - crowding and improper distribution of population are apparent in eastern part of the city even though civic amenities are not available in a proper manner. Overcrowding and unbalanced population distribution is also seen in Central Patna but it is slightly better than in the Eastern. This congestion may be due to various factors such as proximity to the place of work, high land and rental values, poor transport facility and social factors such as community or kinship etc.

The distribution of population is much better in the administrative zone of the city lying mainly in Western Patna. This area has been well planned as compared to other parts of the city which are totally unplanned. The Circuit House, M.L.A. Flats, G.P.O., High Court, several quarters and bungalows for Ministers and government officers and the houses of upper class people are located in this zone. This entire belt in Western Patna gives shelter to a fair amount of population engaged in public administration and various other professions. Besides several residential colonies have sprung up in this part of Patna to accommodate surplus population comprising both migrant and permanent populations.

Southern Patna lying to the south of the main railway line and stretching from Budha Marg in the west to the approach road of Mahatma Gandhi Setu in the east has the largest residential zone. The entire area is given to residential uses with only small patches of land devoted to

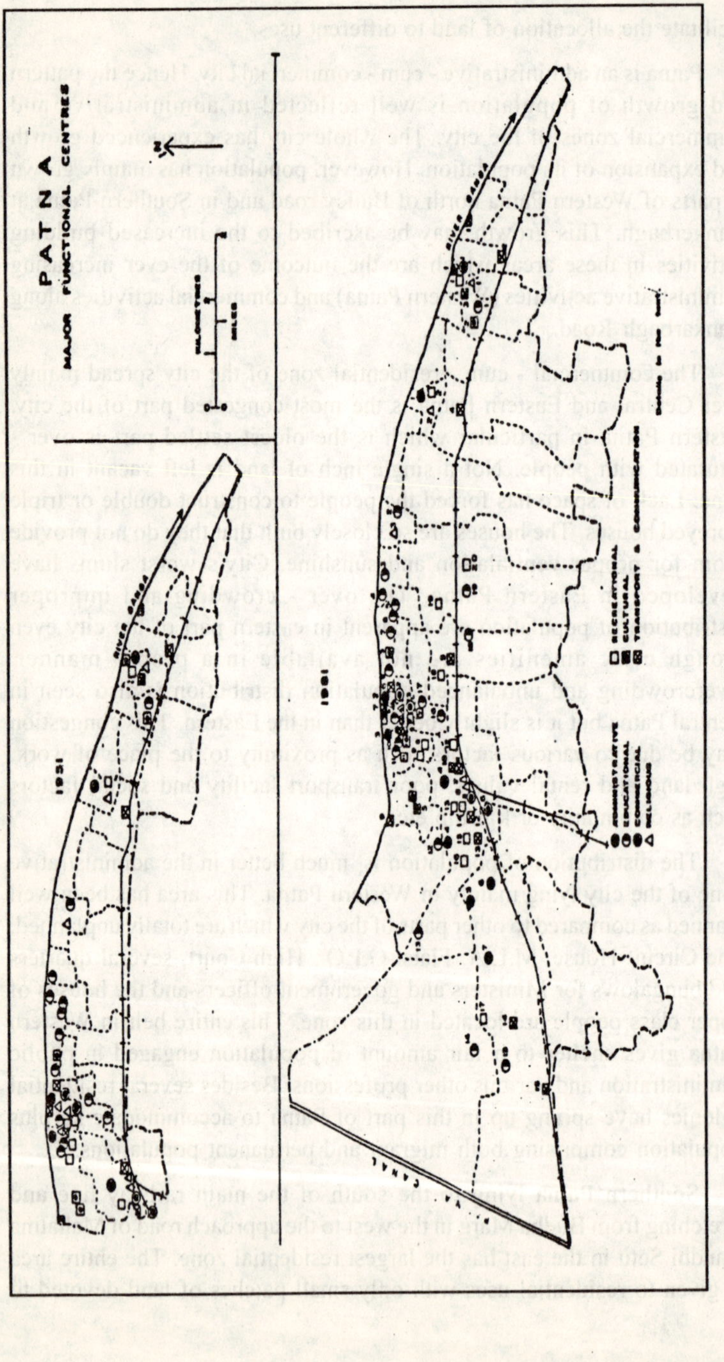

Fig. 28

other uses. Small belts of commercial activity are seen on either side of old bye - pass road and that, too, for a short distance. This zone has spread as far as the new bye - pass road in the south and in the next few years is expected to extend beyond this road. Numerous colonies have been developed and many others are coming up very fast. Although this zone is not very well planned but it is good in the sense that congestion - 'an urban disease' has not been able to breed in so far. This has been possible only because of the availability of large tracts of vacant and agricultural lands now being occupied steadily by residences.

However, it is expected that in the coming years this whole area too will become saturated with houses and people. Still the density of population will continue to be high in the commercial and administrative zones of the city. The construction of Mahatma Gandhi Setu in Eastern Patna is expected to attract a large number of business men and people belonging to other professions to settle in this area. The flood protected areas lying to the south of the railway line will provide space to immigrants and new settlers. Due to the construction of the bridge the land value is also increasing steadily.

References :

1. Chapin,, F. S. (1957) : Urban Land Use Planning, Harper and Brothers, New York, p.3.
2. Ataullah; Md. (1976) : Urban Land Use in Major Towns Along the Ganga in Bihar, Unpublished Ph.D. Thesis, Patna University, p. 93.
3. Smailes, A. E. : op.cit., p.84.
4. Bartholomew, H. and Jackwood (1955) : Land Uses in American Cities, Cambridge, p. 26.
5. Sinha, S. (1981) : Patna : A Study in Urban Renewal and Reconstruction, unpublished Ph. D. Thesis, Patna University, Patna.
6. Sami, A. (1973) : Trend and Growth of Commercial Land Use, Indian Geographical Studies, Research Bulletin No. 5.
7. Dayal, P. and Thakur, B. (1976) : "Commercial Ribbons in Patna : Spatial growth and Functional Structure", National Geographical Journal of India, Vol.22, pp. 166-77.
8. The Industrial Estate is in Pataliputra Housing Colony which is just outside the Municipal Boundary of the city and not in the study area. Even then this colony is very much a part of the urban life in Patna.

5

Urban Development

A modern city is basically an economic entity. It is both an agent as well as instrument of economic growth which transcends physical boundaries and grows under the dual forces of concentration and dispersal. In modern times, a sound economic base is extremely essential for the sustenance of a city. This base is mostly derived from the countryside either in the form of agricultural goods or industrial raw materials. As such a city is not an independent entity in itself, it has to depend on its countryside for its sustenance and growth. In turn the city exercises some kind of 'pull' on its surrounding areas. It has been rightly said that "Cities do not grow of themselves, but countrysides set them up to do tasks that must be performed in central places ".[1] Again as Dickinson[2] puts it " the support of a city depends upon the services it performs not for itself, but for a tributary area". If, however, the countryside is not sound either economically or physically, the situation will not be healthy either for the city or the countryside itself.

It is now being increasingly realized the world over that an economic as well as spatial balance should be created between urban places and their countrysides. Each has to be a viable unit for human habitation within the scope of their resources. This objective, however, cannot be achieved by planning the urban areas in isolation. So, it is essential that a larger area having social and economic interaction and interdependence around the parent city has to be taken as one unit for planning to the extent that the concentration of economic activity is in the parent city which has tremendous potential for advancement of the regional economy and it should not impoverish the hinterland rather diffuse its beneficial effects into the economy of the region. To be precise, urban planning must take into account regional factors.

As such it becomes the first priority for the development of Patna that its entire hinterland be planned and strategy for its development be evolved. For this the influence region of the city and the development of the city must be thought of in consonance with the development of the region.

Patna as a Regional Capital

As the capital of the State of Bihar, Patna enjoys its own regional significance. Being the headquarters of district, divisional and state administration, it acts as an administrative focus for the entire State. The city has a deep association with its hinterland socially, economically, culturally and politically. The hinterland of Patna here, has been delineated by incorporating those places surrounding Patna which can be travelled in an hour irrespective of the distance travelled. So time and accessibility are important parameters for determining the hinterland of Patna (Fig. 29). Thus towns which are covered within this limitation are Hajipur, Sonepur and Dighwara in the north across the Ganga, Fatwa in the east, Marsaurhi in the South, and Dinapur Nizamat, Dinapur Cantonment, Khagaul and Maner in the west. Digha - Mainpura, Pataliputra Housing Colony in the north - west and Phulwari Notified Area Committee in the south - west are out-growths of Patna and form parts of the Patna Urban Agglomeration (Census of India, 1981). Of

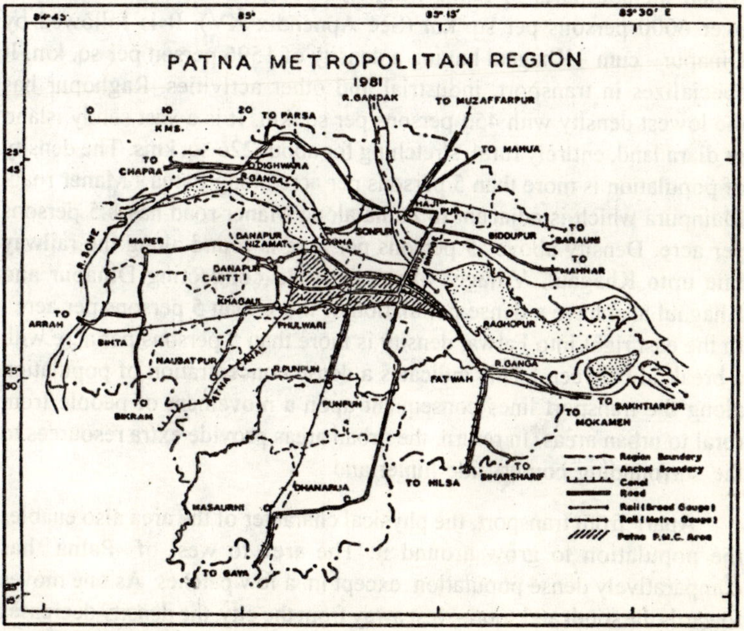

Fig. 29

these Hajipur and Dinapur Nizamat are class II towns having a population of more than 50,000 persons, Sonepur, Khagual, Masaurhi, Dinapur Cantonment and Fatwa belong to Class III towns having a population between 20,000 and 49,999 and Maner and Dighwara fall in the category of class IV towns having a population slightly less than 20,000.

All these towns are distributed among 16 anchals or blocks that come under the hinterland of Patna. They are Patna Rural A and B, Fatwa, Phulwari, Punpun, Dhanarua, Masaurhi, Danapur - cum - Khagaul, Naubatpur, Bihta, Maner, Hajipur, Bidupur, Raghopur, Dighwara and Sonepur. There are 35 villages distributed among these anchals, each having a population of more then 5,000 persons but which have not been considered towns in 1981 Census because three - fourths of their population are engaged in agricultural pursuits (See Appendix No. XV). Dhanarua is the only anchal which is devoid of any such village. This suggests that although the hinterland of Patna is densely settled with many large villages, it is predominantly agricultural.

The density of population is highest in Patna Rural A and B anchals which include parts of Patna Municipal Corporation. This density is over 6000 persons per sq. km (See Appendix XV). It is followed by Dinapur - cum - Khagaul having a density of 1596 person per sq. km. It specializes in transport, industrial and other activities. Raghopur has the lowest density with 453 persons per sq. km. It is a vast sandy island or diara land, entirely rural, stretching for about 226 sq. kms. The density of population is more than 5 persons per acre along Patna - Maner road. Mainpura which is adjacent to Patna along Maner road has 8.5 persons per acre. Density above 5 persons per acre is found along the railway line upto Khagaul. Villages along the road connecting Dinapur and Khagaul also have a dense population of more than 5 persons per acre . In the east right into Fatwa, density is more than 5 persons per acre with a break in between.[3] This indicates a dense concentration of population along the transport lines consequent upon a movement of people from rural to urban areas. In return, the urban areas provide extra resources to the surrounding countryside hinterland.

Apart from transport, the physical character of the area also enables the population to grow around it. The area to west of Patna has comparatively dense population except in a few patches. As one moves towards the south and south-west away from the city, the density decreases gradually because the area is increasingly lowlying and subject to floods from the Punpun river.

The land use of the city's hinterland is primarily agricultural. It is remarkable that the region is pre-eminently rural in character and agriculture remains the mainstay of the people besides having a dominating influence on the regional economy. The hinterland of Patna lacking in minerals and basic industrial resources further confirms that the great bulk of rural folk will cling to the soil.

Table No. 2 makes clear that around 59 percent of the total hinterland is net sown. The land use data for 2 anchals viz, Dhanarua and Fatwa were not available and so the total area for the hinterland in this case has been calculated excluding these 2 anchals and the percentage for each land use category has been calculated accordingly.

Waste land and land given to non-agricultural use account for 16 per cent each. 7 per cent of the total area remains fallow and 3 per cent is given to pasture and orchards. Phulwari has the highest percentage of N.S.A. (88.5%), Masaurhi, Punpun and Nubatpur also have more than 80 % of N.S.A. Patna Rural A and B have low percentage of N.S.A. because most of their area is given to non-agricultural use. N.S.A. in Raghopur and Maner is also low because a large part of their area is sandy waste which is submerged by the Ganga every year.

The land around Patna is given to the cultivation of various vegetables, foodgrains and fodder for animals. Patna is dependent on its hinterland for its requiredments for these perishable goods and as such there is regular exchange of various commodities which makes Patna an important centre for trade and commerce in the region. With the availability of electricity in the rural areas the progressive farmers have installed tubewells to insure intensive cultivation throughout the year. The use of better seeds and fertilizers also adds to crop yields. At places tractors have replaced wooden ploughs. The most important cash crop of the region is potato. The development of cold storage in various parts of the hinterland has intensified the business in vegetables.

The diara lands to the north and the north - east of the city are very fertile in the sense that after the floods, these lands are left covered with silt which produces magnificent crops. Both Bhadai and Rabi crops are grown yielding excellent harvests. In between, cash crops such as vegetables, watermelons, cucumbers etc. are grown. Parts of these diara lands which are not covered by flood water remain sandy and barren.

Patna is well connected with the region by different means of transportation. It is one of the important railway junctions of Eastern

Table 2
Patna Metropolitan Region : Land Use, 1981

Name of the Achal	Total	Waste land	Non-Agricultural land	Pasture & Orchard	Fallow land	N.S.A.
1. Patna Rural	33616	-	17356.4	453.8	5647.1	10158.7
A & B %		-	51.6	1.4	16.8	30.2
2. Phulwari	45532	-	5102.2	-	141.4	40288.4
%		-	11.2	-	0.37	88.5
3. Masaurhi	50110.9	-	9141.0	20.2	240.0	40709.7
%		-	18.2	0.1	0.5	81.2
4. Dhanarua	-	-	-	-	-	-
%	-	-	-	-	-	-
5. Punpun	31795.1	-	4553.3	13.7	1614.3	25613.8
%		-	14.3	0.1	5.1	80.5
6. Maner	43552.9	15290.5	3589.4	4301.7	8400.8	11970.5
%		35.1	8.2	9.9	19.3	27.5
7. Danpur-cum-Khagaul	32890.3	1907.37	3889.0	5246.2	2052.0	19795.8
%		6.8	13.8	1.9	1.3	70.2

8.	Naubatpur	41901.0	-	4596.4	66.7	2190.5	35047.4
	%	-	-	11.0	0.2	5.2	83.6
9.	Bihta	47389.6	68.1	9404.2	362.5	1865.8	35689.0
	%	-	0.1	19.8	0.8	3.9	75.4
10.	Fatwa	-	-	-	-	-	-
	%	-	-	-	-	-	-
11.	Raghopur	65782.3	42046.5	3803.0	-	-	-
	%		63.9	5.8	-	-	-
12.	Bidupur	28599.5	5419.4	3785.0	1255.4	379.5	17760.2
	%		18.9	13.2	4.4	103	62.2
13.	Hajipur	38760.5	1756.1	10781.0	1303.7	2192.8	22726.9
	%		4.5	27.8	3.4	5.7	58.6
14.	Sonepur	44240.5	9021.6	4916.4	34472.0	9149.0	17706.3
	%	-	20.4	11.0	7.9	20.7	40.00
15.	Dighwara	22097.8	6185.8	1962.5	608.7	1740.8	11600.0
	%		28.0	8.9	2.7	7.9	52.5
	Total	525268.4	81695.3	82879.8	10079.8	35164.0	308999.5
	(P.M.R.)		15.52	15.75	3.24	6.77	58.72

India and is a transport node for Chapra, Muzaffarpur, Gaya, Ranchi and Jamshedpur. The main broad gauge railway line of the Eastern Railway which connects Howrah with Delhi runs almost parallel to the Ganga through the southern and central parts of the city. Patna is connected with Gaya and Jehanabad through Patna-Gaya line and also with the industrially rich Chota Nagpur through the South Eastern Railway. Another parallel broad - gauge railway line of North - Eastern Railway runs to the north of Patna across the Ganga. It connects Gorakhpur and Gauhati. Hajipur across the Ganga is linked with Patna through a road bridge. There is a proposal to construct a railway line which will bifurcate from Patna-Gaya line, run parallel to south of Patna/ New Bye-pass road and turn north and again run parallel to Mahatma Gandhi Setu linking Patna with Hajipur.

The city of Patna is also well connected with other cities of Bihar by National and State Highways. The National Highway No. 30 passes through Patna and connects it with Varanasi in the west and Barauni in the east. N.H. 30 meets N.H. 33 at Bakhtiarpur leading to other highways connecting Ranchi, Jamshedpur, Calcutta, Gauhati and Delhi. With the construction of Mahatma Gandhi Setu, Patna has become linked with underdeveloped regions of North Bihar. There are regular bus services plying from Patna to different parts of Bihar in all directions.

Patna has a good aviation service. It is directly connected with Ranchi, Calcutta, Delhi, Lucknow, Gauhati and Kathmandu by air.

As far as communication is concerned Patna has excellent postal services, telegraph, telephone, and teleprinter connections, newspapers and radio and television stations. These have been aided by modern innovations viz. coaxial cables, microwave links, satellite communication etc. Patna is linked with the entire country and abroad through these media. All these have a remarkable bearing on the growth of the city.

Although the city is short of large industries and the pace of industrial development is slow, the region in its immediate vicinity has developed some fairly large industries e.g. Bata Shoe Factory at Digha and Industrial Estate at Pataliputra Colony. This colony is very much a part of Patna, but it has not been incorporated within the Patna Municipal Corporation boundary. There is a huge pipe factory at Phulwari, electric wire and chara machines are manufactured at Khagaul, tiles are manufactured at Maner and Hajipur and there is an Industrial estate at Fatwa. Hajipur also manufactures iron goods. Brick manufacturing at Dhigha and

Sambalpur and several factories at Banka Ghat are notable. All these commodities are fed to the markets at Patna.

Patna, being located in the heart of the agriculturally rich Middle Ganga Plains holds a commanding position in trade of agricultural products. Maroofganj and Mansoorganj are well known wholesale markets in Eastern Patna. Other small marketing centres are at Bihta (rice), Masaurhi and Bakhtiarpur (rice and rabi products), Hajipur (banana, litchi and mango) and Fatwa (rice and milk). Besides Patna also holds a vital position in other services such as health and educational services.

One of the important historical cities of India, Patna has several places of tourist interest around it. To name a few, they are Vaishali, Rajgir, Nalanda, Pawapuri, Gaya, Bodh Gaya and Buxar, all lying within a radius of about 100 kms.

Metropolitan Growth of the City

Within a region one city emerges from the less differentiated groups of villages and country towns. Taking advantage of a strategic location, a larger supply of potable water, a more defensive site, better land for agriculture, easier command of land routes or water routes, a safer harbour - usually with a number of these advantages coming together - one city succeeds in attracting larger number of inhabitants : it becomes the metropolis or "Mother City". In heaping up these advantages, the command of transportation routes probably marks the critical change.[4]

A specialized trade develops with other regions with the surplus of regional products. This brings the necessary food supply to the growing Metropolis along with a host of stimulating goods from other areas. Cross fertilization of culture takes place and gives stimulus to fresh inventions. Long distance trading and administration help it further to grow. A foreign population of traders enter the metropolis. Agriculture tends to become secondary and manufacturing becomes an instrument of trade. Various services tend to bind together the metropolis and the countryside which includes various smaller towns with their own smaller spheres of influence. The potential for metropolitan growth is high in areas characterized by rapid urbanization, high density, large scale rural - urban migration and intense occupational mobility of population.

The city of Patna as its stands today was initially a village on the bank of the Ganga. Later on, people came to realize many advantages offered by the site for carrying on all kinds of economic activities and this has been the principal cause for the growth and expansion for the city. Moreover, it was realized that Patna enjoyed a central position in the Gangetic Plain and commanded a thick population in its neighborhoods. It thus served as a great hinterland. The location of Patna on the bank of Ganga and at a point where the Ganga was joined by a number of major tributaries in its vicinity gave it a unique nodal position. It, thus, became an important transhipping point and a great entrepot. Large amount of commodities that came here were unloaded, stored; marketed and disposed off while others which came here for export were re - loaded and re - shipped. All these combined to give employment to a large number of people leading to a rapid increase in population and development of the city in ancient times.

The nodality of Patna helped to make it an international market place. It served as a permanent market place where trade was conveniently carried on. Gradually, with the growth of city, the trade operations expanded so much so that later, not only goods but 'services' formed part of the manifold economic activities of the people of the city. Thus, people possessing various capabilities immigrated to the city thereby leading to the expansion of the city.

Patna's inland location not only gave advantages of defence and

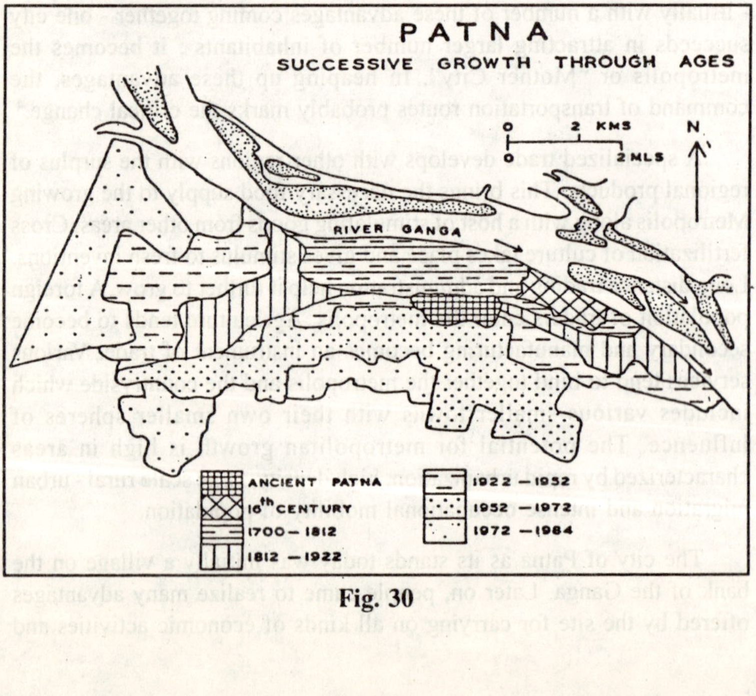

Fig. 30

safety but facilitated it with the convenience of carrying administrative functions and affairs of the government particularly during the medieval times. This in turn, pulled population from the countryside and elsewhere and provided them with employment. With this, the population increased and the city grew. Since independence, Patna has become a multifunctional city with administration, trade and commerce, education and other professional services such as medical and legal services as its principal characteristic (Fig. 30).

All cities have the common function of providing or distributing an array of goods and services to the resident population of that city and to the population of the tributary area. These are functions carried on at centralized locations occurring at local points of the region. There is a spatial relationship between the functional offerings of the local point and their distribution within the tributary area.

Patna acts as a central place within its region. A central place is a locality within which centralized functions are performed, specially the distribution of goods and services for itself as well as the tributary area. Based on differences in range of goods or services, different orders in the functional hierarchy of central places can be discerned.

Table No. 3 shows the functional category of town around Patna.

Table 3

Functional Category of Towns Around Patna

Towns	Total Population 1981	Functional Category, 1971
1. Patna	776371	Services - cum - Trade and Commerce - cum - Industry.
2. Dinapur Nizamat	58684	Primary Activities
3. Dinapur Cantonment	23544	Services
4. Phulwari	22712	Primary Activities
5. Hajipur	62520	Primary Activities
6. Khagaul	34161	Transport
7. Masaurhi	24252	Trade and Commerce
8. Fatwa	21252	Primary activities - cum - Trade and Commerce
9. Bihta*	7684	Primary activities - cum - indus-

		try - cum - Trade & Commerce
10. Maner	19386	N.A.
11. Sonepur	20363	N.A.
12. Dighwara	17062	N.A.

Source : Population - Census Office, Patna.
Functional Category - Town Directory, Census of India, 1971
* Bihta has been declassified as a town in 1981 Census as three - fourths of its population is engaged in agricultural pursuits.

Since data for functional category of towns in 1981 is not available, the classification has been done on the basis of 1971 Census.

The Patna Metropolitans Region has Patna Metropolis as a nodal centre. The region has been delimited empirically. It has 16 anchals and 11 towns within its region. The region being primarily agricultural, has most of its towns engaged in primary activities. These urban centres are not distributed evenly because of the nature of the flood plain and lay-out of transport routes.

The hierarchy of the service centres for Patna Metropolitan Region has been calculated on the basis of the percentage of population engaged in 'other services'. According to 1981 Census, other services category includes all those workers who have been engaged in some economic activity during the last one year and who are not cultivator or agricultural laborers or engaged in a household industry. In all, four orders have been ascertained. Centres having more than 75 per cent of their population engaged in other services are said to be of Ist order, those having between 50 to 75 per cent are said to be of 2nd order, those having between 25 and 50 per cent are said to be of 3rd order and the rest are 4th order centres. In the 4th order centres villages having more than 10,000 population have been included. Sherpur, which falls in Maner anchal has a population of 9,816. Since it is nearer to 10,000 this village has also been included (Table No.4).

A glance at the Table No. 4 reveals that there are three Ist order service centres, five belong to 2nd order, two to 3rd order and the rest six belong to the category of 4th order centres. The most significant of all is Dinapur Cantonment. It lies around 10 miles to the west of the parent city Patna. It has a total population of 23,544 according to 1981 census which is also indicative of its importance. Khagaul and Phulwari which come next, also belong to the Ist order service centre and lie to south-west of the city.

Table 4
Hierarchy of Service Centres, 1981

Towns	Total workers	Persons engaged in other services	% of persons engaged in other services	Hierarchical order
1. Dinapur Nizamat	15530	8870	57.12	2
2. Dinapur Cantonment	7346	7091	96.53	1
3. Phulwari	5311	4024	75.77	1
4. Hajipur	16216	9541	58.84	2
5. Khagaul	8262	7506	90.85	1
6. Masaurhi	5998	3534	58.92	2
7. Fatwa	5853	3531	60.33	2
8. Maner	4967	1726	34.75	3
9. Sonepur	4675	3247	69.45	2
10. Dighwara	4017	1629	40.55	3

Villages	Total Population 1981	Hierarchical Order
1. Pannapur	15329	4
2. Dalipchak	10204	4
3. Kita Chaulishatt	17518	4
4. Sherpur	9816	4
5. Raghopur	11494	4
6. Sabbalpur	13104	4

The 2nd order centres namely, Sonepur, Fatwa, Masaurhi, Hajipur and Dinapur Nizamat are distributed on all sides of Patna. Maner and Dighwara of 3rd order are situated far on the west and the north-west of the city respectively. The six villages belonging to the 4th order situated to the west and north of the city also lie at a distance.

All these service centres are dominated by their mother centre, Patna. The overwhelming importance of these service centres is to be expected and is natural in the region. These centres are marked by changes in population and concentration of public utility services. Trade and commercial activities have also increased in these centres. Modern transportation has changed their appearance. All these indicate that the growth of any urban centre is not due to a single function rather it is the result of cumulative effect of several forces, all of which stimulate different activities and functions.

Patna's metropolitan sphere can broadly be said to be formed of Danapur - Hajipur - Fatwa - Masaurhi - Maner - Khagaul belt. Patna acts as a central place and has its influence over the entire region. The city provides necessary services and facilities to the people in its region. There is a strong relationship between the service centres lying in the region and the city and also among the service centres themselves.

Commuting Population

People from all walks of life, may they by businessmen, government officers, hawkers, labourers, milkmen etc. all come to the city daily, attend to their work and return to their respective places by the evening. There are two types of commuters. One is of regular type who come to Patna every day. This type comprises students, service holders, labourers, milk and vegetables sellers etc. The others are irregular or casual type of commuters. They visit Patna for shopping, for medical treatment or legal problems and also come here for trade of foodgrains and other commodities.

For regular commuters trains are the commonest mode of transport whereas for casual commuters, apart from trains, buses, autorickshaws, taxis, boats and steamers etc. aid in their movement. Daily commuters come as far as from Arrah in the west to Mokameh in the east. During rainy months the percentage of casual commuters decreases. The Mahatma Gandhi Setu which links Patna with Hajipur and the entire North Bihar has tremendously added to the number of commuting population in Patna thereby enormously increasing the day time population of the city. This has made the day time traffic almost unmangeable.

Changing Structural Pattern of Population

The growth of an urban centre, town or city depends on the various functions performed within the town. In fact, the growth of urbanization starts from a focal point. This focal point may either be a business or a public centre which attracts people to settle around it either in a circular or in a sectoral way. There are some theories put forth by urban geographers regarding the growth of urban settlements. These are Concentric Circle Theory by Burgess, Sectoral Theory by Hoyt and Multi - Nuclei theory by Harris and Ullman. The first two theories believe in the growth of settlements from a single focal point, whereas the last one believes in the development of settlement round several nuclei. An attempt has been made here to see whether Patna's structural pattern of population fits with any of the above mentioned types of urban development. It would be proper to review each of these theories separately.

In 1923, E. W. Burgess[5] propounded his Concentric Circle or Zone Theory. According to him, growth of any town or an urban settlement starts from a single point which acts as a centre for attraction for the settlers. Consequently, people from all directions come here for their livelihood and gradually a dense network of transportation develops around this focal point. According to Burgess, the focal point is the Central Business District (C.B.D.) or Down Town District. This zone is an area of divergent activities such as commercial, administrative, industrial, social and civic and also transportation. The most remarkable feature of this zone is that it has minimum residing population with respect to other parts of the city whereas the absolute population during the day is the highest. However, this is true only of American cities and is not strictly applicable to Indian cities because in India the characteristics of a C.B.D. are quite different. Here the density of resident population is highest in the city core and decreases gradually away from the centre. However, in American cities, the density of population increases away from the city centre. Moreover, in India all large cities have mixed land use in their cores i .e., the city centre is given to commercial as well as to residential land use, whereas in American cities, the C.B.D. specializes only in business and commercial activities. This sort of a feature is uncommon in India and so the term C.B.D. does not fit well with Indian conditions. In this case, it would be proper to use terms such as 'Core', 'heart' or nucleus of the city rather than a C.B.D. This would avoid misinterpretations and misapprehensions.

Encircling the C.B.D. is the transition zone. It is a zone of residential deterioration. It is the residence of low income group or the workers engaged in residential activities or commercial and light manufacturing activities. This zone has a number of slums with their submerged regions of poverty, degradation and disease and their underworlds of vice. It presents a mixture of races and immigrants reflecting diversified population structure.

The Zone of Residence is just outside the zone of Transition. It is occupied by the second flow of immigrants who do not get accomodation in the transition zone. The fourth zone is known as the zone of Better

Residence. It houses high income group people and stretches into the suburbs. The last zone is the commuter's zone located outside the city's limits in sub - urban areas. It shows patchy development of high income group residences along some transport routes.

In this way Burgess indicates five zones of urban development all in the form of concentric circles developing one after the other. The land values, accessibility and socio - economic status of the city residents vary directly with distance from the city centre in concentric form.

The second theory is the Sectoral Theory put forward by Homer Hoyt[6] in 1939. It is improvement over the earlier theory. According to him, the growth of a city is not in the form of concentric circles but the entire city is considered as a circle and various areas are sectors radiating out from the centre of that circle. He too, believes in the focal point being the starting point for a city's growth or expansion from where zones given to various land uses migrate outward towards the periphery in the form of sectors along the main radial routes. His assumption is that a town may develop along a number of sectors on all sides, or along some sectors in some parts or only in one part of the town depending on the accessibility to the transport routes. In this theory the high rental sector plays an important role which tends to develop on the farthest existing transport lines. So here, an emphasis is laid on the development of transport lines in the functioning of a city.

This theory is a better indicator to reality than the concentric model because both distance and direction from the city centre are taken into account .

The third theory, the Multiple Nuclei Theory has been enunciated by C.D. Harris and E.Ullman[7] in 1945. Their postulation is that cities are complex organisms. Therefore, land use pattern are built not around a single centre; on the contrary, they are ranged around several centres. Consequently, their model has a cellular structure focused around growth points. The number of nuclei depends largely on the size of the city, its structure and historical background. Unlike Burgess and Hoyt, the growth of an urban area is influenced not only by a single factor but several factors. This theory takes C.B.D. to be the most important factor but not the sole factor in the development of an urban settlement. The urban growth is accentuated by industrial manufacturing zones. However, the growth of all these nuclei depends on intra transportation network. This theory cannot produce a simple model of urban structure, immediately discernible in the form of every city nor does it exclude the probability that elements of concentric and sectoral arrangements will also not be found in particular cities. Thus, this theory is an improvement upon the earlier two theories.

All these theories of urban development depict the growth of cities as a gradual expansion of functional areas from the centre towards the periphery. This expansion, and hence the size and form of a city at ay given time, may be regarded as the resultant of two opposing forces; any centrifugal force derived from the attractions of the periphery and the repulsion from the central area; and a centripetal force derived from a convenience of proximity to the central area.[8] Although centrifugal forces are increasing in strength in the cities the world over, owing to the increase of congestion in the urban core, and to the flexibility of transportation by automobile, the centripetal forces are generally stronger. The tendency of large cities to retain and even increase their primacy is an evidence of the strength of the centralizing forces.

When Patna's modern form of urban development is analyzed it is found that the city in its initial phases of development did grow around a focal point located in the City Chowk area. However, because of physical restraints, the city took a linear shape thereby restricting its cencentric development. Hence, the development of Patna is not compatible with Burgess's theory of concentric circle development. It can be said that Patna's structural pattern is compatible with Hoyt's theory of sectoral development to some extent but not wholly. This is because, Hoyt stresses on one focal point i.e. C.B.D. from where development takes place in the form of sectors. In Patna, sectors of different activities have developed not from a single point but from several points. So, Hoyt's theory is only partially applicable to Patna's urban growth. However, the city's growth fits better with the Multi - Nuclei Theory of Harris and Ullman.

Patna has three nuclei. The first is the City Chowk, the oldest centre located in Eastern Patna. The second nucleus is the Muradpur complex located in Central Patna and the third nucleus is the New Market Area around Mithapur in western Patna. As a matter of fact, all these nuclei happen to be commercial foci. From these focal points the city grew in the form of sectors radiating on all sides. The City Chowk is the original nucleus and the medieval part of the city. In the early period of history the growth of the city started from here and in no time it became densely settled. The areas immediately to the south and extreme east were lowlying, and in the north was the river Ganga, as such further expansion

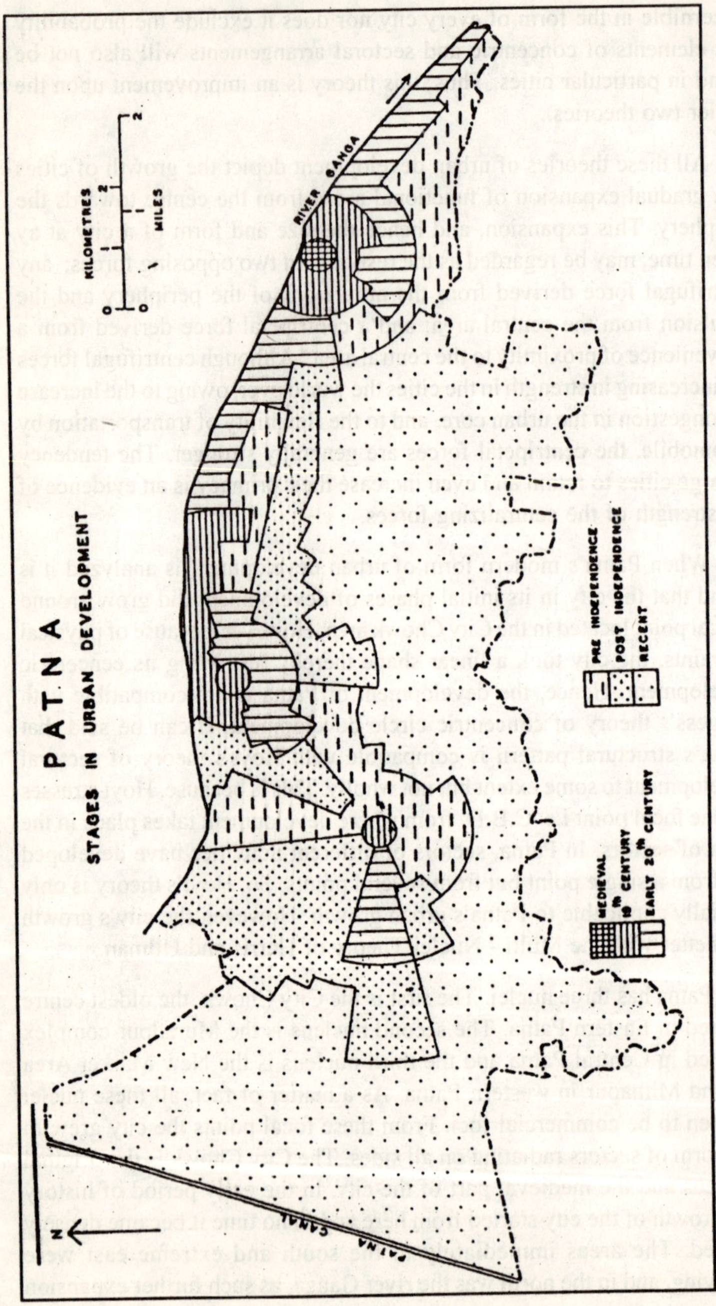
PATNA
STAGES IN URBAN DEVELOPMENT
KILOMETRES 0 1 2
MILES 0 1 2
RIVER GANGA
MEDIEVAL
19th CENTURY
EARLY 20th CENTURY
PRE INDEPENDENCE
POST INDEPENDENCE
RECENT
N
PATNA CANAL

Fig. 31

took place in the west. By the end of the 19th century, another commercial nucleus developed near Muradpur along the Ganga. This pocket was about six kilometers west of the City Chowk. The Muradpur-Bankipore area, because of its favourable location and higher site, became the next attraction for settlers. As a consequence dense network of roads and congested houses developed in this area. During the middle part of the 20th Century a third nucleus came into being near the Patna Railway Junction in the Mithapur area. All these three nuclei developed rather rapidly and haphazardly leading to a dense concentration of population around these nuclei. The density decreases gradually away from these nuclei reflecting the gradual growth and expansion of the city. (Fig. 31).

Rural-Urban Fringe

An important development in urban areas during the past few decades has been the rapid expansion of population into unincorporated areas, outside the municipal limits of the cities and also into the incorporated suburbs. The rural urban fringe is actually an extension of the city itself, real and potential. It is an area where most of the land uses are in flux and therefore subject to planning, direction and control. Rural-Urban fringe according to Andrews[9]," is the intermingling zone of characteristically agricultural and characteristically urban land use structure obtained in the area".

The fringe does not remain static, rather it grows dynamically. A rural area is converted gradually into a Rural-Urban fringe and in due course merges with the parent urban centre. Sinha[10] has demarcated Patna's Rural-Urban fringe. According to him its fringe forms an elongated belt due to the location of the city on a natural levee. The land holdings in the Outer fringe are small, but the pressure of population on land is less because of an increase in non-agricultural employment, even though the density of population is high. In the Inner Fringe, the density of population is increasing, the number of commuting population is greater and the whole area is rapidly getting densely built up. In the outer fringe, the pressure of population is less, but the nature of land use is changing to cash crop cultivation.

On the basis of the continuity of built up area ,the inner fringe of Patna extends upto Banka ghat in the east, Parsa bazar on Patna-Gaya railway line in the south and upto Phulwari and Dinapur in the west. The Outer fringe extends upto Punpun along the railway line in the south, upto Fatwa in the east and a mile beyond Dinapur Khagaul and Phulwari in the west.[11] Now that Patna has been linked with Hajipur and

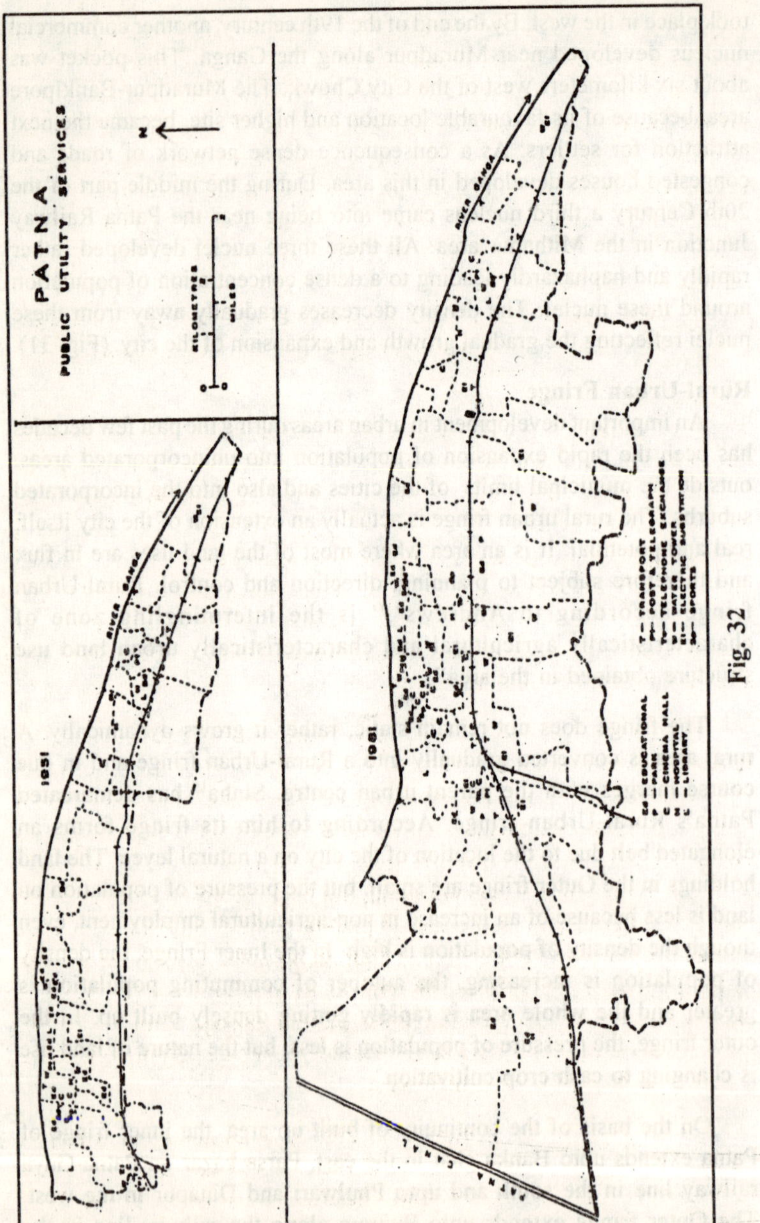

Fig. 32

other towns through the Ganga Bridge, the area around Hajipur has become part of Patna"s Outer rural-urban fringe.

The way of life of the residents of these areas is very much similar to that of purely urban residents, and markedly different from the purely rural countryside.

Civic Services in Patna

The present provision of civic services in Patna as in most other urban centres of the state, is far too short of the requirements. However, as a regional capital it provides facilities not only to its local residents but also the people residing in its hinterland. Important civic services are health, education, recreational, water supply, electricity, sewerage and drainage, transport and communicational etc. (Fig. 32).

Health : Patna is the most important health centre in its entire region. Patna Medical College Hospital located in Central Patna has a number of specialist doctors and it renders services to the people of almost the while state who come here for treatment. There are other hospitals namely, Holy Family Hospital, Padari Ki Haveli Hospital, Patna City Hospital, Tripolia Hospital, Government Ayurvedic Hospital, Rajendra Nagar Hospital and Nalanda Medical College Hospital and T.B. Centre. Besides there are innumerable nursing homes and private health clinics.

Educational : Patna plays a pivotal role in the field of education in Bihar. Patna University is the oldest institution for higher learning in the state and is well recognised all over the country and abroad. There are ten colleges in Patna University belonging to different faculties. They are Patna Law College, Bihar College of Engineering, Patna Science College, Patna College, Vanijya Mahavidyalaya, B.N. College, Magadh Mahila College, Women's Training College, Patna Training College and Patna Women's College. Besides, there are several other degree colleges belonging to the Magadh University. In addition, there are a large number of schools, both private and government . Schools worth mentioning are St. Michael's High School, St. Xavier's, St. Joseph's Convent, Notre Dame Academy, Mt. Carnel, Patna City School, R.M.R. Seminary, Patna Collegiate School, Patliputra High School, Loyala High School, Bankipore Girls High School, and Patna High School etc. All these institutions attract a large number of students from almost all over the State. To meet the growing demand of people, every street is now being occupied by a private institute especially at the primary level. Apart from these, several technical institutions and research institutions have also been established in the city.

Recreational : As regards recreational facilities, it is rather a pathetic sight for the residential as well as the tourist population. Patna has not been able to keep pace with the growing requirements of increasing population. There is an acute shortage of adequate parks, playgrounds, theaters, cinema halls, clubs etc. Moreover, their location is such that they are centralized in the densest parts of the city and just to reach them a lot of patience, time and energy is required. There are 13 cinema halls in the city : 3 in Eastern Patna, 7 in Central Patna and 3 in Western Patna. There are several clubs and theaters. Bankipore Club, New Patna Club, Bhartiya Nritya Kala Mandir and Shri Krishna Memorial Hall are important among them. Sanjay Gandhi Jaivik Udyan also attracts huge crowd especially on weekends and holidays. The old settled areas of Patna do not have any park. Central Patna has Moinul Haque Stadium and Gandhi Maidan where organized games and sports are held. There are several large hotels at Patna led by Patna Maurya Hotel which is claimed to be of 5 star status.

Water Supply : As regards the supply of water, Patna has been blessed by nature and there is plenty of pure drinking water available at a subsoil depth of about 600 ft. The entire water - supply in the city is drawn by tube - wells and works in a decentralized manner. Initially the supply was confined only to government buildings, the University area and a few selected localities. Even today, the water supply does not cover the entire municipal area. For example, half of Western Patna is devoid of piped water supply. Residents of these areas have their own water supply through private borings.

During 1980 - 81 there were 56 tube-wells of different sizes located in different localities of the city. Water used to be supplied through twenty water towers in the town of which the larger ones are named below. Most of them, however, have now gone into disuse, and water is directly pumped into the mains.

The total length of pipelines during 1980-81 was 500 kms. approximately ranging from 300 mm. diameter to 800 mm. diameter. Total installed capacity of all pumps (tube wells + water tower) was about 52 million gallons per day. The average daily supply of water was 20 million gallons. This seems quite adequate but the supply is erratic and ununiform.

Table 5

Location		Storage Capacity in gallons
1.	Amlatola Water Tower	1,00,000
2.	Bailey Road Water Tower	1,00,000
3.	High Court Water Tower	1,00,000
4.	Kadamkaun Water Tower	50,000
5.	University Water Tower	1,00,000
6.	Khajekalan Water Tower	1,00,000
7.	M.L.A. Flat Water Tower	50,000
8.	Mangles Tank Water Tower	1,00,000
9.	Chiraiyatanr Pumping Station	50,000
10.	Digha Pumping Station	1,00,000
11.	Bankipore Water Tower	1,00,000
12.	Simli Water Tower	1,00,000
13.	Rajendranagar Water Tower	1,00,000

Source : Patna Water Board

In several areas of Western, Central and Eastern Patna, the water pressure is much too feeble and inadequate. This is because most of the tubewells and pipes have become old and damaged and are incapable of functioning at peak capacity. The water supply at Patna is looked after by Patna Water Board and Public Health and Engineering Department.

Drainage and Sewerage : The storm drainage system of Patna incorporates a vast network of open drains and conduits with several dewatering pumping stations and multi out-falls. The storm water drains into waterways such as Serpentine Nala, Bakergaj Nala and Kadam Kuan Nala and subsequently water received is discharged directly to the river Ganag through Serpentine Nala and Bakerganj Nala. The Kadam Kaun Nala drains into the Punpun river.

The channel known as Boring Canal was an open drain a few years ago but now it has been converted into an underground drain. It meets Bailey Road on the south and Patna - Dinapur road on the north and flows into the Ganga.

Topographically, Patna is a flat country and the gradient of the city varies roughly between 153 ft. and 179 ft. The provision for proper drainage for the city has been somewhat difficult because of two reasons. First, the city does not have any natural drainage in the north draining into the Ganga because its highest flood level is higher than the general level of the city. Secondly, vast areas to the south of the main railway line are lowlying and given to floods by the Punpun nearly every year. As such, during the monsoon, the main storm water outfall channels are not able to discharge fully into the Ganga as the level of river sometimes rises above the discharge level of the outfall channels, pushing the water back. Therefore, it becomes utmost necessary during floods to close the gates of the affected channels till the subsidence of the water levels. As a consequence, prolonged waterlogging takes place resulting in extreme insanitary conditions.

Sewerage system was first introduced in Patna during 1936-39 when sewer lines were laid in the central eastern part of the city. With increasing demand a sanitary sewerage system was laid out and sewage treatment plants were constructed. At present there are two sewerage treatment plants, one at Saidpur in Central Patna and the other at Beur in South - Western Patna north of the main railway line. In Lohianagar area, in South Patna night soil sewers and storm sewers are interlinked. The sewage from this area is pumped into open channel and discharged into Kadam Kuan Nala without any treatment. This Nala is an open channel carrying foul water passing through the central spine of the dense urban settlement of Patna. On the whole, the existing status of Patna's sewerage is very poor. The sewerage is discharged into the Ganga either by direct pumping or through open channels, nallas and roadside drains. The existing sewerage and drainage network is shown in Fig. 33.

The sanitary conditions in Patna are no better. Everywhere garbage dumps are found, blocking the roads and making the movement of vehicular traffic difficult. Patna Municipal Corporation has not been able to manage proper cleanliness of roads. However, the Government has paid attention to the development of public sewage facility. Public Sulabh Sauchalays have come up at almost all important places in the city. These are basically an adaptation of septic tank system to Indian conditions. Through this electrical energy is also being produced and one-third of the street lighting on Bailey road is provided with this electricity.

Electric Supply : The city gets its entire power supply from the Patna Electricity Supply Undertaking through its own powerhouse at Karbhigia as well as the other power stations of B.S.E. Board and the Damodar Valley Corporation. Patna was electrified in the year 1926. In 1982 - 83 total demand for power was 30,000 K.W. and power available was 26,000 K.W. The number of domestic connections was 60,787, commercial connections 17,739, industrial connections 3,805 and the number of agricultural connection was 1,025.[12] Agricultural connections include private and state tube wells including Water Board and sewerage connections.

More than two - thirds of the total population of the city enjoy electric facilities. The electric supply though erratic in Patna especially during the summer, is much better than in other cities and towns of Bihar.

Transport and Communication

Road Transport : Patna has 290 kms. of metalled road and 150 kms. of unmetalled road. The volume of traffic in Patna is tremendous. Barring a few roads in Western and Southern Patna almost all roads are heavily loaded with traffic. The cheapest mode of traffic is bus. There are four bus depots in the city - one near Malsalami in Eastern Patna, one near Gandhi Maidan owned by Bihar State Rajya Transport Corporation in Central Patna and the other two in Western Patna near the Patna Railway Station. The routes from these bus stands run both within and outside the city. But all areas in the city are not covered by bus service. The bus services are affected by the linear nature of the city, parallel arterial roads and narrow feeder roads between them. Other modes of transport are three wheelers, rickshaws, horse cart etc. Of these rickshaws are the most common. Three wheelers and horse carts are commonly used in Eastern Patna.

Railways : Railways play a vital role in both interstate and intracity transport of Patna. The Eastern Railway passes through the middle part of the city. There are five railway stations, viz., Patna Junction, Patna Sahib, Gulzarbagh, Rajendra Nagar and Phulwari. There is one goods shed opposite Rajendra Nagar Colony which has relieved the pressure on the Junction station yard. The volume of passengers and goods traffic to and from Patna junction is the highest because it is the largest station in the city. Apart from commuter traffic, the railway does play a major role in intracity traffic of Patna.

Waterways : The riverine traffic of passengers and goods has always been a remarkable feature of Patna. From time immemorial, heavy transactions of business used to take place in Patna through the ghats along the Ganga. However, since the opening of Mahatma Gandhi Setu, the importance of ghats has come down. Important ghats of Patna through which traffic is handled by steamers and country boats are Digha Ghat, Mahendru Ghat, Rani Ghat, Khajekalan Ghat and Patna Ghat. There is a proposal to start a goods traffic through barges along the Ganga between Allahabad and Bhagalpur via Patna.

Air ways : Patna airport is situated in western Patna. It is mainly used for civil aircraft namely Indian Airlines, and the aircraft of the Bihar government. The cities directly connected by air are Ranchi, Lucknow, Kanpur, Delhi, Calcutta, Gauhati, Imphal and Kathmandu.

Postal and Telegraph Communication : The expansion of postal service is entirely dependent on the growth of population. There are forty post - offices in the city. Imporant among them are General Post Office and Central Telegraph Office in Western Patna, Bankipore post and Telegraph office in Central Patna and Jhauganj Post and Telegraph Office in Eastern Patna. Patna being the capital city and district headquarters has Quick Mail services facilities. In all post offices, ordinary postal work including money orders are transacted and saving bank facility is provided.

The growth of telegraph services is associated with the growth of postal services. Patna has four booking -cum-delivery offices and seven other booking offices. Since the service range of telegraph office is larger than the postal service in urban centres, fewer telegraph offices are required. On the whole this service is adequate and efficient in the city.

Telephone : The total number of telephone connections given to the people of Patna was 11,659 during the year 1982-83 out of the total capacity of 12,500. The table shows the capacity, working connection and number of people on the waiting list.

Table 6
1982 - 83

	Exchange	Capacity	Working	Waiting List
1.	Patna Main Exchange	6000	5590	821
2.	Rajendra Nagar	5000	4682	644
3.	Patna City	1500	1387	248
4.	Pataliputra Exchange	-	-	-
	Total	12500	11659	1713

Source : District Telephone Exchange. Patna.

Telephones are a common service to people who belong to the upper class, or are business men, professionals and government officers. In 1972 there were only 9,535 telephone connections which increased to 10,718 in 1978 and again 11,659 in 1982-83. This reflects the growth of the city and a general awareness of fast life among the people of Patna. A recent innovation in the telephone system has been the introduction of Subscriber Trunk Dialing System (STD). Through this Patna has been connected with several cities of India and soon will be joined to the All India Grid through the Satellite.

Radio and Television Service : Radio is the most common mass media of communication. Patna has one radio station situated in Central Patna. Since the introduction of a T.V. Relay Centre in 1982, the people of Patna have switched over to T.V. and radio has become of less importance to the affluent. Today roughly one - fifth of the houses of Patna has a T.V. antenna erected on its terrace.

Other Services

Besides there are other important civic services such as newspaper and milk supply and Fire Brigade. All popular newspapers of Bihar such as the Times of India, Hindustan Times, Indian Nation, Aryavarta, Hindustan, Aaj etc. are published from Patna.

Recently milk supply by Patna Dairy Milk Supply Scheme has become very popular in the city. It has taken over in almost all large colonies of Patna uprooting the traditional milkman supply.

The City has two Fire stations. Apart from extinguishing fire, they also help during floods or acute waterlogging by pumping the water out of the area inundated.

Problems

There are many problems related to urban development. The people migrate to urban areas in response to differentials in opportunities. Maximum opportunity, however, also produces maximum friction. Cities are centres of innovation and with modern technology and communication they have enlarged the horizon of the people. The larger the city, the greater the number and diversity of its opportunities. But large cities do require space and so they spread. When the spread is ungraceful, it is termed as 'sprawl'. (See Webster's dictionary).

Urban sprawl in itself is not undesirable; it is manifestation of the urban way of life. Cities will continue to grow and the urban sprawl will expand at an increasing rate. Increasing number of people are attracted to the facilities and amenities of metropolitan living. The problem is not to reduce urban sprawl but rather to reduce its frictions. Perhaps, the most significant problem associated with urban sprawl is in the realm of inefficiency of land use. Also there are problems for the agriculturists caught up in the squeeze of advancing front of urban development, thereby losing their farm lands.

The city of Patna too faces a similar problem. A study of the growth of the city since the very beginning indicates that Patna has always tended to grow westwards. As a consequence the eastern part of the city has suffered from neglect and degeneration. As stated in the earlier chapters the physical factor has always governed the location and the expansion of this city. As the needs grew, people moved outwards from the city centres and began settling in an unplanned manner which led to the irregular or haphazard development of the city. This was mainly the result of the absence of a proper development Plan. Had a Master plan been framed properly and implemented such irregularities in Patna's development and expansion would have been avoided. So it is essential that an overall development plan of the city be drawn up for future growth of the city.

The major problems in Patna's development calling for attention are :

(1) Housing Shortage : There is an acute shortage of housing. The density of occupied residential houses and accommodation density are very high in the old settled parts of the city. (This is discussed in detail in the next chapter). The condition of houses in Eastern Patna, the oldest part of the city, is very poor. This section is on the verge of decay. Most of the houses are degenerated, dilapidated, closely built having poor ventilation and sanitation and are clustered in a contaminated atmosphere. The houses in Central Patna, however, are slightly better, barring a few localities around Muradpur, Pirmohani, Lohanipur etc. where conditions are somewhat poor and houses are old and poorly equipped. Only Western and Southern Patna have well planned colonies with good houses.

In order to meet the housing shortage which has been the result of growing population, new residential areas should be developed and blighted areas should be renewed. This calls for the development of lowlying areas in Southern Patna and open space in Western Patna. The lowlying areas should be made free of waterlogging by improving the drainage system.

(2) Mixed Land Uses : The problem of mixed land use in Eastern and Central parts of the city is the root cause for their improper development. Residential, commercial, administrative, institutional, industrial functions all are seen congregating in one place. This gives the city a jumbled, complicated and complex appearance. It is very difficult to plan these areas. Unless the whole area is demolished completely and planned afresh, no planned layout of separate land uses is possible. Only slight improvements in these areas may be possible. As for example, court, hospital, school and markets are all located next to one another in the central parts of the city. The congestion has become so intense that their expansion is impeded. Hence the hospital which requires a peaceful and tranquil atmosphere, is situated ironically in a congested and noisy part of the city. Thus, the approach should be such that in other areas where new developments are coming up, especially in the western and southern parts of the city, maximum utilization of land through proper distribution and layout of land use be given, so that the development of the city takes place in an organized way.

(3) Deficiency in Civic Services : The provision of civic services to the residents of Patna is quite deficient. These services have not been able to keep pace with the ever increasing population. Water and electricity are consumed heavily which on account of being insufficient are always provided erratically and irregularly. The city is faced with a severe problem of drainage and sewerage. Often during the rains the entire city bears the look of an island surrounded by dirty and filthy water. This problem of drainage has been faced by residents of Patna over the years and it is becoming worse every year. This is a serious problem and has to be looked into thoroughly. Although storm drainage and sewerage lines have been laid to check this acute problem, the attempt is half hearted and disorganized. They are efficient during the dry months but waterlogging becomes uncontrollable during wet months leading to insanitary conditions and leads to the spread of various diseases and epidemics.

Patna has been divided into seven sewerage zones[14] and one more zone for low cost sanitation has been proposed (Fig. 33). This zoning is based upon the habitation densities likely to grow in different areas of the city upto 2011 A.D., topography, road network, natural obstruction, existing and tentatively proposed sites for sewage treatment plants and outfall. The areas which are expected to have densities of 40 to 120

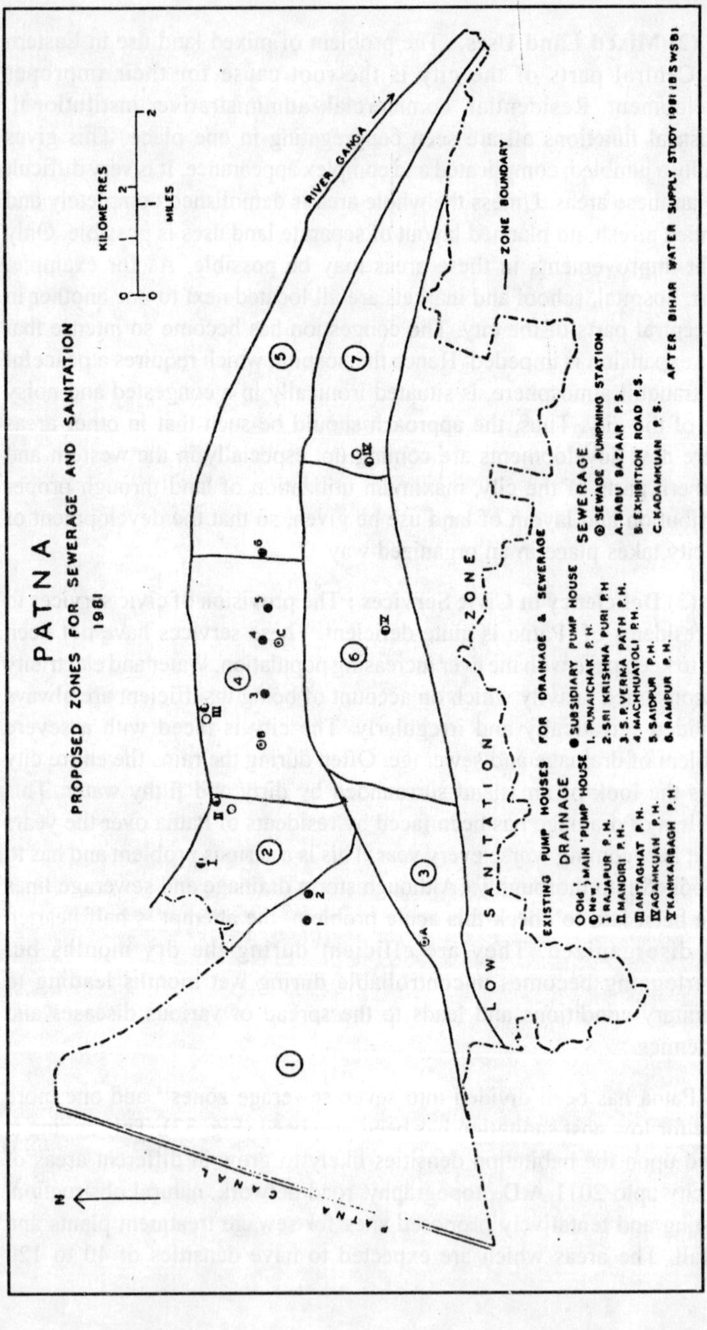
PATNA
PROPOSED ZONES FOR SEWERAGE AND SANITATION
1981
KILOMETRES
MILES
RIVER GANGA
ZONE BOUNDARY
LOW SANITATION ZONE
CANAL
EXISTING PUMP HOUSES FOR DRAINAGE & SEWERAGE
DRAINAGE
OLD MAIN PUMP HOUSE
New
SUBSIDIARY PUMP HOUSE
I RAJAPUR P.H.
II MANDIRI P.H.
III ANTAGHAT P.H.
IV KAGAMKUAN P.H.
V KANKARBAGH P.H.
1. PUNAICHAK P.H.
2. SRI KRISHNA PURI P.H.
3. S.P. VERMA PATH P.H.
4. MACHHUATOLI P.H.
5. SAIDPUR P.H.
6. RAMPUR P.H.
SEWERAGE
SEWAGE PUMPING STATION
A. BABU BAZAAR P.S.
B. EXHIBITION ROAD P.S.
C. KADAMKUAN P.S.
AFTER BIHAR WATER SUPPLY STUDY 1981 (BSWSB)

Fig. 33

persons per acre by 2011 have been considered under these zones. The area to the south of new bye - pass road is mostly rural and lowlying and is often subject to inundation by rainwater during the monsoon. The average ground level of the area is below the high flood level of the river Punpun. It is expected that this area will have a density of 16 persons per acre in 2011 A.D. Owing to the high cost of sanitation accessories, the consultants are of the view that low cost sanitation methods, viz., Sulabh Sauchalay, dug-well latrine, pit privy etc. should be adopted.

Table No. 7 shows the area covered and population served by each zone.

Table 7

Area Covered and Population Served by Proposed Sewerage Zones

Proposed sewerage zone	Area covered by the zone in acres	Total population to be served in 2011	Average - density of population in 2011 (persons per acre)
1	6560	295200	45
2	2422	125944	52
3	1270	76200	60
4	2208	264960	120
5	3328	299520	90
6	2816	112640	40
7	1680	67200	40

Source : Patna Regional Development Authority

It will be seen from the table that the main drawback of the scheme is underestimation of the population to be served. The population of the city proper is likely to be 1.4 million by 2001 as estimated earlier, while this scheme is based on an estimate of 1.3 million by 2001. Obviously the estimates are too low and the whole scheme will have to be recast. However, it is a step in the right disrection, for the city planners are at last awakening to the need for planning.

The city also lacks recreational facilities such as parks and playgrounds. For a healthy atmosphere of the city, open spaces, parks and playgrounds distributed in the residential areas are extremely essential. In the greater part of the city there is no park in residential areas and children use roads and streets for recreational purposes.

The city has large periodic influx of population during marriage and festival seasons. Therefore, in order to accommodate them, many more rest houses, hotels and public conveniences are needed.

(4) Roads : A more serious problem is that of roads in Patna. The arterial roads are so narrow and broken at places, looking more like unmetalled road, that they are incapable of taking the load of the rapidly increasing daytime population and vehicular traffic leading to traffic jams for hours. They need to be widened and repaired properly for convenient movement of traffic in the city. More link roads also need to be provided. Eastern and Central Patna are the worst affected areas. Western Patna, however, has well laid out ring radial road pattern. Traffic jams can also be checked by the enforcement of traffic regulations. Moreover, concrete steps should be taken for removal of encroachment from the roads. A step in the right direction is the construction of two more overbridges on the railway line in Central and Western Patna. These have been just completed. A third bridge is necessary in Eastern Patna.

(5) Slums : The sprawl of slums in the already settled areas of the city poses a serious threat to the city's development. *(This is discussed in the next Chapter).* Slums in Patna which have grown through years and expanded over generations, cannot perhaps be completely eradicated and brought at par with new planned developments. However, general improvement can be brought about by a minimum of changes, acquisition and displacement. Roads and buildings in these areas may be repaired and general civic services may be provided to the slum dwellers. As such, the operation should be for renewal and not clearance which is a difficult task to be performed or rather impossible for any country.

(6) Vacant Land : The existence of vacant pockets within the built up areas, which are mostly used as defecating grounds by town dwellers, is the root cause of unhealthy atmosphere. These areas become waterlogged during the rains creating breeding grounds for mosquitoes and other harmful insects. These grounds can be developed and utilized to meet the deficiencies in various community facilities, particularly playgrounds for children.

(7) Lack of Dumping Ground for Garbage : Inspite of Patna developing so fast, it is a pity that the Municipal Corporation has not been able to provide dumping grounds for the city's garbage. As a result all roads of the city are either lined with garbage dumps or some have hillocks of garbage right in their centre. This is a major reason for traffic jams and traffic bottlenecks especially along the arterial roads. Moreover garbage on roads creates an unhealthy atmosphere for the residents and it becomes worse during the rains polluting the atmosphere with foul smell.

In order to do away with this problem, Municipal Corporation should see that dumping cubicles be provided at places along all the roads. All these should be cleared during the night so that again in the morning, people get cleared cubicles. Moreover, a huge dumping ground should be earmarked so that the garbage collected from the cubicles is dumped here. This ground should be located outside the city for basic reasons such as cleanliness and healthy atmosphere.

(8) Sprawl of Khataals : The city has a large number of Khataals located in its most thickly settled parts. Not a single vacant space in colonies is left open. The milkmen use them for keeping their cattle and later on the whole space is converted into a slum. The growing cattle congestion, coupled with indiscriminate dumping of cattle dung and lack of proper sanitary facilities in the cattle sheds create a serious health problem for the city's population. It would be proper that a separate space facilitated with sanitary equipment away from residential colonies be provided to them. Keeping cattle in densely residential areas should be banned.

Apart from the above stated problems there are other problems as well which call for attention of the planners. To name a few, they are problems of mixed traffic, vehicle parking, unplanned house construction etc.

The problems identified above ask for an immediate action to prepare an integrated urban development plan programmed with a view to achieving maximum good as early as possible. This plan can be divided into phases based on priorities fixed within the frame of the envisaged plan.

References :

1. Jefferson, M. (1931) : "The Distribution of the World's City Folk : A Study in Comparative Civilization", Geographical Review, Vol. 21, p. 453.

2. Dickinson, R. E. (1960) : City, Region and Regionalism. London, p. 49.

3. Sinha, M. M. P. op. cit. p. 122.

4. Mumford, L. (1953) : The Culture of Cities, London, Secker and Warburg, p. 287.

5. Burgess, E. W. (1929) : "Urban Areas in Chicago : An Experiment in Social Research", (Eds.) T. V. Smith and Leonard D. White (Chicago University Press, Chicago), pp. 113 - 38.

6. Hoyt, H. (1939) : The Structural Growth of Residential Neighbourhoods in American Cities U. S. Federal Housing Administration, Washington, pp. 112 - 22.

7. Harris, C. D. (1945) : "The Nature of Cities", Annals of the American Academy of Political and Social Sciences, Vol. 242, pp. 7 - 17.

8. Colby, C. C. (1933) : "Centrifugal and Centripetal Forces in Urban Geography", Annals of the Association of American Geographers, No. 23, pp. 1 - 20.

9. Andrews, Richard (1942) : Elements in Urban Fringe Pattern", Journal of Land and Public Utility Economics, Vol. XVIII, pp. 169 - 83.

10. Sinha, M. M. P. : op. cit.

11. Sinha, M. M. P. (1974) : "Delimiting the Rural Urban Fringe of Patna", Indian Geographical Studies, Research Bulletin No. 3, p. 29.

12. Source : Bihar State Electricity Board and Patna Electric Supply Undertaking.

13. Pataliputra Exchange lies just outside the boundary of Patna and its data is not available.

14. The proposed zoning has been done by the BISWAS Board Consultants as a step towards planning by the Government.

6

Planning

The term 'planning' has different connotations when applied to a city. It is difficult to define planning but it has certain basic attributes. It is future oriented, it is continuous, it is comprehensive; it requires determination of facts and it provides an opportunity for co-ordination. There are various types of planning depending on the various functions performed by the people viz., operational planning, developmental planning and restorative planning.[1]

Operational Planning is connected with the components of the existing city. It is an on going process in the sense that when one operational problem is solved, others take its place so that planning process is continuous. This type of planning has mainly to do with planning of changes in vehicular traffic flow, planning of land use on a group of continuous land parcels, planning of acceptable levels of air pollution, or planning of neighbourhood for possible annexation to the central city.

Developmental Planning is concerned with the development of an area of city which has not been put to urban uses previously or the redevelopment of a blighted area in the city.

Restorative Planning is more or less similar to that of developmental planning in the sense that it deals with redevelopment but through restoration of existing facilities, rather than through construction or creation of facilities.

Planning of the types mentioned deals with organization, development or restoration of components of the existing city, ranging from land use planning in a new development in the city to conversion of an old abandoned warehouse area into a shopping arcade and restaurants.

In other instance, city planning also means the planning, layout, design and location of completely new urban agglomerations on large land areas removed from any existing urban centre.[2] This 'new town' planning is not common at present. However, this approach offers future possibilities.

Planning is not a simple once - and -for all operation to be completed in one step. It is a complex web of a connected series of operations. It has to be done for various time periods, sectors and levels. It has to be given a concrete shape by formulation of policies, programmes and projects.

However, all planning must take into account the human factor, the population to be benefited, and not concentrate on physical planning of land use and services only. This vital fact is often ignored by the city planners who later lament the breakdown of their well laid out town plans and inadequacy of services with the growth of population. It is for the town administration to balance the urban population against planned facilities at later stages of development.

Need For Planning

In modern times, city life is beset with numerous problems. Overcrowding, poor sanitation and lack of adequate services are challenges confronting cities around the world. India has cities populated before the automobile, before electricity, before the machine age - now confronted with the demands for modern amenities. Scarcity of housing has had a detrimental effect on the health of the population. Crime has increased side by side. In sum, city dwellers are subject to increasing physical and psychological difficulties. To overcome these difficulties and problems, planning of the existing city is extremely essential.

The city of Patna is faced with similar problems. Inadequate building space and insufficient civic amenities are problems serious enough to be looked into. These should not be allowed to continue indefinitely and hence call for immediate planning. However, the uncontrolled development and piecemeal planning of Patna entail certain difficulties. It is not a city with modern growth. Its roots lie deep in the historical past. A thorough and proper diagnosis of the city's present status is required regarding commercial, administrative, residential or institutional land use with reference to its original status.

Before going in for planning it is necessary to view the following :

Spatial Pattern of Density and Growth of Population : As stated earlier, the Central Zone is the most densely populated zone in the city with

66.23 persons per acre. The Western Zone has the lowest density namely, 16.63 persons per acre. This can be seen in the following Table No. 8 and Fig. 34.

Table : 8

Zonal Density of Population, 1981

Zones	Area in acres	Total Population	Density of Population per acre
Western	8147.0	135471	16.63
Southern	6347.7	161928	25.51
Central	4102.9	271750	66.23
Eastern	5415.8	207222	38.26
Total Patna M.C.	24013.4	776371	32.33

Source : Calculated by the Author.

Patna as the State Capital obviously attracts people from distant places and has therefore, to bear the burden of regional urban thrust. The city has made rapid strides in its expansion owing to its multifarious developmental activities, not all of which have taken place in a planned manner. The Central Zone at present houses the bulk of population because of the concentration of commercial, institutional - cum - administrative activities in this zone.

Table No. 9 shows zonal growth of population within the city between 1961 and 1981.

Table: 9

Zonal Growth of Population, 1961 - 81

Zones	Total Pop. in 1961 according to 1981 area	Total population 1981	Absolute Change	% of Change
Western	109607	135471	25864	24.00
Southern	15575	161928	146353	940.00
Central	159781	271750	111969	70.08
Eastern	133175	207222	74047	55.00

Source : Calculated by the author.

This table shows that maximum growth has been experienced in the

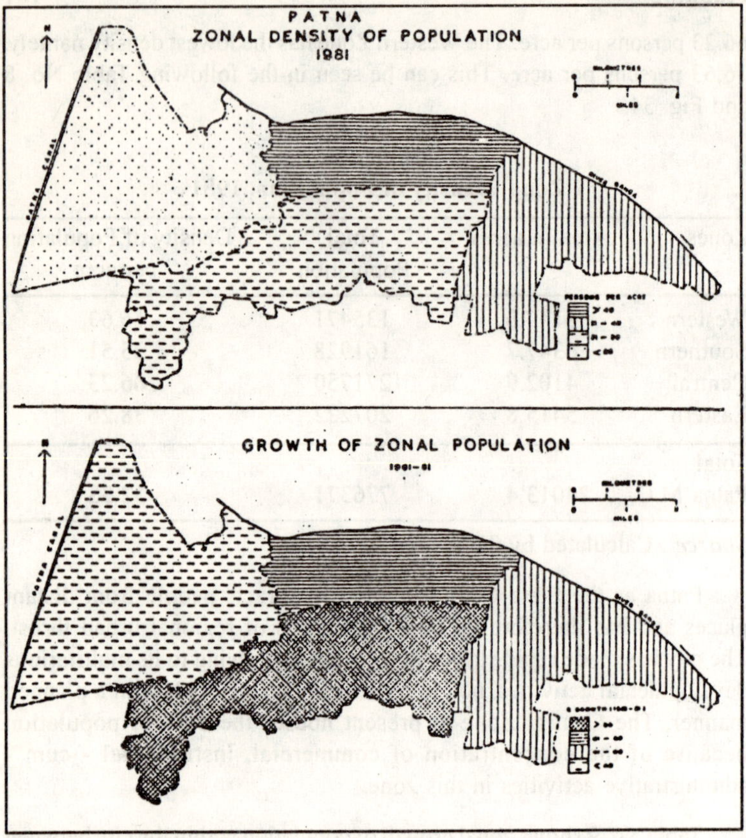

Fig. 34

Southern Zone (Fig. 34). This is because large tracts of vacant land here have been occupied and given to residential purposes. This zone is entirely residential. The Central and the Eastern Zones have also recorded a substantial increase mainly because of their increase in developmental activities. The Western Zone has recorded a small percentage of growth. This reflects that this zone has small residing population because it houses most of the administrative and government offices and large tracts of land are owned by the Government where the density of population is less. It is basically an administrative zone.

On the basis of the above table the growth of population in all the four zones in 1991 and 2001 have been estimated through geometric rate of progression (See Fig. No. 5 given in Chap.3). This can be seen in Table No. 10.

Table : 10
Estimated Population Growth by Zones, 1991 & 2001

Zones	Estimated Pop. 1991	Estimated Pop. 2001	Absolute Change	% of Change
Western	149600	165800	16200	10.83
Southern	308381	587200	278919	90.48
Central	354398	462183	107785	30.41
Eastern	258489	322440	63951	24.74
Total Patna M.C.	1070768	1537623	466855	43.60

Source : Calculated by the Author

This table depicts that the Southern Zone will have maximum growth amounting to 90 per cent in 1991 - 2001 and the Western Zone will experience a low growth of around 11 per cent. The Southern Zone is the main area where the population explosion is taking place as ample virgin land is available for settlement. Hence, such an enormous increase in this zone will not be unusual.

Zonal Literacy : Table No. 11 reveals that in Western, Southern and Central Zones of the city the percentage of total literacy is more or less the same.

Table : 11
Zonal Literacy, 1981

	Figures in Percentage		
Zones	Total Literacy	Male Literacy	Female Literacy
Western	65.21	73.80	53.84
Southern	63.28	72.38	52.04
Central	60.63	68.97	44.58
Eastern	49.26	59.70	37.52
Total Patna M.C.	58.95	68.18	47.54

Source : Calculated by the Author.

However, the Western Zone accounts for the highest literacy. This is because the upper class and upper middle class people including

Government employees and officers live in this zone. Similar is the case with Southern and Central Zone which have middle class people plus educational facilities available at a short distance. The Eastern Zone accounts for low literacy because it has bulk of low income people. Besides, it is the oldest part of the city showing signs of decay. The percentage of male - female literacy follows the same trend as that of total literacy, being higher in Western, Southern and Central Zones and lower in Eastern Zone (Fig. 35).

Zonal Distribution of Total Workers : All four zones of the city have more or less a uniform percentage of total workers ranging between 24 and 28. The Western Zone has the highest percentage of workers with 27.86 and Southern Zone lowest at 23.53. It will be clear from Table No. 12.

Table : 12
Zonewise Total Workers, 1981

Zones	% of total Workers.
Western	27.86
Southern	23.53
Central	26.00
Eastern	25.57
Total Patna M.C.	25.70

Source : Calculated by the Author.

No significant conclusion can be drawn from this pattern of distribution except that the average employment is slightly lower than in other cities because of the large number of student population in Patna.

Housing Pattern

Housing is a problem faced by all growing urban settlements. According to the Census of 1971, Patna had 65,540 houses and 76,276 households which increased to 95,449 and 117,954 respectively in 1981. It will be seen from Appendix Nos. XVI and XVII that the density of occupied residential houses in the city in 1971 was 3.73 houses per acre and in 1981 it was 3.97 per acre. This represents only a slight increase. Figs. 36 and 37 show that in 1971 ward no. 7 had the highest density of houses which is maintained in 1981 as well. These maps reveal that the density of houses is high around the three city cores, decreasing gradually towards the periphery. As stated in earlier chapters, it is common in

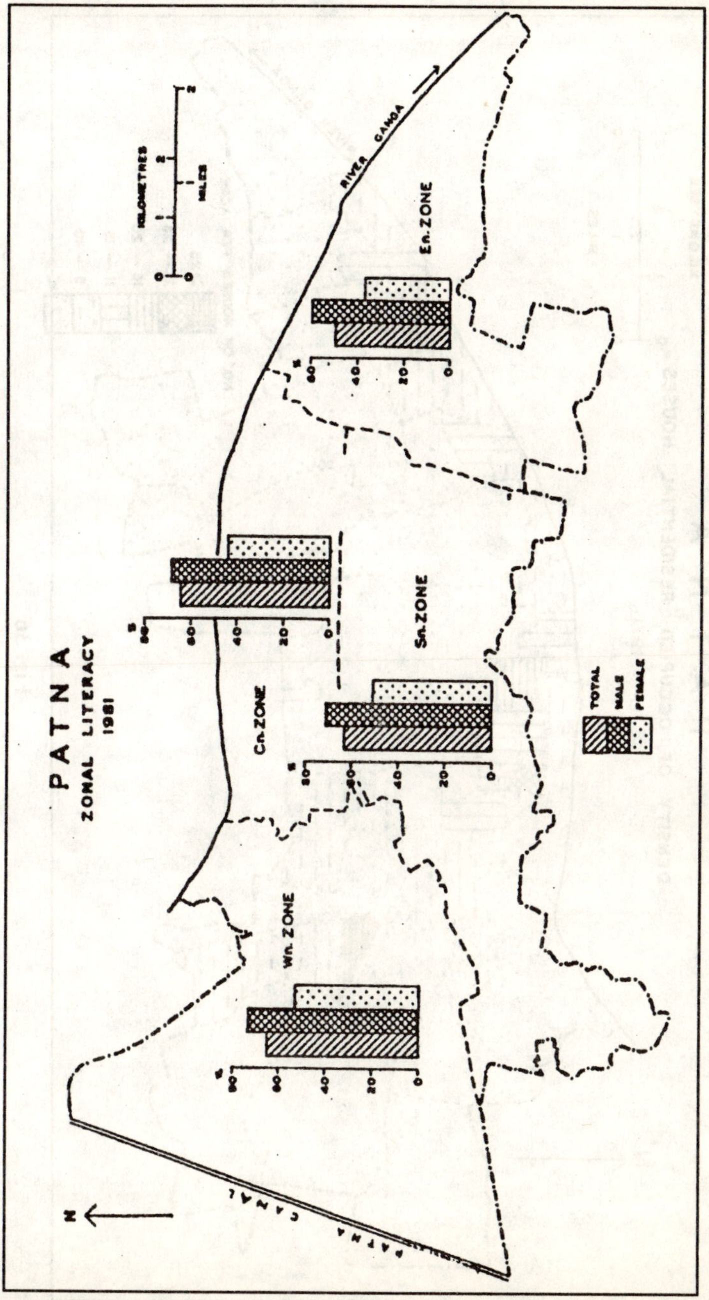
PATNA
ZONAL LITERACY
1981
N
PATNA CANAL
RIVER GANGA
Wn. ZONE
Cn. ZONE
Sn. ZONE
En. ZONE
KILOMETRES
MILES
TOTAL
MALE
FEMALE

Fig. 35

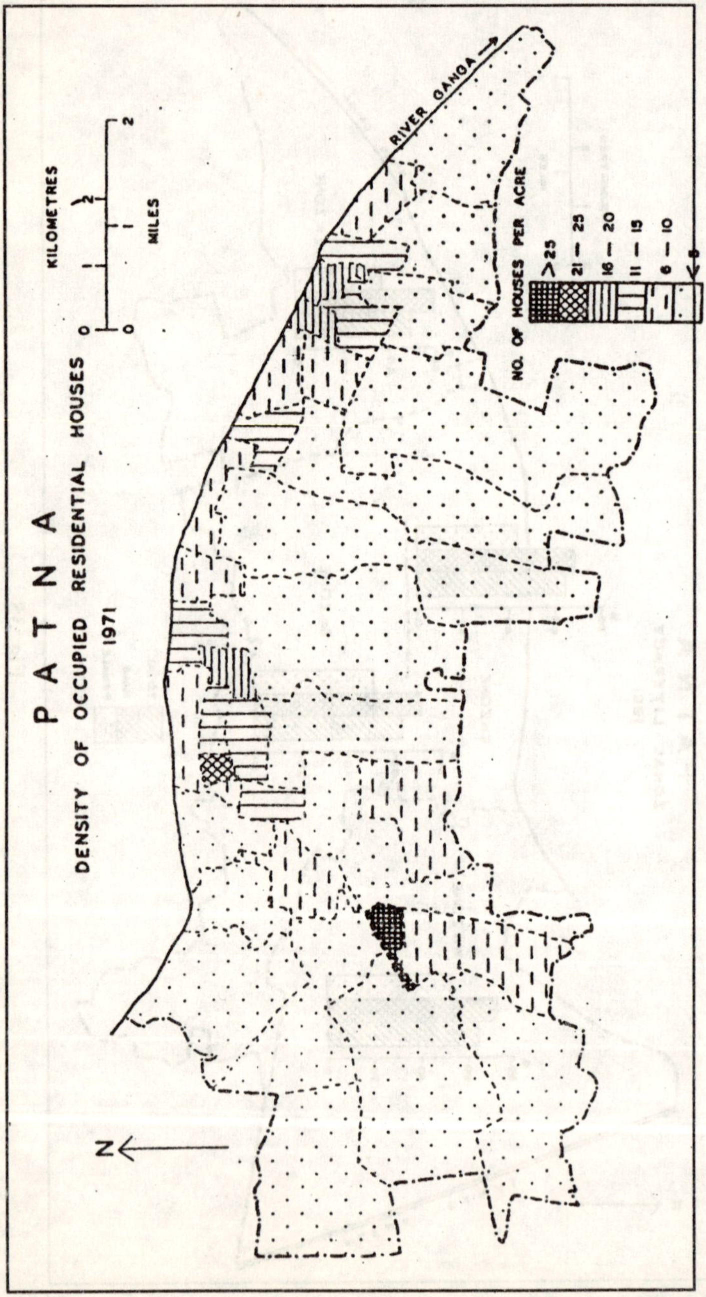
PATNA
DENSITY OF OCCUPIED RESIDENTIAL HOUSES
1971
KILOMETRES
0 1 2
0 1 2
MILES
RIVER GANGA
N
NO. OF HOUSES PER ACRE
>25
21 — 25
16 — 20
11 — 15
6 — 10
<5

Fig. 36

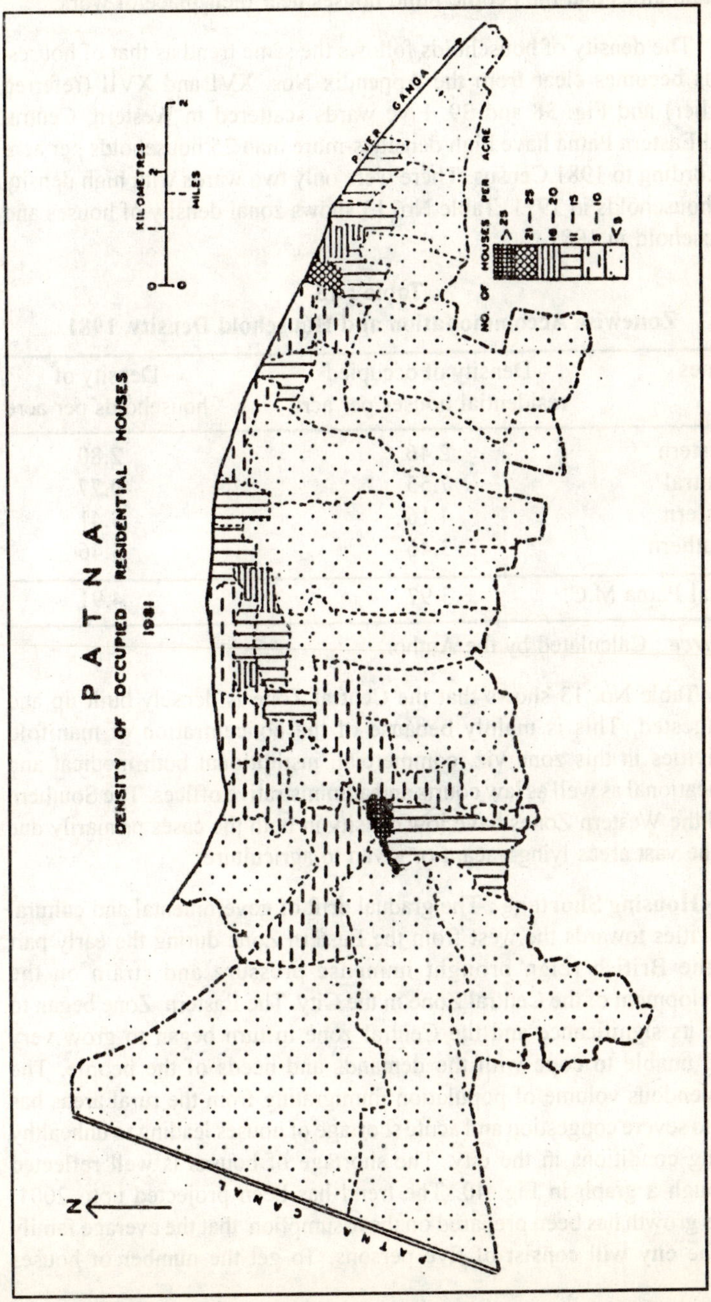
P A T N A
DENSITY OF OCCUPIED RESIDENTIAL HOUSES
1981
KILOMETRES
0 1 2
MILES
0 1 2
RIVER GANGA
PATNA CANAL
N
NO. OF HOUSES PER ACRE
> 25
21 — 25
16 — 20
11 — 15
5 — 10
< 5

Fig 37

Indian cities that the people build houses near their place of work.

The density of households follows the same trend as that of houses. This becomes clear from the Appendix Nos. XVI and XVII (referred earlier) and Fig. 38 and 39. Five wards scattered in Western, Central and Eastern Patna have high densities-more than 25 households per acre according to 1981 Census. There were only two wards with high density of households in 1971. Table No. 13 shows zonal density of houses and household in 1981

Table : 13

Zonewise Accommodation and Household Density, 1981

Zones	Density of occupied residential houses per acre	Density of households per acre
Western	2.46	2.80
Central	7.55	9.77
Eastern	4.16	5.41
Southern	3.46	3.46
Total Patna M.C.	3.97	4.91

Source : Calculated by the Author.

Table No. 13 shows that the Central Zone is densely built up and congested. This is mainly because of the concentration of manifold activities in this zone viz. commercial, institutional both medical and educational as well as law courts and administrative offices. The Southern and the Western Zones have low density in both the cases primarily due to the vast areas lying vacant or given to agriculture.

Housing Shortage : The gradual drift of governmental and cultural activities towards the west from the Eastern Zone during the early part of the British reign brought immense pressure and strain on the development of the Central Zone in the City. The Eastern Zone began to lose its significance and the Central zone in turn began to grow very fast, unable to cope with the demands and needs of the people. The tremendous volume of population immigrating from the rural areas has led to severe congestion and acute shortage of houses leading to unhealthy living conditions in the city. The shortage of houses is well reflected through a graph in Fig. 40. The trend has been projected upto 2001. This growth has been prepared on the assumption that the average family in the city will consist of five persons. To get the number of houses

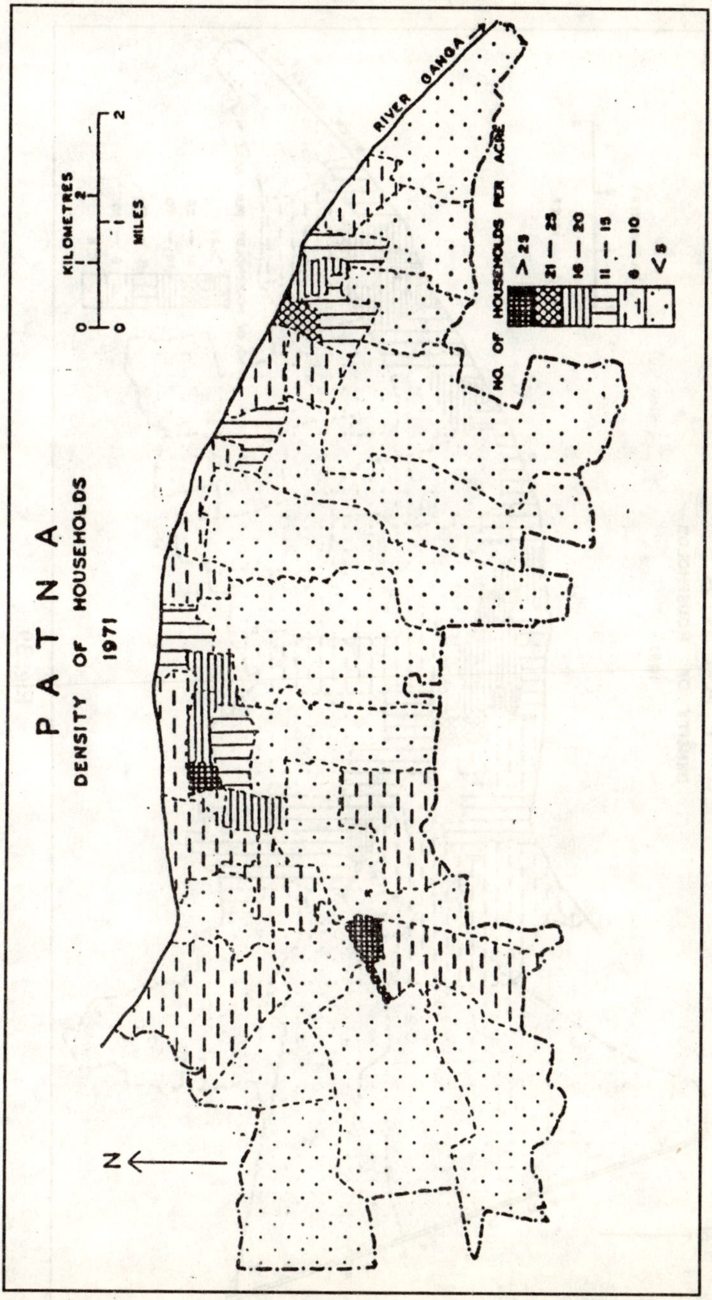
P A T N A
DENSITY OF HOUSEHOLDS
1971
KILOMETRES
0 1 2
MILES
0 1 2
N
RIVER GANGA
NO. OF HOUSEHOLDS PER ACRE
>25
21 — 25
16 — 20
11 — 15
6 — 10
<5

Fig. 38

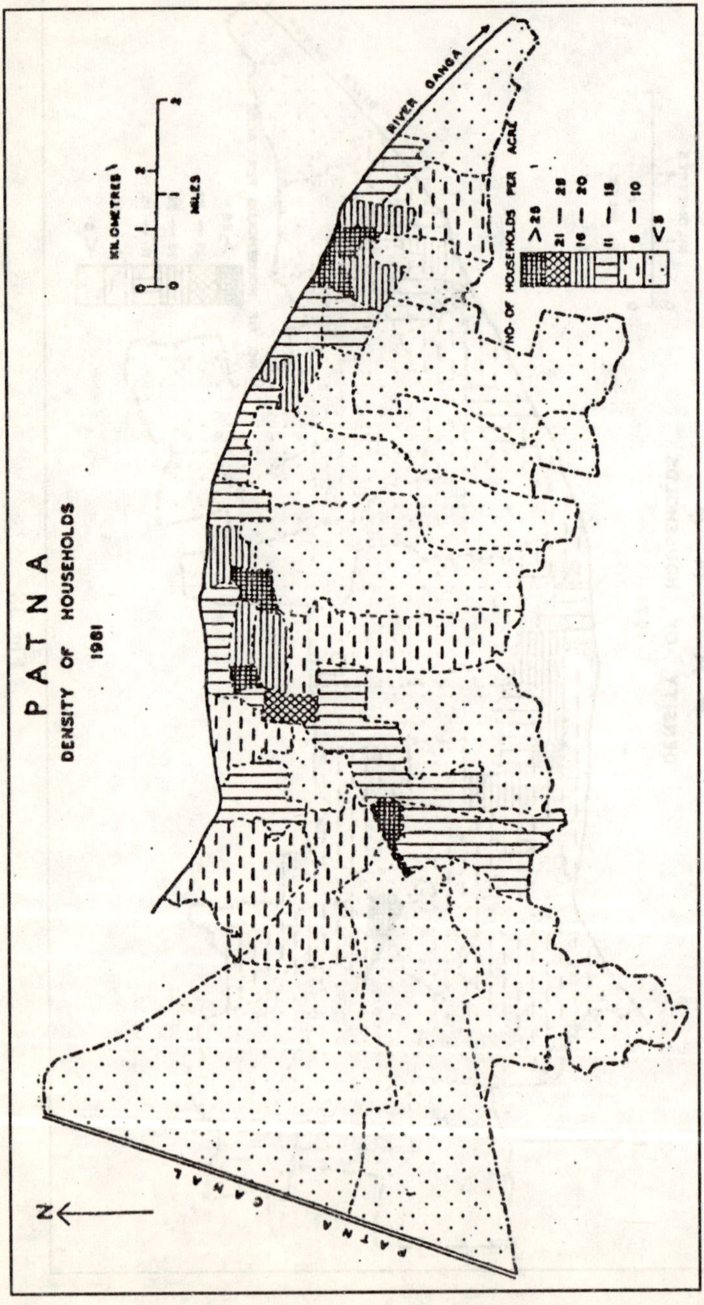

PATNA
DENSITY OF HOUSEHOLDS
1981
KILOMETRES
MILES
RIVER GANGA
NO. OF HOUSEHOLDS PER ACRE
>25
21 — 25
16 — 20
11 — 15
6 — 10
<5
N
PATNA CANAL

Fig. 39

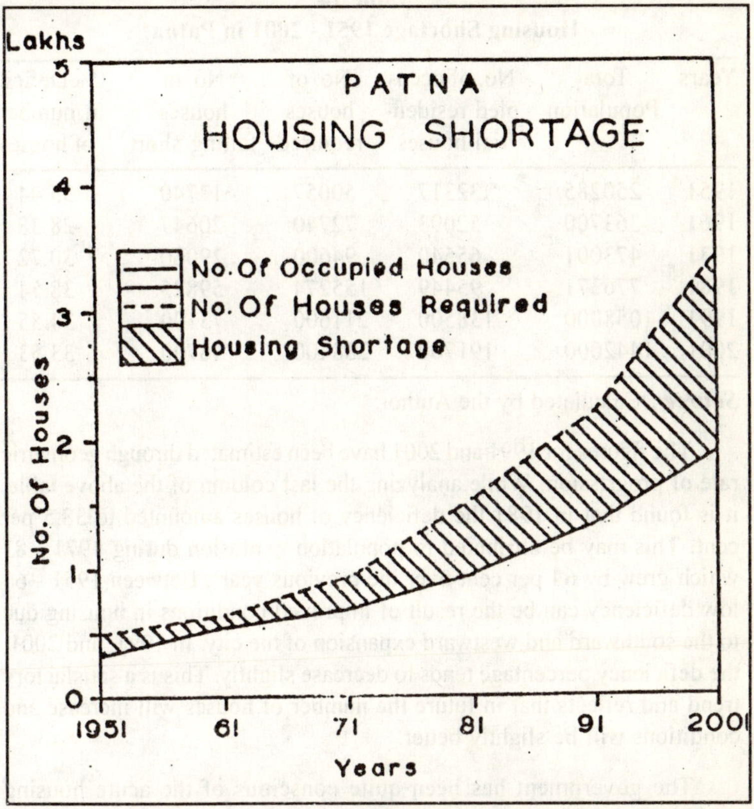

Fig. 40

required, total population in various decennial years was thus divided by 5. The gap between the number of occupied residential houses and the number of required houses represents the housing shortage. This gap has been increasing with time. This shows that in future the housing problem will be more intense and severe and hence calls for immediate and proper planning and action. The shortage, however, does not include the requirements that will be created by the demolition of dilapidated and obsolete houses, or due to the thinning or clearance of overcrowded areas or even due to change in land use from residential to nonresidential uses. The shortage, thus represents only the effect of immigration and natural increase in population. The shortage of houses in Patna through years can be seen in Table No. 14.

Table 14
Housing Shortage 1951 - 2001 in Patna

Years	Total Population	No. of occupied residential houses	No. of houses required	No. of houses falling short	% Deficit in number of houses
1951	250285	32317	50057	17740	35.44
1961	363700	52093	72740	20647	28.38
1971	473001	65540	94600	29060	30.72
1981	776371	95449	155274	59825	38.54
1991	1058000	138500	211600	73100	34.55
2001	1442000	191700	288400	96700	33.53

Source : Calculated by the Author.

The figures for 1991 and 2001 have been estimated through geometric rate of progrfssion. While analyzing the last column of the above table, it is found that in 1981 the deficiency of houses amounted to 38.5 per cent. This may be attributed to population explosion during 1971 - 81 which grew by 64 per cent over the previous year . Between 1951 - 61 low deficiency can be the result of improved conditions in housing due to the southward and westward expansion of the city. In 1991 and 2001, the deficiency percentage tends to decrease slightly. This is a satisfactory trend and reflects that in future the number of houses will increase and conditions will be slightly better.

The government has been quite conscious of the acute housing problem in Patna. During the last few years a number of housing projects were taken up both by the government and the Patna Improvement Trust (now Patna Regional Development Authority) to alleviate the housing shortage in the city. Furthermore, several cooperative housing societies have done substantial work and inspite of the problem of land acquisition, a substantial number of houses have been built in the city.

Private housing development has not been encouraging mainly because of the paucity of developed land in the city. The cost of building material has also accentuated the problem. Hence, provision of developed land is indeed urgently needed to meet the acute shortage of houses in Patna. Due consideration should be given to the needs of the economically weaker sections. The crux of the problem here is that this section of population cannot afford to build houses on their own nor can they afford to pay the prevailing rates of rent. Thus they are forced to live in clusters leading to the development of slums.

To meet the shortage of houses, it is extremely essential that the duplication of authorities and their rules and regulations and building bye - laws should be simplified in order to increase the building activities. This can be done by putting the existing resources to maximum use and giving co-ordinated direction to the entire programme and also by gearing up the administrative machinery for full implementation of housing schemes.

However, the conditions prevailing in the city have become so acute and problematic that it is beyond the capacity of local authorities to tackle the problem effectively. It is essential that urban local bodies may clear the slums and bligthed areas and improve density of population to the normal standards. The land in and around the city has to be so well planned as to check the growth of encrochments leading to the formation of slums as well also to check the addition of more population to the already thickly populated areas.

Slum Development

In India as well as elsewhere, the slums present a scene of fifth and squalor of dingy streets and unkempt zones of delapidated and obsolete houses, of overcrowding in tiny rooms and of totally inadequate civic services. In addition to pucca built slums comprising mostly of over congested single room tenements, ill ventialated and in poor state of habitation without proper services, every city has the horizontal slums of hutment colonies which pockmark the surface all over.[3].

They are the result of continuing influx of population from the rural areas. Slums are generally associated with industrial development. In the case of Patna, the reasons for their development are entirely different. Patna does not have large industries. Hence the main reason for slum development is the old age of the city. To meet the needs of migrants, chawls or bustees emerged which have later degenerated into slums. Many social vices viz., gambling, drinking, juvenile delinquency etc. are common among the people living in slums.

The slums of Patna can be divided into four types.[4] First type comprises rural - cum - urban pockets in the city where the pattern of life and physical conditions resemble rural conditions, e.g. Mandiri, Rajapur, Punaichak, Bahadurpur and Sandalpur.

The second type comprises areas where there is no regard for planning standards and housing regulations. The residents do not belong to lower class. Only the houses are built haphazardly without proper street layout and sanitary conditions. Slums of this type have developed in parts of Mithapur, Jakanpur, Yarpur, Lohanipur and Chiraiyantar.

The third type of slum areas has an extreme overcrowding of building on land and of persons in buildings. Lack of sanitary facilities leads to unhealthy conditions. Educational, recreational and other civic amenities are also sadly absent. Bakerganj, Sabzibagh, Darzitola, Goriatoli, Lalbagh, Mahendru, Shahganj and Sultanganj belong to this type of slum. All these areas together form the commercial core of the city and also contain the University and the Civil Courts.

The fourth types of slums include areas which have degenerated due to obsolence and negligence. This type has developed in parts of Sadar Gali, Bari Patan Devi, Lodi Katra and areas behind the main streets and the lanes. There are innumerable pockets of temporary thatched huts of scavengers, milkmen and washermen. Moreover, animals and human beings share the same roof. The shift of the centre of gravity from this area to the west of the city led to the degeneration of this area thereby resulting in obsolescence.

The worst slums of the City are the areas around Mithapur, Jakkanpur, Mandiri, Salimpur Ahra, Lohanipur, Sabzibagh, Musallahpur, Langertoli and Nawab Bahadur Road. Basically these are rural enclaves in the city which have been saddled with dense population without commensurate civic amenities.

The problem of these slums should be tackled in totality with a view to determining their deficiencies in respect of the physical environment and the socio-economic needs of the slum dwellers.

Slum prevention is as important as slum clearance and improvement. As such steps have to be taken to eradicate and improve the existing slums and also to ensure that the planned areas do not degenerate into slums in due course. For prevention therefore, it is necessary that proper building code be enforced, planning regulations, proper provision and maintenance of sanitary lay out also be enforced effectively.

As regards clearance and improvement of slums, measures will vary as per their type. In Patna, this problem is so acute that it is very difficult to clear and redevelop slum areas of the city. So it would be proper, instead of uprooting these areas, to improve upon these areas by providing them with basic amenities such as roads, electricity, water supply, parks etc. There are a few areas which require complete renovation. In such cases, the population to be displaced should be offered with shelter before implementation of this operation.

In the Central Zone, the areas around Muradpur are very densely populated, the density reaching more than 250 persons per acre at some places. This has been mainly due to the availability of basic amenities in earlier times. However, these amenities now fall short of requirement and are unable to meet the demands of the growing population in these areas. As such these areas require to be improved upon regarding basic amenities.

The Eastern Zone of the city is the main sufferer from this disease. The entire area is deteriorating rapidly because of negligence and old age. The area needs to be provided with employment opportunities in the shape of new small scale industries and institutions in this part of the city. Measures should also be taken to improve street pattern, housing condition and sanitary conditions, which in turn will infuse a new life into the dwellers of this area.

Setting up of Centrifugal and Centripetal Forces

The development of function, form and pattern is governed by a set of forces which are definite yet imperfectly recognized. These are termed Centrifugal and Centripetal forces. The centrifugal forces impel functions to migrate from the central part of a city towards or beyond its periphery while the centripetal forces hold certain functions in the central part of the city and attract others to it.

The existing land use in most parts of Patna is the result of uncontrolled sprawl which has consolidated over a period of time. Therefore, the problem is more acute regarding urban renewal and redevelopment of existing area, than that of controlling the haphazard development of new areas. In order that the urban development of the city takes place in an organized manner and the plan be comprehensive and economic, it is essential that there be a balance between the centrifugal and centripetal forces. For this dispersal of different activities and their proper allocation is necessary to be done. For instance the Central Zone of the city has mixed land uses. It is very congested, leaving no space for further development and expansion of any activity.

To make the Central Zone and other congested areas of the city relieved of the burden of ever increasing population density, a dispersal of different activities should be enforced.

The suggestions made below should be strictly adhered to in the interest of future development of the city.

1. The Government buildings such as the Courts, Collectorate and Divisional Offices are located in haphazard manner in the Central Zone and have no space for further expansion. It is proposed to shift all of them to the Western or the Southern zone of the city. If all these offices are at one place., the efficiency increases and maneuverability of work becomes easier. This will also result in the shift of population from the Central Zone to the Western or Southern parts of the city.

2. The locations of the General Hospital in the heart of the city is rather ironical. Situated along the Ganga, its location was favorable in an earlier period but now as it stands in the busiest and noisiest part of the city, its location does not seem proper. It would be proper if the entire hospital unit is shifted closer to the river bank leaving a belt of vacant land between the hospital buildings and the arterial road namely Ashok Raj Path and the entire campus landscaped. The hospital should be in the midst of tranquil atmosphere, pure air and green background. The development of Indira Gandhi Institute of Medical Science in Western Patna which is already going on will help move the people from central part of the city.

3. Patna University and most of its colleges are situated in the Central Zone of the city, north of the Ashok Raj Path, along the bank of the Ganga. Owing to congestion its further expansion is restricted. It is desirable that the whole campus be shifted to the Western Zone, north of Bailey Road in Sheikhpura area. Large tracts of land are lying vacant in this part of the city which can be used for the University Campus. The serene and calm atmosphere of the University has also been lost due to growing congestion and noise of automobile moving in this zone. In order to restore its serenity, a new educational campus should be created. If this happens, it will attract population to settle around it and in turn help to reduce the density in the Central Zone. The existing building can be used for specialized research and vocational training.

When all these institutions are shifted to the southern and the western parts of the city, ample land will be available for the development of the river front and by widening of the Ashok Raj Path a new CBD can be created. A convenient mobility of traffic and their parking can also be made possible.

No doubt, the whole affair will be costly but seen from the other side, the face of the city will change completely. The river - front with parks and gardens will add to the beauty of the city. The Central Zone will be given solely to commercial use.

The shifting of administrative and educational functions from Central Zone to Western and Southern Zones will act as a centrifugal force and their congregation in the respective zones act as a centripetal force.

4. The present commercial activities in the Central, Eastern and Western Zones of the city are mostly carried along the street. This is hazardous and undesirable as far as traffic is concerned. Since they have been existing from a long time, their removal will create a lot of problems such as displacement of a large number of shopkeepers and their relocation in a consolidated form. It is proposed that they be left alone, and the condition may be improved upon with slight changes to provide parking for vehicles and safety to pedestrians.

Shopping Centres should be planned in the Western and the Southern Zones to meet the demands of the local residents. This would also help in relocation of the population.

5. Patna has a large number of small and medium sized industries and unfortunately it has never given birth to any large industry. To strengthen the economic base of the city and to enhance employment potentialities, it is necessary to establish some industries in an organized manner. It is proposed to develop such industries in the western part of the city near Digha and also in the eastern part of the city south - east of the Patna Sahib Railway Station. These two pockets will serve as centripetal nodes and may eventually provide employment to more than 50,000 persons. Besides other small industrial sectors can also be opened to the north of Phulwari Sharif Railway Station and to the east of the Patna Gaya railway line in Western Patna. These will also provide employment to a fair amount of people and consequently will favour relocation of population.

6. Some parts of Central and Eastern Patna are very densely populated with densities of more then 200 persons per acre. Most of the densely populated area have degenerated into slums and are marked by obsolete conditions of living. Especially in Eastern Patna, the housing conditions are very poor and primitive. They need to be improved upon thoroughly. In order to attain a balanced population distribution, relocation of the population is necessary. The people from these areas can be shifted to

other parts of the city, say in the southern zone. It is proposed that the government should construct multi - storeyed buildings with two roomed flats fitted with basic necessities and amenities. These should be provided to the population shifted from the slums. This seems a bit difficult and costly but at the same time this will check the city from further degeneration. Examples of such an exercise can be cited from Delhi and Chandigarh. Several degenerated colonies and slums have been demolished in these cities and new colonies have been set up in providing a fresh look to the urban landscape. Of course, the dislocated people were provided with accommodation by the government.

It is emphasized that inspite of the tremendous finance involved, planning and future development of the city can be guided by the above suggestions if a 'beautiful Patna' is to be conceived and presented to the public.

The Old Master Plan for Patna

The Master Plan for Patna[5] was presented in two volumes in 1962 to enforce control on the development of the city based on certain imperatives. They were :

1. The character of the city.
2. Provision for accommodation such as hotels, rest houses etc. to the large seasonal floating population.
3. Economy of the city.
4. Measures for provision of work opportunities to the people.
5. Provision for housing the growing population of the city.
6. Provision for places of learning, cultural activities and recreation for all age groups and for all classes of people.
7. To decrease the problem of transportation and
8. The implementation of the Master Plan.

The plan has been prepared for a period of two decades. The city, however, could not cease to grow after twenty years and therefore, the various projections had been made within reasonable limits of accuracy only for that period. The projections had been made based on the past trend and certain premises for the foreseable future.

The inherent drawbacks of the urban structure of the city were the lack of basic medium of cohesion and of common civic interests among the people. The Master Plan envisaged the creation of planned neighbourhood units. The concept of neighbourhood units emerged from technical considerations. As Singh[6] points out, " the present tendency of urban development is to decentralize the urban population into different communities or districts sub-divided into neighbourhood units".

In recent years experiments with neighbourhood units have been tried with a fair amount of success in many countries of the world and in India as well in the planning of the new cities e.g. Chandigarh. The concept of neighbourhood units in its subsequent applications was found to be well-founded in as much as it also sought to solve some of the dangerous social tendencies of unrestrained development of rapidly growing cities.

The basic concept of the emerging urban pattern for Patna was based on the principle of 'organic growth', that is, growth related and geared to the day to day living needs of the people. The physical manifestation of this principle can be found in the 'cellular form' which envisages that the city should be comprised of a number of 'cells' each within a distinct identity and function of its own, but coherently integrated with each other to give the city its total form and function.[7]

As proposed in the Master Plan, the neighbourhood was to be a self contained unit where a group of people were to reside and within which all day to day needs of those living were to be met. The optimum size of the neighbourhood depends on two factors :

(a) Desired 'limits of walkability', and

(b) The size of group within which a sense of neighbourhood is experienced and which is able to sustain the minimum basic units of all the social service elements that are required for day to day living.

The limits of walkability is relatively easier to determine. It depends on time, distance and desirability. The size of the group cannot be determined with precision.

The proposed population in all new neighbourhoods have been kept at multiples of 7500 so that they can support one or more complete units of the basic social service elements. However, where the neighbourhood population is less or more than the required for optimum neighbourhood the sizes of the social services elements as well as their numbers can be suitably adjusted to meet the requirement of the population. The master plan proposed to divide the city into 27 neighbourhood units.

There is generally shortage of urban land in many cities and a general trend has been to obtain as high a density as possible by constructing tall multi-storeyed building. In the case of Patna, this, however, was not possible. This may be ascribed to various reasons. First, the city lies in the seismic belt; Secondly, the soil is not suitable for multi - storeyed structure and thirdly, multi - storyed buildings require quite a large sum of money for special services such as lifts etc., and fourthly, with the non - mechanized system of building construction, the cost of construction per unit floor area is much higher for multi - storyed building. In view of these limitations the buildings in Patna were assumed to be restricted to two or three storeys only.

Studies in the residential densities in relation to height (storeys) of buildings indicate that with two or three storeyed buildings, optimum gross residential densities vary between 45 to 75 persons per acre. The high figure in exceptional cases such as for redevelopment of existing congested areas can however, be exceeded to a gross residential density of 100 persons per by reducing to a certain extent, the width of the roads and size of social service elements. But for new residential development of the city, the gross density must be between 45 and 75 persons peracre. As such the optimum size of the neighbourhood in terms of population works out to be 15,000 persons and in terms of physical extent between 200 and 300 acres. It is clear that one neighbourhood will have two sub-units having a population of 7,500 each. This figure seemed desirable to the framers of the Master Plan as it was large enough to give a neighbourhood an urban character and small enough to stimulate social relationship.

The old Master Plan also made certain proposals for a limited change in traffic pattern, civic services and institutional planning. More particularly it laid emphasis on future land use for the city taking into account mainly the new and vacant space around the city.

Unfortunately the proposed Master Plan became out-dated even before it reached the stage of execution. This was partly on account of government's intransigence because of paucity of funds, and partly because the growth of population was phenomenal and outstripped all estimate. In fact, the city sprawl continued unhindered and its pace was so rapid that planning for all neighbourhood units became awry and went unimplemented. Thus slums grew unchecked, the civic services fell short and the population density increased enormously all over the city.

Present Development Proposals

Public policy objectives concerning urban population distribution often are achieved through residential land use regulation. Control over population distribution also can be exerted indirectly through the selection of employment sites. If population policy goals can be expressed as target for each zone of the urban area, then it is possible to determine that spatial distribution of employment for which population distribution comes as close as possible to these targets.[8]

It has been suggested in the New Master Plan for Patna, which is under preparation by the P.R.D.A. that the city is expected to expand 600 yards beyond the New Patna Bye Pass Road in the South and 100 yards beyond Patna Canal in the west.

Keeping this in the view, following policies for the future development of the city may be suggested here :

1. It is essential that any development taking place in future be guided by proper organization of land uses in Patna. For implementation of any urban development programme, availability of land and its control are essential prerequisites. Control such as zoning regulations, subdivision rules, buildings bye - laws and authority to approve layouts are means of directing urban growth. Uncontrolled settlements and squatting on public lands pock-marks the urban landscape and attempts to control their growth are doomed to failure. Acquisition of land and creating an adequate stock of urban land would be essential not only for future growth but also for a large number of public use and slum clearance programmes.

2. Proper allocation of land of a particular use should be the first priority of planning. For this land use zoning has to be initiated. Zoning is the legal regulation of the use of land. It is for the protection of public health, welfare and safety. The regulation includes provisions for the use of property and limitations upon the shape and bulk of buildings that occupy the land. Zoning is not a substitute nor an alternative for the general plan. The general plan expresses basic policies which shapes the community character, the general land use, circulation and relationship among the variety of urban facilities. The zoning plan establishes the

specific limitations which apply to the use of land as an instrument for achieving the goals set forth in the general plan. Serving as a comprehensive guide for urban development, the general plan is usually adopted as a 'resolution' by the legislative body. The zoning plan is adopted and rendered effective as a legal 'ordinance'. So zoning only provides the framework within which planning is undertaken and is an essential part of any comprehensive plan but is not a substitute.

3. As suggested in the old master plan 'the neighbourhood concept' for the future development of he city will be helpful and appropriate and will lead to a planned development of the city. There will thus be easy availability of education, health, shopping and recreation facilities because all will be served within the neighbourhood itself. As a result, loss of time and energy will be checked. It is proposed that vacant land of the city be divided into adequate number of neighbourhoods (approximately 60) each accommodating a population of 10, 000 persons and each provided with all basic and utility services. The existing colonies should be developed and fitted into this overall pattern. This concept has been discussed in detail earlier in this chapter.

4. Encroachment often takes place on vacant land and leads to substandard development of the area. This should be thoroughly checked. These encroachments are generally done by migrant rural population. Since the city is growing rapidly housing schemes should be implemented so that the immigrating population is provided with accommodation. The local authority should take an initiative to construct single room flats accommodating migrant population.

5. Large tracts of land are lying vacant in Western and Southern Patna. Apart from developing residential, commercial and recreational complexes, it would be proper to leave open spaces in between which should be developed later into parks and playgrounds. This would be beneficial to the residents of the area and provide them with a healthy environment. Such planned developments have taken place in a few cities of the country namely Jamshedpur, Bokaro, Chandigarh, New Delhi, Bangalore etc.

The open space in a residential area should be in proportion to the density of that area. As suggested by the Planning Standards framed by the Government of Bihar, the open space exclusive for active recreation and breathing place, shall be worked out on proposed population of the area. The following criteria may be adopted for arriving at open space depending on density.[9]

Persons per acre	Persons per hectare	Open Space in percentage
100	250	15
150	325	18
200	500	22
250 & above	625 & above	25

However, open spaces provided in the proposed land use plan of a Master Plan, shall be over and above this minimum open space and shall not be counted under the density ratio mentioned above.

6. The very basis of planning lies in the functional relationship between total land and various uses to which it is put. It is felt that undesirable mixing of land uses all over the city should be thoroughly checked.

7. All urban settlements tend to engulf the surrounding agricultural land. In order to check this unwarranted urban growth it is necessary that green belt be provided around the city. This will allow to shape the expansion of the city as well as act as a restrictive measure to urban sprawl. In the case of Patna, a green belt should be created to the south and west of Patna.

Apart from the suggestions made above for the future development pattern of the city, the author feels it appropriate to make a few more suggestions regarding the improvement of certain services existing within the city.

(a) Most of the roads in the city are narrow and encroached upon on either side by shops and other commercial buildings and offices on account of which they are congested and are often faced with traffic jams. This calls for a better alignment and adequate width of roads in future so that these problems may not be repeated. The roads should be of four lane or six lane width as necessary to hold easy movement of two -way traffic. Besides, sufficient space should be left open on either side of the roads for their future widening. This should be strictly followed.

(b) Mixed traffic is a serious problem in the city's life. Strong measures have to be taken to arrest this problem. After all population is bound to increase and so will the associated problems. Dividing the slow moving vehicles such as rickshaws and thelas (cart) from fast moving cars and scooters will be a proper step. It is difficult to do away with rickshaws altogether, but separate traffic lanes can be reserved for them. The frequency of buses, minibuses, three-wheelers, etc. should be increased to cope with the increasing population and cause a fast movement of traffic. Once this task is done, chances of traffic jams will be less. It will also be essential to remove traffic bottlenecks caused by narrow road widths at certain points, such as near Kulharia house, southern Exhibition Road and near the Hospital. There are numerous such points in Eastern Patna.

(c) Another serious problem is that of drainage of Patna. Unless a severe measure is undertaken and implemented thoroughly the future development of the city will remain threatened. The city slopes from north to south and from west to east. The city has always faced drainage problems because nearly all drainage lines open into the Ganga in the north. During the monsoon season, when the river is in spate, the level of the river rises above the level of the natural drainage lines and these are unable to discharge slush and sullage into the Ganga. This results in the back flow through the manholes, thereby flooding the low lying areas. Therefore, in order to check this, it would be proper that all drainage channels are taken to the south with outfalls into the Punpun. No doubt, this project will involve a huge amount of money but at the same time it will turn into a cheaper exercise in the long run as pumping of water out of the choked drains also involves an enormous expense on electricity.

Besides, there are several other problems such as housing shortages, slum clearance and commercial development etc. which have already been discussed in the earlier chapter to which reference may be made. This also involves urban renewal and reconstruction leading to a reallocation of population between these areas.

The problem of population redistribution has already been discussed in earlier pages. We have seen that the density of population is high in Central and Eastern Zones and low in the Western and Southern Zones. The population density., however, is rapidly rising in Southern Patna, where ample land is available for private construction. Expansion in the west is restricted because most of the land is owned by the Government and earmarked for specified institutions. It is for this reason that the city is expected to expand in the west beyond Dinapur Khagaul road by the year 2001.

By this year, a greater Patna is likely to emerge with a population of over 2 millions which will have a continuous urban tract between Hajipur and Parsa Bazar from north to south and between Fatwa and Dinapur - Khagual from east to west. Development of these satellite towns as dormitory towns will reduce the influx of people into Patna. It is, therefore, desirable that centripetal forces be set up in all satellite towns mentioned in Chapter V by developing them and providing them with civic amenities and new housing colonies. The industrial estate at Hajipur in the north and at Banka Ghat/Fatwa in the east are steps in this direction. At the same time these towns should have adequate transport connection with Patna.

Within Patna itself, centrifugal forces should be set up in the Central Zone and centripetal forces developed in the Southern and Western Zones. This can be done by shifting certain institutions from Central Patna to Western or Southern Patna, as discussed earlier. All this will lead to better coordination between different parts of the city and a better redistribution of population. The attempt should be to reduce and keep in check the population density to less than 100 persons per acre as envisaged in the planning standards.

***References* :**

1. Northam, R. N. : op. cit. p. 393.
2. Ibid : p. 393.
3. Bhardwaj, R. K. : op.cit. p. 279.
4. Master Plan for Patna : op. cit. p. 76.
5. The Master Plan for Patna : op. cit.
6. Singh, U. (1961) : "Allahabad : A Study in its Planning and Development", National Geographical Journal of India, Vol. VIII, p. 108.
7. Master Plan for Patna : op. cit., p. 61.
8. Barber, G. M. (1977) : Urban Population Distribution Planning in Hudson, J. C. (ed.) Annals of the Association of American Geog., Vol. 67, No. 2. p. 239.
9. Planning Standards and Building Bye - Laws for cities with population more than 1,00,000 of Bihar 1976, prepared by Bihar Govt. Building Bye - Law's Committee.

7

Summary and Conclusion

General Summary

An immense areal expansion of cities has taken place during this century all over the world. However, the magnitude of a real expansion is a matter of degree and varies from country to country. Immigration is the main reason for increase in urban population, and it has led to several problems associated with civic life.

Very simply, urban sprawl or areal expansion of cities or urban development refers to the spatial expansion of urban concentrations beyond the limits of the city, thus occupying rural pockets in the periphery.

A number of research work has been done in several countries of the world. Geographers have studied the general pattern of urban development in its various stages, causes of development, the problems associated with it and the solutions of these problems. However, very few authors have tried to put forth and suggest ways for controlling urban development. The pattern of growth of cities has been studied by Burgess, Hoyt and Harris and Ullman. Sinclair, Shipton and Willi have studied the stages of urban expansion and problems associated with them. In India, Bhardwaj has dealt with the problems faced by Indian cities in the way of their expansion and also their solutions. Other important works have been done by Dann, Ujagir Singh, R.L. Singh, Bonifatieva and others in this field.

In the present work an attempt has been made to view the pattern of urban development in Patna through years as also the pattern of population distribution within the city. The city's development has been compared with the theoretical models.

Problems related to the development of the city have been analyzed. Finally, the author has suggested measures to overcome these problems so that the development of the city in future may take place in a planned manner.

The city of Patna stands on the levee of the Ganga in the north. The Sone lies to the west and the Punpun is in the south. The confluence of the Punpun and the Ganga is in the east. The general slope of the city is from north to south and from west to east. These restrictions have inhibited the growth of Patna and have confined the city to a linear shape. Patna M.C. has an area of 79.42 sq. kms. with a population of 7,76,373 persons according to 1981 census, the corresponding density being 32.23 persons per acre. It has 37 Municipal wards.

Patna's history goes back to 2500 years. Its growth has mainly been guided by the physical character of its site right from the beginning. The northward expansion of the city has always been restricted by the presence of river Ganga, and the southward expansion has been restricted because of the low level of the land and the fear of its being flooded by the Punpun. The city has thus developed and expanded along the levee of the Ganga in a restricted manner taking a linear shape. In 1911-12, it became the capital of the newly formed Province of Bihar and Orissa. After independence the city started growing rapidly in terms of both people and space. The main contribution for this population growth has been made by migrants coming from the surrounding rural areas. This feature is likely to continue in the future.

Patna can be divided into four zones - Eastern, Central, Western and Southern. The Eastern and the Central Zones were built during the medieval times while the Western and the Southern Zones have developed entirely during the 20th century. The Eastern Zone is the oldest part, haphazardly developed and densely populated. The Central Zone being that of British origin is slightly better though still unplanned and densely populated. The Western Zone was particularly planned as new capital by the Britishers after 1911. In the Southern Zone the development is most recent, but unfortunately it is largely unplanned.

Patna is a very old city and its earlier population is not known. The population figures mentioned in the chronicles of various travellers cannot be taken as authentic. Since 1872 the census figures reveal that the population of Patna has been growing save between 1881 and 1901 when it declined by 21 per cent. Till 1921, the population kept fluctuating but thereafter it has grown steadily. During 1921-31 the population increased by 33 per cent. It has maintained almost the same rate of growth with slight fluctuations till 1971. However, the growth rate has been exemplary during 1971 - 81 being over 64 per cent. This has occurred mainly because of progress and advancement in various services viz. medical, educational, commercial and other civic amenities. These have acted as a magnet for the rural population. This tremendous increase in population has resulted in the failure of civic resources and has led to a type of urban chaos. As such several problems such as housing shortage, traffic problem, lack of basic amenities and slum development have come into existence.

The pattern of distribution of population in the city has been uneven. During pre-independence period, the population was concentrated in Eastern Patna, the chief centre for wholesale trade in the city. Then the people moved west, although still preferring to live near their place of work. Lately, the trend has been to settle away from the city's congestion, noise and pollution. Thus the people are now settling in the Western and Southern parts of the city, quite distant from the city's centre. The Eastern and Central parts of the city are more densely settled while the Western and Southern parts are still relatively free from congestion.

The ward level figures for various decadal years are difficult to compare because of the enormous changes brought about in the municipal area and ward boundaries in the city. However, for the purpose of study, data for 1971 has been recalculated by wards on the basis of the area and location of the wards in 1981.

There is a marked contrast in the intra -city distribution of population during 1981. Ward No. 15 lying in Central Patna, covering Muradpur area has the highest density of more than 225 persons per acre. This is the commercial focus of the city. In contrast Ward No.1 falling in Western Patna has the lowest density of 8.39 persons per acre. Throughout the city the commercial areas are more densely populated and the density decreases towards the agricultural and low lying areas in the west and the south.

In all the four zones of the city male population is slightly higher than female population in all age groups. Broadly speaking, female population is concentrated more in the Eastern Zone and gradually decreases towards the west. This is probably because this part is the oldest in the city and provides job opportunities for lower class people. Low female ratio in the western part is mainly because of administrative functions dominating in the area.

The level of literacy in the city has increased from 53.36 per cent in 1971 to 58.95 per cent in 1981. This may be ascribed to the growing general awareness among the urbanities, as well as better educational facilities available in this city. The literacy is well over 60 per cent in the western half of the city and well below 50 per cent in the eastern half. Male literacy is also higher in the west because of the concentration of upper class people. Low female literacy here may be because of the presence of uneducated female migrants from rural areas.

'The growth of the city's population has been influenced by various physical, social, economic and political factors in varying degrees of their complexity. The future growth is also likely to be affected by these factors. However, the growth of Patna will always be restricted in the north and the east.

Mahatma Gandhi Setu built over the Ganga linking Patna with Hajipur has led to a substantial increase in the commuting population, making the city more congested during the day. The present population of 7.6 lakhs is estimated increase to 1.4 millions by 2001 A.D.

Patna with its long history of evolution and development has areas given to mixed land uses. However, three land use categories predominate in the city. These are : residential, commercial, administrative - cum - institutional. Residential areas are spread all over the city but Kankerbag Colony is South Patna in the largest residential area in the city. It mostly houses middle class people. The commercial concentration is highest in the City Chowk in Eastern Patna specializing in wholesale trade. Muradpur in Central Patna is the second important commercial centre specialising in retail trade while the third market is around Mithapur in Western Patna. The administrative sector falls in the Western part of the city which is marked by the Raj Bhawan, Old and New Secretariats, Circuit House, High Court, General Post Office etc. The institutional sector is confined more to the central part of the city. This part forms a compact administrative - cum - institutional zone and has colleges, University and various government and judicial offices located in this part. The city, apart from these land uses, is also given to other functions such as recreational, industrial and transportational. Patna may be said to be an administrative - cum - institutional - cum - commercial city.

The effect of land use on population is reflected in the occupational structure of the city. The highest concentration of workers in 1971 was found in the Central Zone which is the centre of multi - functional activities which gradually shifted to the Western Zone in 1981 because of the increase in administrative activities. The percentage of working force is highest in these services being over 36 per cent followed by employment in commercial activities.

Since Patna is an unplanned city and a city of mixed land uses, demarcation of clear-cut functional zones becomes difficult. However, broad functional zones have been demarcated on the basis of dominant functions of the city. Four zones, namely residential, commercial, administrative and institutional have been recognized.

The residential zone occupied most of the urban land in the past and continues to do so even today. The oldest part of the city had maximum concentration of houses. Then the buildings spread along the Ashok Raj Path in the early 20th century. The growing congestion in these areas forced the occupants to move out which led to the expansion of the residential zone upto Sheikhpura in the west and New Bye - Pass Road in the South. The upper class residential areas have mainly sprung up in the west. The middle class residential houses are found throughout the city.

There are three commercial nuclei in the city. The City Chowk, the oldest part has been the commercial core of the city since the beginning. The second commercial core developed around Muradpur retail complex and the third has sprung up around Mithapur. All these cores are in a way continuous except one or two breaks in between. The entire commercial zone appears like a narrow ribbon because shops are aligned along the roads. Retail trading is busiest and most important along the Ashok Raj Path. Maroofganj and Mansoorganj in Eastern Patna are renowned wholesale grain markets. Shopping ribbons are seen flanking almost all roads. These commercial areas have developed adjacent to residential areas and cater to the basic requirements of the residents.

Patna has been an administrative focus right from the beginning. The new Capital City was laid out in Western Patna when Patna became the capital of the Province of Bihar and Orissa in 1911-12. This part was outside the municipal limit of the city. With the passage of time, the city grew and took within its limit this administrative area. Now, it serves as the capital city, and headquarters of district and divisional administration. The second major concentration is in Central Zone where the Courts, the Collectorate and divisional offices are located. The third concentration is found in Eastern Patna where sub-divisional courts and jail and other government offices are located.

Modern Patna became the cultural focus and a seat of learning since the establishment of the Patna University in 1917 in the Central Zone. Most of the constituent colleges of this University are located in this zone. Some colleges are also found in other parts of the city. Schools are located particularly everywhere in the city especially at the primary level.

Apart from these three functional zones there are other functional zones such as medical, industrial, transportational, recreational etc., but they form small patches.

The pattern of distribution and growth of population is well reflected in the administrative and commercial zones of the city. It is expected that in the coming years the density of population will continue to be high in the commercial and the central administrative zones of the city.

Patna being centrally located in the Middle Ganga Plain has command over the entire region. A regular transaction of industrial and agricultural goods and services takes place between the capital city and its hinterland. Being connected with the region by various means of transportation, the city acts as a node for the entire region. This nodal character of the city has helped Patna to expand its trade and services, which subsequently have made it attain a metropolitan character. Patna's Metropolitan Sphere can be broadly said to bee formed of Danapur - Hajipur - Fatwą - Masaurhi - Maner - Dighwara belt.

The city expanded gradually and swallowed up several rural pockets lying on its periphery. The development of the city can be shown to be in consonance with three traditional theories of urban growth . It has been found that since the development of the city of Patna is linear, it cannot be explained in terms of the theory of concentric development advanced by Burgess. However it can be explained partly through the theory of Hoyts and partly through that of Harris and Ullman's. The sectors of various activities have developed in Patna not from a single point but from several points . Thus the multi nuclei theory is more applicable to Patna's form of development . The city has three nuclei - City Chowk, Muradpur and Mithapur - all of which happen to be commercial foci . From these points the city has grown in sectors of various sizes and radii. The density of population also decreases gradually away from these nuclei reflecting and proving the growth pattern and expansion of the city .

The city has been growing on account of its multifarious services being provided to the entire region, such as medical ,educational , recreational, water supply, drainage, and sewerage ,electricity, transport and communication etc. However these have been short of requirements and have been unable to cope with the growing demands of increasing population of the city thereby creating several complex problems . Some of the major problems include housing shortage, development of slums and transport bottlenecks.

The city has been growing in a haphazard manner. The problem is not of 'growth' but of 'unplanned growth' which spreads like an unchecked disease and creates problems for future development of the city. This is a serious matter to be looked into and calls for stern measures that would ensure proper and fruitful development of the city.

Setting up of centrifugal and centripetal forces is extremely essential for the dispersal of different activities within the city which may lead to a more balanced distribution of population in future. A number of suggestions have been made regarding physical planning and land use as well as policies to be adopted in this connection. These are given in Chapter VI.

A comprehensive Master Plan for Patna had been prepared in 1962 for its future development. Unfortunately, it was not fully implemented. In the meanwhile the growth of population outstripped the estimates made by planners. The present population of Patna is likely to grow to 1.4 million and a Greater Patna is likely to emerge with a population of over 2 millions by 2001. There is now need to prepare a new Master Plan with the guidelines suggested above and it should be enforced by the authorities in right earnest.

Conclusion

The intra-city distribution and growth of population in Patna has been guided mainly by the configuration of site and physical environment of the city . The growth and expansion of Patna has been restricted because of the rivers Ganga, Punpun and Sone lying to the north, south and west of the city respectively.

The general slope of the city is from north to south and from west to east . However the levee of the Ganga slopes from east to west . As such, right from the beginning, the population was concentrated mainly in eastern Patna. Gradually when this part of the city became overcrowded, the people shifted towards west and south . The present trend of growth is along the transport lines viz. Patna -Dinapur road along the Ganga, along Bailey road towards Phulwari and Khagaul and in areas between the railway line and the new bye pass road in the south, where the density of population has already become high. The commercial areas of Patna form the more densely populated nuclei and the density decreases gradually towards the lowlying and agricultural areas in the south and west.

The distributional pattern of the city's population and functional character of the urban land are very closely associated with each other and the effect of land use on population is reflected in the occupational structure of Patna. The percentage of total workers went down slightly in 1981 as compared to 1971 figures, mainly on account of the large influx of persons in search of jobs. The rate of growth of employment opportunities has not kept pace with the tremendously growing population of the city. This may be traced to the absence of significant industrial development in the city.

Till 1971, the workers were concentrated mainly in Central Patna but lately they have spread towards western Patna because of an increase in administrative activities.

It was expected that with the growth of population during 1971-81, the pattern of land use and population character would change. However, the overall picture continues to be the same with only small changes in respective percentages.

It has been found that Patna in its initial phases grew around a single nucleus around the Chowk area of Eastern Patna. However, because of the physical constraints, the city took a linear shape, thereby restricting its concentric development. As such the growth of Patna is not compatible with Burgess's Theory of concentric development. The city's structural growth pattern is compatible with Hoyt's theory of sectorial development to some extent. However, in Patna, sectors of various activities have developed not from single nucleus but radiate outwards from several nuclei. As such Hoyt's theory is only partially applicable to Patna's form of urban growth. Thus, the present growth pattern fits better with the Multi - Nuclei Theory of Harris and Ullman, and the nuclei and their sectors fall in an overall linear pattern.

Patna has three nuclei viz. City Chowk (Eastern Patna), Muradpur Complex (Central Patna) and the New Market Area (Western Patna). All these happen to be commercial nuclei. From these points the city has grown in sectors expanding on all sides. They have developed rather rapidly and haphazardly leading to a dense concentration of population around them. The density decreases gradually away from these nuclei.

The mutual growth towards two nuclei which lie in a linear fashion has imparted an elongated shape to the city. The developments of sectors towards north and south have been restricted by the riverine tracts.

Patna has been growing rapidly because of the various civic amenities being provided to its entire region. However, they have not been able to meet the ever increasing demands of the growing population, thereby creating several complex problems such as housing shortage, slum development, traffic bottlenecks etc.

In order to overcome these problems stern measures should be taken which may ensure dispersal of various activities within the city and may lead to a more balanced distribution of population. The existing mixed land use in most parts of Patna is the result of uncontrolled sprawl which has consolidated over a period of time. Therefore, the problem is more intense regarding urban redevelopment and urban renewal of the existing areas than that of controlling the haphazard development of new areas. This can be done by creating a balance between centripetal and centrifugal forces generated within the city.

The Old Master Plan for Patna envisaged the creation of 27 planned neighborhood units. As proposed, it was supposed to be a self-contained unit where a group of people were to reside and within which all day to day needs of living were to be met.

The Old Master Plan also made certain proposals regarding traffic pattern, civic services and institutional planning. The Plan could not be executed because of paucity of funds and unexpected growth of population which outstripped all plan estimates. As a matter of fact, the city continued to expand unhindered and its pace was so rapid that planning for all neighbourhood units failed and could not be implemented. As such slums have developed, civic amenities have fallen short and the population has increased enormously during the last thirty years.

A number of suggestions have been made regarding future physical development and land use in Patna. For implementation of any urban development programmes, availability of land and its control are essential prerequisites. Controls such as zoning regulations, sub - division rules, building bye - laws and authority to approve layouts are means of directing urban growth. Acquisition of land would be essential not only for future growth but also for a large number of public use and slum clearance programmes. Construction and allocation of single room flats to migrant rural population would check the growing encroachment on roads caused by them.

Space should be left open in the residential areas for parks and playgrounds and this should be in proportion to the density of population of the areas.

The synthesis of planning lies in the functional relationship between total land and various uses to which it is put. Hence undesirable mixing up of land uses should be checked thoroughly.

The shifting of certain institutions to outlying areas has been advocated. Lastly, in order to shape the city's growth, it is suggested that a green belt to be created around the Western and Southern parts of the city.

Apart from the above suggestions the author has suggested improvements of certain basic civic amenities existing within the city such as better alignment and adequate widths of roads, an arrest of the problem of mixed traffic and an increase in the flow of fast moving vehicles, transfer of all drainage lines from the Ganga to the Punpun etc.

The present study is an attempt to examine the pattern of population distribution in the city in relation to the city's haphazard and unchecked urban sprawl. The author has tried to suggest ways for the future development of the city in a planned and proper way. However, a detailed zonal plan and physical planning proposals have been left out. These may form part of future studies as a continuation and extension of the work already done.

Bibliography

Books

Abercombie, P. (1961) : Town and Country Planning, London Oxford University Press.

Adams, T. (1935) : Outline of Town and City Planning, New York : Russel Sage Foundation.

Ahmad, E. (1965) : Bihar : A Physical, Economic and Regional Geography, Ranchi : Ranchi University.

Ahmad, Q. (1965) : Indian Cities, : Characteristics and Correlates, Hyderabad : University of Sind.

Alam, S. M. (1972) : Metropolitan Hyderabad and Its Region, London : Asia Publishing House.

Alam, S. M. (1965) : Hyderabad and Secunderabad : A Study in Urban Geography, Hyderabad : Allied Publishers Pvt. Ltd., Osmania University Press.

Alam, S. M. & Khan, W. (1972) : Metropolitan Hyderabad : A Strategy for Development, Hyderabad : Asia Publishing House, Osmania University Press.

Alankar, S. V. (1949) : Pataliputra - Ki - Katha, Allahabad : Hindustan Academy.

Ali, A. F. M., Abdul (1931) : Patna : Her Relation with the John Company Bahadur etc. Calcutta.

Anderson, N. (1959): The Urban Community : A World Perspective, New York : Henry Holt & Co.

Anderson, W. et. al. (1950) : City Planning : Selection of Readings in its

Theory and Practices, Minneapolis.

Bapegamage, A. (1957) : Delhi : A Study in Urban Sociology, Bombay, University of Bombay.

Brtholomew, H. (1955) : Land Uses in American Cities, Cambridge Harvard University Press.

Bekinsale, R. P. & Houstan, J. M. (eds.) (1968) : Urbanization and its Problems, Essay in J. Honour of E.W. Gilbert, Oxford Baseo Black Well.

Berry, B. J. L. & Houstan, F. E. (1970) : Geographic Perspective on Urban Systems, New Jersey : Prentice Hall Inc. Engelwood Cliffs.

Beyer, G. H. (ed.) (1967) : The Urban Explosion in Latin America, Ithaca : Cornell University Press.

Bhat, L. S. (1972) : Regional Planning in India, Calcutta : Statistical Publishing Society.

Bhardwaj, R. K. (1974) : Urban Development in India, Delhi : National Publishing House.

Bijlani, H. U. (1977) : Urban Problems, New Delhi : Indian Institute of Public Administration.

Bogue, D. J. & Harris, D. L. (1954) : Comparative Populations and Urban Research viz. Multiple Regression and Covariance Analysis, Ohio, U.S.A.

Bose, A. (1970) : Urbanization in India : An Inventory of Source Materials, Delhi : Institute of Economic Development.

Bose, A. (1973) : Studies in India's Urbanization 1901 - 1971, Bombay - New Delhi : Tata McGraw Hill Publishing Co. Ltd.

Bourne, L. S. (ed.) (1970) : Internal Structure of the City, New York : Oxford University Press.

Buchanan, C. & Patterns (1969) : Regional Studies in Ireland, Dublin : An Foras Forbarths.

Buchanan, F. (1812) : An Account of District of Bihar and Patna in 1811 - 12, Calcutta : Bihar and Orissa Research Society.

Carter, H. (1973) : Urban Planning and Local Authorities, Lucknow :

Lucknow University.

Chapin, F. S. (1957) : Urban Land Use Planning, New York : Harper and Brothers.

Chatterjee, S. P. (1949) : 24 Parganas and Calcutta (Bengali Edition) Calcutta : City Book Co.

Chatterjee, S. P. (1964) : Fifty years of Science in India (Geography), Calcutta : Indian Science Congress Association.

Chatterjee, S. P. (1968) : Progress of Geography in India (1964 - 68), Calcutta : Indian Science Congress Association.

Clark, J. I. (1973) : Population Geography, Oxford : Pergamon Press.

Das, R. B. (1970) : Urban Planning and Local Authorities, Lucknow : Lucknow University.

Dayal, P. (1953) : Bihar in Maps, Patna, Kusum Prakashan.

Dickinson, R. E. (1952) : City, Region and Regionalism, London : Routledge and Kegan Paul Ltd.

Diwarkar, R. R. (ed.) (1958) : Bihar Through the Ages, Calcutta : Orient Longmans Pvt. Ltd.

Donald, H. W. (1958) : Urban Planning and Municipal Public Policy Zoning, New York : Harper and Brothers.

Duncan, O. D. et.al (1960) : Metropolis and Region, Baltimore : John Hopkin Press.

Duncan, O. D. & Reiss, A. J. Jr. (1956) : Social Characteristics of Urban and Rural Communities, New York, John Wiley and Sons Inc.

Dutta, K. K. (1946) : An Introduction of Bihar, Patna : Indian Historical Congress, IX Session.

Dutta, K. K. (1957) : Unrest against British Rule in Bihar (1831 - 1839), Patna : Superintendent, Secretariat Press.

Dutta, K. K. (1967) : The Life and Thought of the People of Bihar, Calcutta : Scientific Book Agencies.

Freeman, T. W. (1967) : Geography and Planning, London : Hutchinson.

Gallion, A. B.& Eisner, S. (1963) : Urban Pattern, New York : Van Nostrand Reinhold Co.

Gamer, R. E. (1972) : The Politics of Urban Development in Singapore, Ithaca : Cornell University Press.

Garnler, B. J. (1967) : Urban Geography, London : Longmans, Green and Co. Ltd.

Geddes, P. (1949) : Cities in Evolution, London : Williams and Norgate Ltd.

Ghosh, M. (1919) : Pataliputra Patna : Law Press.

Ghosh, M. et. al. (1972) : Calcutta : A Study in Urban Growth Dynamics, Calcutta : Firma K. L. Mukhopadhyay.

Gibbs, J. P. (1966) : Urban Research Methods, Indian Edition, New Delhi : Affiliated East - West Press Pvt. Ltd.

Gillie, F. (1971) : The Cork Sub - regional Planning Study, An Foras Forbartha.

Govindraj, A. S. (1963) : Bangalore City Central Area Development, New Delhi : School of Planning and Architecture.

Gowda, K. S. R. (1972) : Urban and Regional Planning Mysore : University of Mysore.

Greer, G. (1942) : The Problems of the Cities and Towns, Conference on Urbanism, Harvard University.

Haig, R. M. (1927) : Major Economic Factor in Metropolitan Growth and Arrangement, Regional Survey of New York and its Environs.

Hubbard, T. K. & Hubbard H. V. (1929) : Our Cities Today and Tommorrow, Cambridge : Harvard University Press.

Hauser, P. M. & Schnore, L. F. (eds.) (1967) : The Study of Urbanisation, New York : John Wiley and Sons Inc.

Hawley, A. H. (1955) : The Changing Shape of Metropolitan America : Deconcentration since 1920, Illinois, U.S.A.

Jackson, J. N. (1968) : Survey for Town and Country Planning, London : Hutchinson University Library.

Jackson, V. M. (1925) : Journal of Francis Buchanan (Afterwards Hamilton), Patna and Gaya : Bihar and Orissa Government Printing.

James, H. R. & Johnes (1966) : Urban Geography : An Introductory Analysis, Oxford : Pergamon Press.

Johnson, J. H. (1967) : Urban Geography : An Introductory Analysis, Oxford : Pergamon Press.

Jones, E. (1966) : Towns and Cities, London : Oxford University Press.

Lal, D. N. (1973) : Patna in 1955 : A Demographic Sample Study Patna : Demographic Research Centre, Department of Statistics, Patna University.

Lewis, H. M. (1961) : Planning the Modern City (Vol. One), London : John Wiley and Sons Inc.

Mayer, H. M. and Kohn, C. F. (eds.) (1967) : Readings in Urban Geography, Allahabad : Central Book Depot.

Mayer, J. R. Kain, J. F. & Wohe, M. (1966) : The Urban Transportation Problem, bridge : Harvard University Press.

Mishra, R. P. (ed.) (1978) : Million Cities of India, New Delhi : Vikas Publishing Co.

Modak, M. V. and Ambedkar, V. N. (1971) : Town and Country Planning and Housing Bombay : Orient Longmans Ltd.

Mumford; L. (1961) : The City in History : Its Origin, its Transformation and its Prospects, Harcourt, New York; Brace and Co.

Mumford, L. (1968) : The Urban Prospect, Harcourt, New York : Brace and World Inc.

Murphy, R. E. (1966) : The American City - An Urban Geography, New York : McGraw Hill Book Co.

Noble, A. G. & Dutt, A. K. (1977) : Indian Urbanization and Planning : Vehicles of Modernization, New Delhi : Tata McGraw Hill Publishing Co. Ltd.

Northam, R. M. (1975) : Urban Geography, New York : John Wiley and Sons, Inc.

Park, R. E. (1967) : The City, Chicago : Chicago University Press.

Prakasarao, V. L. S. (1964) : Towns of Mysore State, Bombay : Asia Publishing Co.

Queens, S. & Thomas, L. F. (1939) : The City, New York.

Robinson, C. M. (1916) : City Planning, New York.

Rodwin, L. (1970) : Nations and Cities : A Comparison of Strategies of Urban Growth, Boston, Houghton, Mifflin.

Saaviner, E. (1943) : The City, its Growth, its Decay and its Future, New York.

Samaddar, J. N. (1927) : The Glories of Magadh, Calcutta.

Sami, A. (1980) : Intra Urban Market Geography : A Case Study of Patna, New Delhi : Concept Publishing Co.

Sarkar, J. (1932) : Bihar and Orissa during the Fall of Moghal Empire, Patna.

Sert, J. (1942) : Can Our Cities Survive, Cambridge : Harvard University Press.

Singh. H. H. (1972) : Kanpur : A Study in Urban Geography, Varanasi : Davis Publishing Agency.

Singh. L. R. (ed.) (1981) : New Perspectives in Geography, Prof. P. Dayal Felicitation Volume, Allahabad : Thinkers Library.

Singh, R. L. (1964) : Bangalore : An Urban Survey, Varanasi : Tara Publication.

Singh, R. L. (ed.) (1973) : Urban Geography in the Developing Countries, I.G.U. Symposium, 1968, Varanasi : National Geographical Society of India.

Singh, R. L. (1961) : Banaras : A Study in Urban Geography, Varanasi : Nandkishore Publications.

Singh, R. P. & Kumar, A. (1970) : Monography of Bihar Patna : Bharati Bhawan.

Singh, U. (1966) : Allahabad : A Study in Urban Geography, Varanasi, Banaras Hindu University.

Sinha, M. M. P. (1980) : The Impact of Urbanization on Land Use in the Rural - Urban Fringe : A Case Study of Patna, New Delhi : Concept Publishing Co.

Smailes, A. E. (1953) : The Geography of Towns, London : Hutchinson University Library.

Taneja, K. L. (1971) : Morphology of Indian Cities, Varanasi : National Geographical Society of India.

Taylor, G. (1948) : Urban Geography, London : Methuen & Co. Ltd.

Turner, R. (ed.) (1962) : India's Urban Future, Bombay : Oxford University Press.

Waddel, L. A. (1903) : Report on Excavation at Pataliputra, Calcutta.

Weaver, R. C. (1969) : The U· ban Complex : Human Values in Urban Life, Ludhiana : Lyall Book Depot.

Weber, A. F. (1964) : The Growth of Cities in the Nineteenth Century, New York : Cornell University Press.

Woodbury, C. (ed.) (1962) : Urban Redevelopment : Problems and Prospects, Chicago; University of Chicago Press.

Articles And Journals

Adhikari, S. (1978) "Origin and Evolution of Capital Cities in Ancient India : A Politico - Geographical Analysis, Geographical Bulletin of India. No. III.

Ahmad, E. & Spate, O. H. K. (1950) "Five Cities of Ganga Plain", Geographical Review, Vol. XI.

Alam, S. M. (1965) : Hyderabad - Secunderabad Cities - A Study in Urban Geography, Bombay.

Andreus, R. B. (1942) : "Elements in the Urban Fringe Pattern", Journal of Land and Public Utility Economics, Vol. 18, pp. 169-83.

Arriga, E. E. (1968) : "Components of the City Growth in Selected Latin American Countries", Milbank, Memorial Fund Quarterly, 46, Part I, pp. 237-52.

Ataullah, M. (1982) : "Urban Land Use Pattern in Ganga - Side Cities :

A Case Study of Patna" Indian Geographical Studies, Research Bulletin No. 18, pp. 45-52.

Aurousseau, M. (1921) : "The Distribution of Population : Geographical A Constructive Problem" A Geographical Review of India, Vol. 11, pp. 363-92.

Bagchi, K. & Sen, U. (1963) : "Giridih - Its Growth and Land Use", Geographical Review of India, Vol. 25, No. 4.

Barber, G. M. (1977) : "Urban Population Distribution Planning", in Hudson, J.C. (ed.), Annals of the Association of American Geographers, Vol. 67, No. 2.

Berry, B. J. L. & Garrison, : "Alternate Explanations of Urban Rank Size Relationships", Annals of the Association of American Geographers, Vol. 48, pp. 83-91.

Berry, B. J. L. Simmons, J. W. & Tenant, R. J. (1963) : "Urban Population Densities : Structure and Change', Geographical Review, Vol. 53, pp. 389-405.

Bhat, D. R. & Sharma, A. N. (1974) : "The Pattern of Urban Development in Karnal District, Geographical View Point, Vol. V, Nos. 1 and 2.

Bhattacharya, M. (1975) : "Urbanisation and Urban Problems in India's Some Policy Issues", Nagarlok, pp. 1-14.

Bhattacharya, S. & Basak, T. (1970) : "The Morphology of Chittaranjan Township, Geographical Review of India, Vol. XXXII, pp. 262-68.

Bonifatieva, L. I. (1971) : "Problems of Urban Planning in India", In Economic and Socio - Cultural Dimensions of Regionalization, Office of Registrar General of India, pp. 343-63.

Bose, M. S. G. (1970) : "Development of Unplanned Capital Towns", Nagarlok, Vol. 2, No. 2, pp. 11-17.

Boyce, R. R. (1966) : "The Edge of the Metropolis : The Wave Theory Analog Approach", British Columbia - Series, No. 7, pp. 31-40.

Brush, J. E. (1962) : " The Morphology of Indian Cities", in Turner, R. (ed.), India's Urban Future, California : University of California Press.

Brush, J. E. (1968) : " Spatial Pattern of Population in Indian Cities",

The Geographical Review, Vol. 58.

Burgess, E. W. (1925) : " The Growth of the City", In Park, R. E.; Burgess, E. W. and Mckenzie, R. D. (eds.), The City, Chicago : Chicago University Press, pp. 47-62.

Burgess, E. W. (1929) : "Urban Areas in Chicago : An Experiment in Social Science Research", (eds.) T. V. Smith and Leonard D. White, Chicago : Chicago University Press, pp. 113-138.

Chatterjee, A. B. (1955) : "Demographic Features of Howrah City", Geographical Review of India, Vol. 20.

Chari, C. S. S. (1927) : "Stages in the Growth of the City of Madras" Journal of Madras Geographical Association, Vol. 2, pp. 74-104.

Colby, C. C. (1933) : "Centrifugal and Centripetal Forces in Urban Geography", Annals of the Association of American Geographers, No. 23, pp. 1-20.

Dann, R. (1931) : "A Note on Urban Geography of Malabar", Journal of Madras Geographical Association, Vol. 2, No. 3.

Davie, M. R. (1937) : "The Pattern of Urban Growth" in Murdock, G. P. (ed.), Studies in the Science of Society, New Haven : Yale University Press, pp. 133-161.

Dayal, P. (1968) : "The Bihar Plain : A Regional Study", Transactions of the Indian Council of Geographers, Vol. 5, pp. 1-29.

Dayal, P. (1972) : "Evolution and Spatial Structure of Retail Functions in Patna". First Indian Geographical Congress, New Delhi.

Dayal, P. & Thakur, B. (1976) : "Commercial Ribbons in Patna : Spatial Growth and Functional Structure", National Geographical Journal of India, Vol. 22 pp. 166-77.

Deshpande, C. D. (1941) : "Cities and Towns of Bombay Province : Aspects of Urban Geography", Journal of Madras Geographical Association, Vol. 16, No. 3.

Devgun, S. K. & Agarwal, S. K. (1971) : "Levels of Urbanisation in India", The Geographical View Point, October, pp. 15-22.

Dhabriya, S. S. (1964) : "Evolution of Cultural Landscape in Udaipur City", National Geographical Journal of India, Vol. 10, No. 2.

Dhabriya, S. S. (1976) : "Centrifugal and Centripetal Forces and City Expansion", Indian Journal of Geography, Vol. XI, No. 1, pp. 68-78.

Dickinson, R. E. (1934) : The Metropolitan Regions of the United States, "The Geographical Review, Vol. 24, pp. 278-291.

Dickinson, R. E. (1942) : "The Distribution of Functions of Smaller Urban Settlements of East Anglia", Geography, Vol. 17, pp. 19-31.

Dikshit, K. R. (1970) : "Evolution of Cities in Maharashtra : An Analysis of Phases of Urbanization", Indian Geographical Journal, Vol. XLV, pp. 53-64.

Dixit, K. R. (1961) : "The Concept of Functional Zones", National Geographical Journal of India, No. 7, pp. 191-205.

Dogra, B. B. (1974) : "Crisis in Our Cities", Civic Affairs, Vol. 22, No. 2, pp. 5-9.

Dutt, A. K. Barari, D. & Sami, A. (1984) : "Changes and Characteristics of Colonial and Traditional Cities of India", Asian Geographer, Vol. 3, No. 2, pp. 103-109.

Dwivedi, R. L. (1965) : "Demographic Features of Allahabad City", Geographical Review of India, Vol. 27, No. 4.

Ellefson, R. A. (1962) : "City - Hinterland Relationship", in Turner, R. (ed.), India's Urban Future, California : University of California Press, pp. 94-116.

Fry, M. E. & Drew : "Chandigarh and Urban Development in India", Asian Review, Vol. XLI.

Fryer, D. W. (1953) : "The Million City in S. E. Asia", Geographical Review, Vol. XLIII.

Ganguli, B. N. (1963) : "Some Characteristics of Population of Cities, Town Groups and Towns with Population of 50,000 and over", A.U.J.R., Vol. 11, No. 2.

Ghosh, B. (1976) : "Trend and Pattern of Population Growth of Calcutta City", Geographical Review of India, Vol. XXXVIII, No. 1, pp. 85-90.

Goryacheva, A. M. (1977) : "Factor Analysis of the Growth of India's

Largest Cities and Differentiation of Economic Functions", Soviet Geography, Vol. XVIII, No. 6, pp. 384-395.

Green, F. H. W. (1961) : "Urban Hinterlands in England and Wales "An Analysis of Bus Services : in Theoderson, G. A. (ed.), Studies in Human Ecology, New York : Row, Peterson and Co.

Green, H. L. (1955) : "Hinterland Boundaries of New York City and Boston Southern New England", Economic Geography, Vol. 31, pp. 283-300.

Guha, M. (1953) : "Morphology of Calcutta", Geographical Review of India, Vol. 15, No. 3.

Harris, C. D. (1943) : "A Functional Classification of Cities in the United States", Geographical Review, Vol. 33, pp. 86-99.

Harris, C. D. (1943) : "Suburbs", American Journal of Sociology, No. 49, pp. 1-13.

Harris, C. D. (1945) : "The Nature of Cities", Annals of American Academy of Political and Social Sciences, Vol. 242, pp. 7-17.

Harris, C. D. & Ullman, E. L. (1951) : "The Nature of Cities", In Mayer, H. M. and Kohn, C. F. (eds.), Readings in Urban Geography, Chicago : Chicago University Press, pp. 277-286.

Hart, J. F. (1955) : "Functions and Occupational Structure of Cities of the American South", Annals of the Association of American Geographers, Vol. 45, pp. 269-286.

Holzner, L. (1966) : "Urban Geography without a Regional System", The Professional Geographer. Vol. 18, No. 3, pp. 129-131.

Hoselitz, B. F. (1959) : "The Cities of India and their Problems", Annals of the Association of American Geographers, No. 49, pp. 223-231.

Hoyt, H. (1939) : "City Growth and Mortage Risk", Insured Mortage Portfolio, Vol. 1, Nos. 6-10 (Dec. 1936 - Apr. 1937), Passim; and Idem (U.S. Federal Housing Administration), The Structure and Growth of Residential Neighbourhoods in American Cities (Washington : Government Printing Office, 1939) Passim.

Hussain, M. L. (1980) : "Urban Expansion or Encroachment", Geographical Review of India, Vol. 42, No. 2, pp. 131-139.

Jauhari; A. S. (1968) : "Urban Development in Sutlej -Yamuna Divide", in Singh, R. L. (ed.), Urban Geography in Developing Countries, Proceedings of I.G.U. Symposium, No. 15, Varanasi, pp. 65-71.

Kar, N. R. (1960) : "Urban Characteristics of Calcutta", Indian Population Bulletin, Vol. 1, pp. 35-67.

Karan, P. P. (1952) : "Patna and Jamshedpur", Geographical Review of India, Vol. 14, No. 2.

Karan, P. P. (1957) : "The Pattern of Indian Towns, A Study in Urban Morphology", Journal of American Institute, Vol. XXIII.

Karimi, S. M. (1973) : "Origin and Evolution of Towns in Ancient Bihar", The Journal of Bihar Research Society, Vol. 59, pp. 75-92.

Karimi, S. M. (1977) : "Floods in Patna : Reasons and Remedies", Indian Geographical Studies, No. 9, pp. 58-69.

Kollmorgen, W. M. and Jenks, G. F. (1951) : "A Geographic Study of Population and Settlement Changes in Sherman Country, Kansas", Transactions of the Kansas Academy of Science, Vol. 54, pp. 449-494.

Kuriyan, G. (1941) : "Distribution of Population in the City of Madras", Indian Geographical Journal, Vol. 16, No. 1.

Lahiri, T. B. (1963) : "Calcutta Metropolitan District", Proceedings of the Indian Sciences Congress.

Mahto, K. (1964) : "Pattern of Population Growth in Bihar", Indian Geographical Studies, No. 2, pp. 28-35.

Mathur, S. P. (1968) : "The Growth of Functional Structure of Dehradun : A Case Study of an Indian Resort Town", in Singh R. L. (ed.) Urban Geography in Developing Countries, Proceedings of I.G.U. Symposium No.15, Varanasi, pp. 234-243.

Maxwell, J. W. (1967) : "The Functional Structure of Canadian Cities : A Classification of Cities", Geographical Bulletin, Vol. 9, No. 4, pp. 61-87.

Mayer, H. M. (1967) : "Urban Geography", in James, P. E. and Jones C. F. (eds.) American Geography : Inventory and Prospect, Syracuse : Syrecuse University Press.

Mayer, H. M. (1967) : "A Survey of Urban Geography", in Manser, P. M. and Schnore, L. P. (eds.), The Study of Urbanization, New York : John Wiley and Sons Inc.

Mayer, H.M. (1969) : "Making a Living in Cities : The Urban Economic Base", Journal of Geography, Vol. LXVIII, No. 2, pp. 70-87.

Morill, R. (1968) : "Expansion of Urban Fringe : A Stimulation Experiment", Papers of Regional Science Association, No. 15, pp. 185-202.

Mukerji, A. B. (1953) : "Modinagar - A Study in Urban Geography" Geographical Review of India, Vol. 15, No. 4.

Milkh, R. (1973) : "The Housing and Urban Development Corporation : A New Dimension in Housing", Nagarlok, pp. 47-51.

Murphy, R.E. and Vance, T.E.Jr. (1954) : "Delimiting the C.B.D.", Economic Geography, Vol. 30, pp. 199-222.

Murphy, R. E. (1966) : "Urbanization in Asia", Ekisties, Vol. 21, No. 122.

Pal, S. K. (1970) : "Changing Role of Urbanization of Central Cities in India : A Study in Spatial Redistribution of Population 1901-61", Geographical Review of India, Vol. 32, No. 2, pp. 97-112.

Park, R. E. & Newcomb, C. (1933) : "Newspaper Circulation and Metropolitan Regions", in McKenjie, R. (ed.) The Metropolitan Community, New York : McGraw Hill Book Co.

Pathak, C. R. (1980) : "Urban Problems and Politics in India" Indian Journal of Regional Sciences, Vol. 12. No. 1. pp. 71-90.

Patil, S. R. (1968) : "Moment Analysis of the Distribution of Urban Settlements and Population of Mysore State", I.G.U. Special Number, National Geographical Journal of India, Vol. 14, Part 2-3, pp. 214-222.

Payne, G. (1973) : "Scatter Housing and Urban Growth in India", Social Science Research Council Monograph, pp. 162-181.

Pickard, J. P. (1959) : "Metropolitanization of U. S. ", Urban Land Institute, Research Monograph 2.

Pickard, J. P. (1962) : "Urban Regions of the U.S.", Urban Land, Vol.

21, No. 4, pp. 3-10.

Prasad, A. (1958) : "Double Towns of India : A Problem in Urban Morphology", Geographical Outlook, Vol. 2, No. 1.

Prasad, B. (1981) : "Role of Master Plans in Urban Development", Indian Geographical Studies, Research Bulletin No. 16, pp. 6-14.

Prasad, K. (1978) : "The Impact of Ganga Bridge on the Circulation System of Patna and its Environs", Geographical Bulletin of India, No. 4, pp. 35-44.

Ram, L. N. & Sinha S. (1981) : "Historical Evolution of a Capital City : Patna", Indian Geographical Studies, Research Bulletin No. 17, pp. 41-49.

Ram, L. N. & Thakur, B. (1973) : "The Ecological Structure of Gaya", Geographical Outlook, 9, pp. 89-91.

Raza, M., Kundu, A. & Nangia, S. (1975) : "Urban Rural Continum in India", Indian and Foreign Review, Vol. XII, No. 15 and 16 pp. 13-14 & 16.

Reddy, N. B. K. (1968) : "Occupational Structure of the Urban Centres in Krishna and Godavari Deltas", in Singh, R. L. (ed.) Urban Geography in Developing Countries, Proceedings of I.G.U. Symposium, No. 15, Varanasi, pp. 119-136.

Reddy, N. B. K. (1970) : "Moment Analysis and Centographic Study of the Spatial Distribution of Urban Settlements and Population of the Krishna and Godavari Deltas", Geographical Review of India, Vol. 32, No. 1. pp. 14-28.

Saxena, P. B. (1972) : "The Changing Pattern of Demographic Structure of Dehradun City", The Deccan Geographer, Vol. X, No. 2, pp. 51-71.

Schnore, L. F. & Paterson, G. D. (1958) : U.S. and Canada; Annals of American Academy of Political and Social Science, No. 316, pp. 60-68.

Shah, K. K. (1969) : "Housing and Urban Development in India" Civic Affairs, Vol. 16, No. 12, pp. 5-11.

Shastri, P. (1973) : "Growth and Distribution of Population in Nagpur

City", National Geographer, Vol. VIII, pp. 63-70.

Sinclair, R. (1978) : "Spatial Change and the Urban Landscape', Geographic Polonica, Vol. 80, pp. 33-46.

Sinclair, R. Shipton, R. and Willis, M. (1971) : "A Case Study of Urban Expansion in South Western Macomb Country, Michigan : Michigan Academician, Vol. 4, No. 2.

Singh, D. K. (1972) : "Kerakat : A Urban Service Centre : Lower Gomati Valley", National Geographical Journal of India, Vol. XVIII, pp. 28-41.

Singh, L. R. & Singh, R. D. (1980) : "Spatio Demographic Structure of Patna in its Ecological Setting", Erkunde, Vol. 34, No. 4, pp. 281-87.

Singh, R. L. (1961) : "Evolution of Bangalore City", National Geographical Journal of India, Vol. 5, No. 4.

Singh, S. P. (1959) : "Demographic Features of Lucknow", National Geographical Journal of India, Vol. 5, No. 3.

Singh, R. P. & Dabral, M. P. (1970) : "A Comparative Analysis of Growth and Functional Characteristics of the Towns of Ganga - Yamuna Doab", The Indian Geographical Journal, Vol. XLV, Nos. 1 and 2, pp. 40-45.

Singh, U. (1961) : "Allahabad : A Study in its Planning and Development", National Geographical Journal of India, Vol. VII.

Singh, U. (1962) : "Role of Geographers in Town Planning with Special Reference to KAVAL Towns", Proceedings S.S.G.

Singh, U. (1963) : Changes in Built - Up Area in KAVAL Towns in the Ganga Plain", National Geographical Journal of India, Vol. 12, pp. 203-271.

Singh, U. (1968) : "Cities of the Ganga Plain - Their Problems and Planning", in Singh, R. L. (ed.) Urban Geography in Developing Countries, Proceedings of I.G.U, Symposium No. 15, Varanasi, pp. 343-350.

Singhal, G. D. (1980) : "Spatial Growth of Gaya and its Impact on Fringe Settlements", Indian Geographical Studies, Research Bulletin No.

14, pp. 24-28.

Sinha, B. N. (1962) : "The Bearing of Population Growth on the Economy of Orissa", The Deccan Geographer, Vol. 1, No. 2.

Sinha, M. M. P. (1974) : "Delimiting the Rural - Urban Fringe of Patna", Indian Geographical Studies, Research Bulletin No. 3, pp. 28-32.

Sinha, M. M. P. (1971) : "Rural - Urban Fringe", A Geographical Approach, Indian Geographical Studies, Research Bulletin No. 9, pp. 50-57.

Sinha, S. (1983) : "Patna : A Study in Urban Morphology", Indian Geographical Studies, Research Bulletin No. 20, pp. 61-70.

Smailes, A. E. (1947) : "The Analysis and Delimitation of Urban Field", Geography, Vol. 32, pp. 151-161.

Smailes, A. E. (1969) : "The Indian City : A Descriptive Model", Geographische Zeitschrift, 57, pp. 177-190.

Srinivasachari, C. S. (1927) : "Growth of City of Madras", Journal of Madras Geographical Association, Vol. 2, No. 3.

Srinivasachari, C. S. (1939) : "Growth of Madras City", Journal of Madras Geographical Association, Vol. 14, No. 2.

Srivastava, V. K. (1967) : "Sidhi District Headquarters", Transition, Geographical Thought, Vol. 3, No. 1.

Stanislawski, D. (1946) : "The Origin and the Spread of the Grid Pattern Towns", Geographical Review, Vol. 36, pp. 105-120.

Subramanyam, N. (1938) : "Some Aspects of the Growth of Greater Madras", Journal of Madras Geographical Association, Vol. 13, No. 1.

Sundaram, K. V. & Chandrashekhar, C. S. (1968) : "Urban Morphology and Internal Structure of Towns : Some Case Studies", National Geographical Journal of India, 14, pp. 55-64.

Swaminathan, N. (1928): "Sewage and City Geography", Journal of Madras Geographical Association, Vol. 2, No. 4.

Taylor, G. (1945) : "The Seven Ages of Towns", Economic Geography, Vol. 31, pp. 157-160.

Thakur, B. (1972) : "The Central Business District of Patna", Proceedings of Symposium on Urban Land Use (21st International Geographical Congress. 1963) Hyderabad National Committee for Geography, Calcutta, pp. 77-84.

Thapan, D. (1968) : "Evolution of Steel Towns" in Singh, R. L. (ed.) Urban Geography in Developing Countries, Proceedings of I.G.U. Symposium, No. 15, Varanasi, pp. 55-66.

Todaro, M. P. (1980) : "Urbanization in Developing Nations : Trends, Prospects and Policies, Journal of Geography, Vol. 79, No. 5.

Trewartha, G. T. (1953) : "A Case for Population Geography", Annals of the Association of American Geographers, Vol. XLIII.

Tripathy, R. R. (1970) : "Functional Analysis of the Towns of Maharastra State", Geographical Review of India, Vol. 32, No. 1, pp. 41-46.

Tripathy, S. N. & Sinha, B.N. (1976) : "An Investigation into Urban Growth Through Applications of Employment and Location Quotients : Bhubaneshwar - A Case Study", Research Bulletin, Eastern Geographical Society, No. 2.

Turner, J. F. C. (1968) : "Housing Priorities, Settlements Patterns and Urban Development in Modernising Countries", Journal of the American Institute of Planners, No. 34, pp. 354-363.

Ullman, E. L. (1941) : "A Theory of Location for Cities", American Journal of Sociology, Vol. 46, pp. 853-864.

Vagale, L. R. (1959) : "Trends of Housing Needs in India", Urban and Rural Planning Though, Vol. 11.

Vagale, L. R. (1961) : "Bangalore : A Study of its Planning Problems", Journal of the Institute of Town Planners, India, pp. 84-89.

Verma, K. N. (1962) : " Jabalpur : A Study in Urban Geography and Town Planning", Deccan Geographer, No. 1, pp. 40-52.

Vining, R. (1955) : "A Description of Certain Special Aspects of an Economic System"; Economic Development and Cultural Change, Vol. 3, pp. 147-195.

Vishwanath, V. (1981) : "Growth and Development of Towns in Tamilnadu, 1901-1981", The Indian Geographical Journal, Vol. 56, Nos. 1 & 2, pp. 43-53.

Whebell, C. F. F. J. (1969) : "Corridors : A Theory of Urban Systems", Annals of the Association of American Geographers, No. 59, pp. 1-56.

Wingo, L. Jr. (1969) : "Latin American Urbanization - Plan or Process", in Frieden, B. J. and Nash, W. (ed.) Shaping an Urban Future, Cambridge Mass, Mit Press, pp. 115-116.

Wirth, L. (1938) : "Urbanization as a way of life", American Journal of Sociology, 44, pp. 1-24.

Woodridge, S. W. (1938) : "Town and Rural Planning — the Physical Factors in the Problem", Geography, Vol. 22, pp. 90-93.

Government Publications

A Survey of Research in Geography (1972), New Delhi : Indian Council of Social Science Research.

Basic Development Plan for Calcutta Metropolitan District 1966-86, C.M.P.O., Government of West Bengal, 1966.

Bombay's Development and Master Plan : A 20 Years Perspective (1970), Bombay : The Bombay Civic Trust.

Census of India (1951), District Census Handbook, Patna District, Part X - A, Patna : Superintendent, Secretariat Press.

Census of India (1961) : District Census Handbook, Patna District, Part X-A, Patna : Superintenden, Secretariat Press.

Census of India (1971), District Census Handbook, Patna District, Part X - A Patna : Superintendent, Secretariat Press.

City Development Plans and their Implementation (Papers and Proceedings of the Seminar) (1977), Centre for Urban Studies, Indian Institute of Public Administration, New Delhi.

Hauser, A & Green; G. (1941) : Urban Development of Cities in the U.S. Federal Housing Administration, Washington.

Hoyt, H. (1939) : The Structure and Growth of Residential Neighbourhood in American Cities, Washington : U.S., Federal Housing Administration.

Hunter, W. W. (1877) : A Statistical Account of Bengal, Vol. XI, District of Patna and Saran.

Hunter, W. W. (1908) : Imperial Gazetteer of India, Vol. 7 and 20, Oxford : The Clarendon Press.

Kumar, N. (1970) : Bihar District Gazetteer, Patna : Patna District, Government Press.

Kumar, N. (1971) : Image of Patna, Government of Bihar, Patna.

Master Plan for Delhi (1962) Delhi Development Authority, New Delhi.

Master Plan for Delhi (1963), Parts I & II, Patna : Patna Improvement Trust.

O'Malley, L.S.S. (1909) : Impartal Gazetteer of India, Bengal Series, Bengal, Vol. II, Calcutta.

O'Malley, L. S.S. (1924) : Bihar and Orissa District Gazetter Patna District , Superintendent, Bihar and Orissa, Patna : Government Printing Press.

Plan and Progress (1964) : Patna Improvement Trust, Patna.

Planning Standard and Building Bye - Laws for Cities with Population more than 1,00,000 of Bihar (Finalized), (1976), Prepared by Bihar Government Building Bye - Laws Committee.

Report on Land Use Pattern of India's Cities and Towns (1966), Town and Country Planning Organization (Ministry of Works, House and Urban Development), New Delhi.

Social Aspects of Housing and Urban Development (1967), New York : United Nations Research Council Publication.

The Ganga Bridge at Patna (1967), The National Council of Applied Economic Research, New Delhi.

The Science of Geography (1877, 1965), National Academy of Science, National Research Council Publication.

Town Planning in Bihar (1966), Town Planning Section, L.S.G. Deptt. Patna.

Traffic and Transportation Problems in Metropolitan Cities (1967), Metropolitan Transport Team Committee on Plan Projects, New Delhi : Planning Commission.

Bibliography

Urban Planning and Development Authorities (Papers and Proceedings of the Seminar) (1978), Centre for Urban Studies, Indian Institute of Public Administration, New Delhi.

Others

Ataullah, Md. (1979) : "Urban Land Use in Major Towns along the Ganga in Bihar", Unpublished Ph.D. Thesis, Department of Geography, Patna University.

Dube, K. K. (1966) : "Use and Misuse of Land in KAVAL Towns", Unpublished Ph.D. Thesis, Banaras Hindu University.

Dwivedi, R. L. (1958) : "Allahabad : A Study in Urban Geography" Unpublished Ph.D. Thesis, Allahabad University.

Narayan, N. (1968) : "Patna : A Study in Urban Morphology", Unpublished M.A. Dissertation, Department of Geography, Patna University.

Penguin Books (1965) : Cities, A Scientific American Book, London : C. Nicholls and Co. Ltd.

Prasad, K. (1981) : "Evaluation and Growth of Urban Transport and Communication of Ganga Side Cities of Bihar", Unpublished Ph.D. Thesis, Patna University, Patna.

Sharma, K. D. (1972) : "Transport and Communication System of Patna", Unpublished M.A. Dissertation, Department of Geography, Patna University.

Singh, L. P. (1967) : "Patna : A Study in Public Utility Services", Unpublished M.A. Dissertation, Department of Geography, Patna University.

Singh, N. (1977) : "Factors Affecting Population Distribution in Patna", Unpublished M.A. Dissertation, Department of Geography, Patna University.

Sinha, K. (1970) : "Patna : A Study in Urban Land Use", Unpublished M.A. Dissertation, Department of Geography, Patna University.

Sinha, M. K. (1968) : "Spatial Distribution of Retail Trade : A Case Study of Patna", Unpublished M.C.P. Thesis, Department of Architecture and Regional Planning I.I.T., Kharagpur.

Sinha, S. (1981) : "Patna : A Study in Urban Renewal and Reconstruction", Unpublished Ph. D. Thesis, Department of Geography, Patna University.

Sinha, S. K. N. (1963) : "The Umland of Patna", Unpublished M.A. Dissertation, Department of Geography, Patna University.

Thakore, M. P. (1962) : "Aspects of Urban Geography of New Delhi", Ph.D. Thesis, Queen Mary College, University of London.

Tiwari, A. R. (1957) : "Urban Geography of Agra", Unpublished Ph.D. Thesis, London University.

Appendix - I

Patna : Growth of Population, 1971-81

Ward No.	Total Population Total of 1971 calculated on the basis of the area in 1981	Growth of population (1981)	% age of population	growth
1	22110	28500	6390	28.90
2	22240	28286	6046	27.19
3	22704	32476	9772	43.04
4	22599	29268	6669	29.51
5	8465	23667	15202	179.59
6	7730	33371	25641	331.71
7	11691	16046	4355	37.25
8	16931	34242	17311	102.24
9	10226	12351	2125	20.78
10	11840	13680	1840	15.54
11	17634	53466	35832	203.20
12	13702	16937	3235	23.61
13	13510	16232	2722	20.15
14	26453	35744	9291	35.12
15	12096	13226	1130	9.34
16	12457	15801	3344	26.84
17	16081	22103	6022	37.45
18	16270	30739	14469	88.93
19	10550	17147	6597	62.53
20	10558	16030	5472	51.83
21	14570	27975	13405	92.00
22	10340	16025	5685	41.52
23	11298	17084	5786	51.21
24	12302	18753	6451	52.44
25	12321	18353	6032	48.96
26	13819	19905	6086	44.04
27	10732	14799	4067	37.90
28	11840	16288	4448	37.57
29	10679	13773	3094	28.97
30	10274	13174	2900	28.23
31	12471	18999	6528	52.35
32	9723	13468	3745	38.52
33	9076	12473	3397	37.43
34	10911	15454	4541	41.62
35	10205	17240	7035	68.94
36	13701	18232	4531	33.07
37	9969	15046	5077	50.93
Total Patna (P.M.C.)	514944	776371	261427	50.77

Appendix - II

Patna : Density of Population, 1951

Ward No.	Total Population of 1971	Area in acre	Density of population per acre
1	12530	385.8	32.48
2	7773	364.7	21.31
3	8753	271.1	32.29
4	5435	50.0	108.70
5	7174	25.6	280.23
6	6256	41.2	151.84
7	2876	164.5	17.48
8	10386	50.0	207.72
9	10490	65.1	161.14
10	16295	120.5	135.23
11	10596	194.5	54.48
12	7353	273.2	26.92
13	8009	192.7	41.56
14	5700	110.0	51.82
15	7867	688.4	11.43
16	7224	146.2	49.41
17	7985	173.9	45.92
18	6004	431.0	13.93
19	5060	100.6	50.30
20	9576	265.8	36.03
21	9931	174.4	56.94
22	9300	183.8	50.60
23	5777	67.3	85.84
24	8164	108.0	75.59
25	7929	709.6	11.17
26	7415	90.1	82.30
27	5965	113.2	52.69
28	6190	108.1	57.26
29	7995	388.9	20.56
30	7093	153.6	46.18
31	6054	245.8	24.63
32	5130	654.3	7.84
Total Patna (P.M.C.)	250285	7111.9	35.19

Appendix - III
Patna : Density of Population, 1961

Ward No.	Total Population	Area of the ward in acre	Density of population per acre
1	7516	385.8	18.55
2	16240	364.7	45.53
3	11984	271.1	44.20
4	6327	50.0	126.54
5	9200	25.6	359.38
6	11279	41.2	273.76
7	6440	164.5	39.15
8	10796	50.0	215.92
9	9120	65.1	140.09
10	5837	120.5	48.44
11	12812	194.5	65.87
12	10189	273.2	37.30
13	13029	192.7	67.61
14	11967	110.0	108.79
15	8532	688.4	12.39
16	8514	146.2	58.24
17	8921	173.9	51.30
18	8072	431.0	18.73
19	10100	100.6	100.40
20	5820	265.8	21.90
21	8667	174.4	49.70
22	11122	183.8	60.51
23	8078	67.3	120.03
24	7954	108.0	73.65
25	8077	709.6	11.38
26	8883	90.1	98.59
27	6082	113.2	53.73
28	8801	108.1	81.42
29	7791	388.9	20.03
30	7420	153.6	48.31
31	6727	245.8	27.37
32	7140	654.3	10.91
33	16140	677.0	23.84
34	12040	1640.0	7.34
35	11259	1222.0	9.21
36	11792	124.0	95.10
37	23033	594.0	38.78
Total Patna (P.M.C.)	363700	11227.05	32.40

Appendix - IV
Patna : Density of Population, 1971

Ward No.	Total Population	Area in acre	Density of population per acre
1	15099	828.4	18.23
2	10766	1282.6	8.39
3	18665	1051.2	17.76
4	22599	729.2	30.99
5	8465	306.6	27.61
6	7730	815.6	9.48
7	11691	76.8	152.23
8	16931	442.6	38.25
9	10226	261.2	39.15
10	11840	280.4	42.23
11	17634	828.4	21.29
12	13702	208.4	65.75
13	13510	122.6	110.20
14	23090	471.2	49.00
15	12096	51.8	233.51
16	12457	109.8	113.45
17	16081	171.6	93.71
18	15957	673.8	23.68
19	10550	97.0	108.76
20	10558	138.6	76.18
21	13693	1373.2	9.97
22	10340	148.2	69.77
23	11298	171.6	65.84
24	12302	1361.4	9.04
25	12321	152.4	80.85
26	13819	1194.0	11.57
27	10732	165.2	64.96
28	11840	174.8	67.73
29	10679	1590.8	6.71
30	10274	64.0	160.53
31	12471	149.2	83.59
32	9723	70.4	138.11
33	9076	376.4	24.11
34	10911	112.4	97.07
35	10205	177.0	57.66
36	13701	473.8	28.92
37	9969	715.4	13.93
Total Patna (P.M.C.)	473001	17556.5	26.94

Appendix - V
Patna : Density of Population, 1981

Ward No.	Total Population	Area in acre	Density of population per acre
1	28500	3398.4	8.39
2	28286	3127.0	9.05
3	32476	1836.2	17.69
4	29268	729.2	40.14
5	23667	306.6	77.19
6	33371	815.6	40.92
7	16046	76.8	208.93
8	34242	442.6	77.37
9	12351	261.2	47.29
10	13680	280.4	48.79
11	53466	828.4	64.54
12	16937	208.4	81.27
13	16232	122.6	132.40
14	35744	1240.2	28.82
15	13226	51.8	255.33
16	15801	109.8	143.91
17	22103	171.6	123.81
18	30739	889.8	34.55
19	17147	97.0	176.77
20	16030	138.6	115.66
21	27975	1784.2	15.68
22	16025	148.2	108.13
23	17084	171.6	99.56
24	18753	1361.4	13.78
25	18373	152.4	120.56
26	19905	1194.0	16.67
27	14799	165.2	89.58
28	16288	174.8	93.18
29	13773	1590.8	8.66
30	13174	64.0	205.84
31	18999	149.2	127.34
32	13468	70.4	191.31
33	12473	376.4	33.14
34	15452	112.4	137.47
35	17240	177.0	97.40
36	18232	473.8	38.48
37	15046	715.4	21.03
Total Patna (P.M.C.)	776371	24097.9	32.22
Total of Area of wards		24013.4	32.33

Appendix - VI

Patna : Age-Sex structure, Sample Survey, 1983

Age-group	Western Zone		Central Zone		Eastern Zone		Southern Zone	
	% of male population	% of Female population	% of male population	% of Female population	% of male population	% of Female population	% of male population	% of Female population
0-4	48.27	51.73	50.97	49.03	52.75	42.25	48.65	51.35
5-9	50.57	49.43	50.47	49.53	54.22	45.78	55.89	44.11
10-14	58.55	41.45	58.27	41.73	57.12	42.88	59.04	40.96
15-19	56.44	43.56	61.15	38.85	55.99	44.01	61.50	38.50
20-24	56.44	43.56	62.72	37.28	63.15	36.85	65.90	34.10
25-29	48.51	51.49	51.15	48.85	57.49	42.51	49.25	50.75
30-34	41.29	58.71	43.43	56.57	42.97	57.03	44.12	55.88
35-39	51.25	48.75	51.26	48.74	42.97	57.03	46.12	53.88
40-44	64.20	35.80	57.60	42.40	51.40	48.60	57.91	42.09
45-49	59.18	40.82	61.40	38.60	60.26	39.64	55.52	44.48
50-54	72.38	27.62	66.46	33.54	60.81	39.19	65.72	34.28
55-59	68.37	31.63	52.87	47.13	62.18	37.82	64.29	35.71
60-64	49.21	50.79	65.59	34.41	64.34	35.66	51.28	48.72
65-69	54.29	45.71	57.14	42.86	56.70	43.30	51.28	48.72
70 & above	59.26	40.74	62.69	37.31	67.10	32.90	54.35	45.65

Appendix - VII
Patna : Sex Ratio, 1971 & 1981

Ward No.	No. of females per thousand males 1971	No. of females per thousand males 1981
1	791	796
2	706	732
3	830	846
4	751	789
5	683	733
6	616	679
7	767	812
8	790	817
9	747	702
10	581	678
11	738	776
12	770	774
13	742	768
14	748	819
15	761	801
16	763	771
17	753	754
18	719	785
19	731	759
20	720	769
21	813	813
22	882	887
23	859	887
24	880	863
25	851	881
26	883	903
27	873	884
28	948	920
29	893	907
30	886	875
31	871	905
32	844	861
33	863	901
34	863	866
35	846	889
36	888	900
37	886	855
Total Patna (P.M.C.)	793	810

Appendix - VIII
Patna : Literacy, 1971

Ward No.	Total Population	Total literates	% age of literates
1	15099	8980	59.47
2	10766	7378	68.53
3	18665	9754	52.26
4	22599	13717	60.70
5	8465	4692	55.43
6	7730	4618	59.74
7	11691	7254	61.62
8	16931	10167	60.05
9	10226	6138	60.02
10	11840	7195	60.77
11	17634	10497	59.53
12	13702	8146	59.45
13	13510	8845	65.47
14	23090	13265	57.45
15	12096	7475	61.80
16	12457	7493	60.15
17	16081	9594	59.66
18	15957	11013	69.02
19	10550	5247	49.74
20	10558	6264	59.33
21	13693	5042	36.82
22	10340	4776	46.19
23	11298	5107	45.20
24	12303	4971	40.41
25	12321	5836	47.37
26	13819	57017	41.30
27	10732	5679	52.92
28	11840	4865	41.09
29	10679	3173	29.71
30	10274	4799	46.71
31	12471	5693	45.65
32	9723	6260	64.38
33	9076	4335	47.76
34	10911	4862	44.56
35	10205	4779	46.77
36	13701	5484	40.03
37	9969	3269	32.79
Total Patna (P.M.C.)	473001	252369	53.36

Appendix - IX
Patna : Literacy, 1981

Ward No.	Total Population	Total literates & educated	% of literates & educated to the total population
1	28500	19285	67.67
2	28286	16106	56.94
3	32476	18538	36.34
4	29268	19985	68.28
5	23667	14878	62.96
6	33371	22576	67.75
7	16046	10386	64.73
8	34242	22980	67.11
9	12351	7531	60.98
10	13680	9112	66.61
11	53466	33740	63.12
12	16937	10838	63.99
13	16232	11137	68.81
14	35744	24136	67.53
15	13226	7666	57.96
16	15801	8126	51.43
17	22103	15197	68.76
18	30739	21498	69.94
19	17147	9865	57.53
20	16030	9166	57.18
21	27975	15189	54.29
22	16025	8596	53.64
23	17084	9694	56.74
24	18753	9342	49.82
25	18373	10337	56.26
26	19905	9127	45.85
27	14799	8023	54.21
28	16288	8382	51.46
29	13773	4725	34.31
30	13174	6359	48.26
31	18999	9680	50.95
32	13468	8858	65.77
33	12473	6338	50.96
34	15452	8100	52.42
35	17240	8339	48.37
36	18232	8113	44.50
37	15046	5692	37.83
Total Patna (P.M.C.)	776371	457640	58.95

Appendix - X
Patna : Male-Female Literacy, 1971

Ward No.	Male population	Female population	No. of literate males	No. of literate females	% of male literacy	% of female literacy
1	8430	6669	5800	3180	68.80	47.68
2	6310	4456	4840	2538	76.70	56.96
3	10199	8466	6583	3171	64.55	37.46
4	12909	9690	8903	4814	68.97	49.68
5	5029	3436	3058	1634	60.81	47.56
6	4784	2946	3221	1397	67.33	47.42
7	6615	5076	4697	2557	71.01	50.37
8	9461	7470	6690	3477	70.71	46.55
9	5854	4372	4061	2077	69.37	47.51
10	7489	4351	4857	2338	64.86	53.73
11	10148	7486	7031	3466	69.22	46.30
12	7740	5962	5285	2861	68.28	47.99
13	7755	5755	5670	3175	73.11	55.17
14	13205	9883	8824	4441	66.82	44.94
15	6869	5227	4815	2660	70.10	50.89
16	7067	5390	4893	2660	69.23	49.35
17	9175	6906	6351	3243	69.22	46.96
18	9283	6674	6892	4121	74.24	61.75
19	6095	4455	3725	1522	61.12	34.16
20	6139	4419	4190	2074	68.25	46.93
21	7554	6139	3623	1419	47.96	23.11
22	5495	4845	3013	1763	54.83	36.39
23	6077	5221	3331	1776	54.81	34.02
24	6542	5760	3360	1611	51.36	27.97
25	6656	5665	3892	1944	58.47	34.32
26	7337	6482	3848	1859	52.45	28.68
27	5730	5002	3591	2088	62.67	41.74
28	6077	5763	3001	1864	49.38	32.34
29	5641	5038	2392	781	42.40	15.50
30	5448	4826	3122	1677	57.31	34.75
31	6664	5807	3653	2040	54.82	35.13
32	5274	4449	3767	2493	71.43	56.04
33	4871	4205	2889	1446	59.31	34.39
34	5856	5055	3171	1691	54.15	33.45
35	5527	4678	3233	1546	58.49	33.05
36	7255	6446	3823	1661	52.69	25.77
37	5286	4683	2370	899	44.84	19.20
Total (P.M.C.)	263848	209153	116465	85904	63.09	41.07

Appendix - XI
Patna : Male-Female Literacy, 1981

Ward No.	Male population	Female population	No. of literate males	No. of literate females	% of male literacy	% of female literacy
1	15868	12632	12153	7132	76.60	56.46
2	16323	11963	11254	4882	68.95	40.56
3	17590	14866	11991	6547	68.17	43.98
4	16358	12910	12281	7704	75.08	59.67
5	13649	10018	9479	5399	69.45	53.89
6	19741	13630	14752	7824	74.73	57.40
7	8852	7194	6492	3894	73.34	54.13
8	18836	15406	14357	8623	76.22	55.95
9	7256	5095	4940	2591	68.08	50.85
10	8149	5532	5794	3318	71.11	59.98
11	30195	23271	21939	11801	72.66	50.71
12	9542	7395	6916	3922	72.48	53.04
13	9177	7055	6734	4403	73.38	62.14
14	19695	16049	14794	9342	75.12	58.21
15	7341	5885	4161	3505	56.68	59.56
16	8919	6882	6963	1163	78.07	16.90
17	12598	9505	9944	5253	78.93	55.27
18	17269	13470	13007	8491	75.32	63.04
19	9803	7344	6708	3157	68.43	42.99
20	9061	6969	5549	3617	61.24	52.99
21	15427	12548	9616	5573	62.33	44.31
22	8488	7537	5325	3361	61.68	44.59
23	9100	7984	5946	3748	65.34	46.94
24	10062	8691	5997	3345	59.60	38.49
25	9765	8608	6430	3907	65.85	45.39
26	10460	9445	6065	3062	57.98	32.42
27	7855	6944	4903	3120	62.42	44.93
28	8480	7808	5016	3366	59.15	43.03
29	7220	6553	3411	1314	47.24	20.05
30	7024	6150	4503	1856	64.11	30.18
31	9974	9025	5974	3706	59.90	41.06
32	7212	6256	5256	3602	72.88	57.58
33	6559	5914	4024	2314	61.35	39.13
34	8279	7173	5171	2929	62.46	40.83
35	9122	8118	5303	3036	58.13	37.40
36	9594	8638	5371	2742	55.98	31.74
37	8109	6937	4041	1651	49.83	23.80
Total Patna (P.M.C.)	428951	347420	292470	165170	68.18	47.54

Appendix - XII
Patna : Occupational Structure, 1971

Ward No.	% age of total workers	% age of commercial workers	% age of industrial workers	% age workers engaged in other services	% age of workers under construction	% age of workers under transport storage and Communication
1	26.64	5.15	3.83	50.71	3.21	4.80
2	28.41	2.84	1.80	80.06	4.18	8.96
3	24.91	14.86	7.79	43.86	6.32	6.35
4	27.86	14.23	8.88	48.23	6.12	9.96
5	33.93	17.83	11.11	39.66	4.32	25.04
6	32.19	12.58	2.29	67.08	7.92	8.72
7	27.73	25.14	11.41	44.85	3.09	12.74
8	25.44	17.01	7.85	48.63	5.92	10.28
9	28.25	31.33	12.53	40.00	2.49	11.77
10	35.73	30.38	12.51	28.09	2.93	7.66
11	26.45	24.07	15.97	37.41	4.16	15.24
12	27.59	19.84	9.20	61.54	2.12	6.43
13	28.13	33.65	12.02	40.28	2.39	8.18
14	27.06	18.77	9.72	46.91	5.38	10.02
15	26.61	35.82	26.87	25.26	2.24	6.83
16	24.97	29.70	19.03	39.38	1.96	7.23
17	28.01	27.44	17.63	38.18	2.04	4.95
18	28.95	24.87	10.00	50.39	1.88	7.47
19	26.53	24.33	15.79	29.15	3.79	12.04
20	24.79	23.00	13.45	40.47	3.52	12.30
21	27.73	13.54	10.77	22.33	3.35	5.14
22	25.56	17.93	25.20	37.46	3.03	7.11
23	23.61	15.29	32.76	27.74	3.15	8.88
24	26.07	15.25	22.67	16.84	3.15	7.11
25	24.63	23.23	22.67	24.38	4.38	7.32
26	27.88	17.96	18.40	18.84	2.28	4.26
27	24.58	18.92	28.66	36.09	3.64	8.19
28	25.06	19.48	37.61	25.01	3.03	7.01
29	31.71	6.11	12.73	7.17	1.24	3.99
30	27.19	36.45	25.06	25.85	2.22	6.84
31	25.29	22.35	34.94	24.03	3.33	10.11
32	25.75	43.37	19.41	23.04	1.64	9.12
33	25.79	21.66	23.49	17.77	2.22	9.14
34	25.88	28.01	31.09	20.72	3.33	11.58
35	26.85	32.81	26.61	17.48	1.75	14.45
36	28.14	12.66	13.54	9.39	0.75	7.42
37	29.99	13.31	10.67	9.06	2.34	4.82
Total (P.M.C)	27.23	20.93	15.87	36.00	3.38	8.79

Appendix - XIII

List of Major Functional Centres shown in Figure No. 28

ADMINISTRATIVE

Nos. on the Map	Name of the Centres
1	City Court
2	Civil Court
3	Collectorate
4	High Court
5	New Secretariate
6	Old Secretariate
7	Raj Bhawan

EDUCATIONAL/INSTITUTIONAL

Nos. on the Map	Name of the Centres
1	Guru Govind Singh College
2	B.N.R. Training College
3	Patna Law College
4	Bihar College of Engineering
5	Patna Science College
6	Patna University
7	Patna College
8	Patna Medical College
9	B. N. College
10	Patna Women's Training College
11	Magadh Mahila College
12	Patna Women's College
13	A. N. College
14	Indira Gandhi Institute of Medical Sciences
15	Bihar Veterenary College
16	Ayurvedic College
17	Patna Training College
18	Commerce College
19	Nalanda Medical College

COMMERCIAL

Nos. on the Map	Name of the Centres
1	City Chowk market
2	Muradpur Market

3	Bakerganj Market
4	Dak Bungalow Road Market
5	New Market
6	Mithapur Market

RELIGIOUS

Nos. on the Map	Name of the Centres
1	Har Mandir
2	Bari Patan Devi
3	Pathar Ki Masjid
4	Bishop's Church
5	Birla Mandir
6	Protestant's Church
7	Mahavir Asthan (near Patna Jn.)
8	Mosque near Patna Junction

RECREATIONAL

Nos. on the Map	Name of the Centres
1	Krishna Talkies
2	Anand Talkies
3	Bankipore Club
4	Elphinstone (Cinema Hall)
5	Mona (Cinema Hall)
6	Regent (Cinema Hall)
7	Rupak (Cinema Hall)
8	Chanakya (Cinema Hall)
9	Apsara (Cinema Hall)
10	Gandhi Maidan
11	Golghar
12	Veena (Cinema Hall)
13	Ashok (Cinema Hall)
14	Pearl (Cinema Hall)
15	Hardinge Park
16	New Patna Club
17	Sanjay Gandhi Jaivik Udyan
18	Vaishali (Cinema Hall)
19	Moniul Haque Stadium
20	Kumhrar

CULTURAL

Nos. on the Map	Name of the Centres
1	Jalan Museum
2	Bihar Hitashi Pustakalaya
3	Khuda Bakhsh Oriental Public Library
4	Sinha Library
5	Patna Museum

TRANSPORT AND COMMUNICATION

Nos. on the Map	Name of the Centres
1	Patna Ghat
2	Patna Sahib Railway Station
3	Jhauganj Post Office
4	Gulzarbagh Railway Station
5	Rajendranagar Railway Station
6	Bankipore Post and Telegraph Office
7	Mahendru Ghat
8	Bankipore Bus Stand
9	Digha Ghat
10	Station Bus Stand (Frazer Road)
11	Patna Junction
12	General Post Office
13	Hardinge Park Bus Stand
14	Patna Aerodrome
15	Phulwari Sharif Railway Station

Appendix - XIV

Patna : Metropolitan Region, Classes of Town, 1981

	City/Towns	Total Population	Class of Town (according to Population)
1	Patna M. C.	773720	Class I (1 lakh & above)
2	Hajipur	62509	Class II
3	Dinapur Nizamat	58632	(50,000-99,999)
4	Khagaul	34124	
5	Masaurhi	24233	
6	Danapur Cantonment	23468	Class III
7	Phulwari Sharif	22753	(20,000-49,999)
8	Fatwa	21183	
9	Maner	19364	Class III
10	Dighwara	17072	(10,000-19,999)

Appendix - XV

Patna : Metropolitan Region, List of Villages under (P.M.R.) having more than 5000 population in 1981 (Anchal wise)

Name of the Anchal		Name of the Village	Population over 5000
1. Patna Rural A		Fatehpur	6646
		Sabbalpur	8325
2. Patna Rural B	(i)	Pannapur	6925
3. Fatwa	(i)	Jethuli	5932
	(ii)	Hansipur Machhariyawan	5646
	(iii)	Jaitya	5283
4. Phulwari	(i)	Alampur Ganpura	8506
	(ii)	Bariya	5508
5. Punpun		Lakhana	9249
6. Dhanapura		Nil	-
7. Masaurhi		Shahabad	7145
8. Danapur-cum-Khagaul	(i)	Pannapur	15329
	(ii)	Dalipchak	10204
9. Naubatpur	(i)	Chesi	5256
10. Bihta	(i)	Painal	5597
11. Maner	(i)	Kita Chaulishatt	17518
	(ii)	Beapur	6218
	(iii)	Sherpur	9816
12. Hajipur	(i)	Dihi Kalan	8185
	(ii)	Pannapur	5445
	(iii)	Dayal pur Sakha	6290
13. Bidupur	(i)	Daudnagar	5809
	(ii)	Bidupur	5631
	(iii)	Kuhibpur	6292
14. Raghopur	(i)	Tehrasia	5970
	(ii)	Rampurshan	5430
	(iii)	Raghopur	11494
	(iv)	Fatehpur Sabbaz	5806
	(v)	Paharpur	8694
	(vi)	Birpur	7254
	(vii)	Zarmanpur Karai	6386
15. Dighwara	(i)	Sitapur	5228
	(ii)	Jhaua	5273
16. Sonepur	(i)	Sabbalpur	13104
	(ii)	Shahpur	6903

Source : Census Office opp. B.N. College, Patna

Appendix - XVI
Patna Metropolitan Region, 1981

	Name of the Anchal/ Block	Total Population	Area in sq. km.	Density of population per km^2
1& 2	Patna Rural A+B	860721	136.04	6326.87
3	Fatwa	119697	252.8	473.48
4	Phulwari	159200	179.2	888.39
5	Punpun	81141	128.8	629.8
6	Dhanarua	114971	185.6	619.46
7	Masaurhi	131207	202.4	648.26
8	Dinapur-Cum-Khagaul	206998	129.7	1595.97
9	Naubatpur	119037	167.7	709.82
10	Maner	124903	170.7	731.71
11	Bihta	141987	193.9	732.27
12	Hajipur	200587	156.8	1279.25
13	Bidupur	131462	114.5	1148.14
14	Raghopur	102315	225.8	453.12
15	Sonepur	134152	167.9	799.0
16	Dighwara	70968	88.9	798.29

Appendix - XVII

Patna : Accommodation density and Household density, 1971

Ward No.	Area of the ward in acre	No. of occupied residential houses	No. of households	Density of occupied residential houses per acre	Density of households per acre
1	828.4	2179	2348	2.63	2.83
2	1282.6	1617	1896	1.26	1.48
3	1051.2	2472	2757	2.35	2.62
4	729.2	3704	4069	5.08	5.58
5	306.6	1174	1327	3.83	4.33
6	815.6	1396	1571	1.71	1.93
7	76.8	1974	2086	25.70	27.16
8	442.6	2450	3143	5.54	7.10
9	261.2	1263	1658	4.84	6.35
10	280.4	1693	2005	6.04	7.15
11	828.4	2919	3205	3.52	3.87
12	208.4	1298	1962	6.23	9.42
13	122.6	1475	2066	12.03	16.85
14	471.2	3585	4304	7.61	9.13
15	51.8	1289	1553	24.88	29.98
16	109.8	1390	1818	12.66	16.56
17	171.6	2155	2633	12.56	15.34
18	673.8	3686	2838	3.99	4.21
19	97.0	1562	1789	16.10	18.44
20	138.6	1456	1582	10.51	11.41
21	1373.2	1859	2119	1.35	1.54
22	148.2	1412	1509	9.53	10.18
23	171.6	1344	1600	7.83	9.32
24	1361.4	1649	1887	1.21	1.39
25	152.4	1598	1900	10.49	12.47
26	1194.0	1935	2110	1.62	1.77
27	165.2	1368	1558	8.28	9.43
28	174.8	1545	1806	8.84	10.33
29	1590.8	1576	1691	0.99	1.06
30	64.0	1298	1562	20.28	24.41
31	149.2	1611	1973	10.80	13.22
32	70.4	1172	1438	16.65	20.43
33	376.4	1226	1387	3.26	3.69
34	112.4	1344	1692	11.96	15.05
35	177.0	1495	1705	8.39	9.63
36	473.8	1924	2207	4.06	4.66
37	715.4	1457	1522	2.04	2.13
Total Patna (P.M.C.)	17556.5	65540	76276	3.73	4.34

Appendix - XVIII

Patna : Accommodation density and Household (family) density, 1981

Ward No.	Area of the ward in acre	No. of occupied residential houses	No. of households	Density of occupied residential houses per acre	Density of households per acre
1	3398.4	3878	4529	1.14	1.33
2	3127.0	4184	4659	1.34	1.49
3	1836.2	4093	4715	2.23	2.57
4	729.2	3854	4819	4.87	6.08
5	306.6	3194	4088	10.42	13.33
6	815.6	5630	6197	6.90	7.60
7	76.8	2457	2615	31.99	34.05
8	442.6	5078	6716	11.45	12.91
9	261.2	1782	2000	6.82	7.66
10	280.4	1749	2169	3.23	4.01
11	828.4	6862	8914	8.28	10.77
12	208.4	1702	2381	8.17	11.43
13	122.6	1887	2537	15.39	20.69
14	1240.2	5121	5757	4.13	4.64
15	51.8	1006	1519	19.42	29.32
16	109.8	1378	2159	12.55	19.66
17	171.6	2232	3360	13.01	19.58
18	889.8	4237	4975	4.76	5.59
19	97.0	1739	2531	17.93	26.09
20	138.6	1929	2210	13.92	15.95
21	1784.2	3544	3850	1.99	2.16
22	148.2	1695	2023	11.44	13.65
23	171.6	1465	2136	8.54	12.45
24	1361.4	2249	2820	1.65	2.07
25	152.4	1972	2564	12.94	16.82
26	1194.0	2338	2966	1.96	2.48
27	165.2	1591	1910	9.63	11.56
28	174.8	1692	2260	9.68	12.93
29	1590.8	1712	2026	1.08	1.27
30	60.0	1315	1797	20.55	28.08
31	149.2	1766	2450	11.84	16.42
32	70.4	1267	1877	18.00	26.66
33	376.4	1391	1743	3.70	4.63
34	112.4	1511	2248	13.44	20.00
35	177.0	1936	2529	10.94	14.29
36	473.8	2179	2610	4.60	5.51
37	715.4	1844	2295	2.58	3.21
Total Patna (P.M.C.)	24097.9	95449	117954	3.96	4.89
Calculated total of all wards	24013.4 acre			3.97	4.91
Diff.	84.5 acre				

Appendix XIX

Population of Patna and Agglomeration, 1991, with Variation since 1971

Town/ Urban Agglomeration	Year	Status	Area in Km²	Persons	Decade Variation	%Decade Variation	Males	Females
(i) Patna	1981	Municipal Coporation	79.42	776,371	+303370	+64.14	428.951	347.420
	1991	"	99.45	917,243	+140,872	+18.14	502,748	414,495
(ii) Digha Mainpura (Outgrowth)	1981		6.99	33,856	-	-	18.184	15,672
	1991		6.99	34,770	+914	+2.70	18,770	16,000
(iii) Pataliputra Housing Colony (Outgrowth)	1981		0.64	3,736	+1437	+62.51	2,180	1,556
	1991		0.64	4,404	+668	+17.88	2,455	1,949
(iv) Dinapur Nizamat	1981	Municipality	11.63	58,684	+15,990	+37.45	31,171	27,513
	1991	"	11.63	84,616	+25,932	+44.19	45.474	39,142
(v) Phulwari Sharif	1981	Notified Area	6.48	22,717	+6,795	+42.69	12,091	10,621
	1991	"	6.48	35,123	+13,411	+54.65	18,605	16,518
(vi) Dinapur Cantonment	1981	Cantonment	3.42	23,544	+6,245	+36.10	13,666	9.878
	1991	"	3.42	23,491	- 53	- 0.23	13,192	10,299

The Urban Agglomeration represents a continuons Urban spread constituting a town and its adjoining urban outgrowth or two more physically Contiguous towns together with Contiguous urban outgrowth which may actually fall within the revenue limits of a village.

Source : Census of India 1991 Genaral Population Tables, Bihar Series 5, Part II- A, Published, 1998.

Appendix -XX

Area and Population of Patna-Dinapur Standard Urban Area, 1981- 1991 with Nature and Reason of Change

Name of SUA	Name (Status)	1981 Area	1981 Urban Population	1991 Area	1991 Urban Population	Nature and Reason of Change, 1981-91
Patna-Dinapur	1. Patna(M.C.)					
	(i) Digha-Mainpura (Outgrowth)	79.42 6.99	776,371 33,856	99.45 6.99	917,243 34,770	Rural Components Viz, Villages Khajepur and Amukurtha of Patna Rural (a) CD
	(ii) Pataliputra Housing Colony (Outgrowth)	0.64	3,736	0.64	4,404	Block which were partly included in Patna Municipal Corporation in 1981
	2. Dinapur Nizamet (Municipality)	11.63	58,684	11.63	84,616	have been wholly included in Patna M.C. in 1991. Further,
	3. Khagaul (Municipality)	3.66	34,161	3.66	40,453	some changes in the area of Patna M.C. have
	4. Phulwari Sharif (N.A.)	6.48	22,712	6.48	35,123	occurred due to revised compantation.
	5. Fatwah (N.A.)	4.90	21,252	4.90	20,668	
	6.Dinapur Cantonment (Cantt)	3.42	23,544	3.42	23,491	

The Concept of Standard Urban Area was adopted in 1971 census for spatially continuous set of Urban and Rural settlements. It was defined as the projected growth area of a city/town having 50,000 or more population in 1971. It includes not only town and village which will get merged but also the intervening area having potentiality for urbanisation for all. It is supposed to have one or all of the following characteristics - (a) Predominant Urban and land use , (b) Intensive inter-action with the urban Centres, (c) Anticipated Urban growth as a result of locatianal decisions (d) Existence of big villages large proportion of working force engaged in non agricultural activities

Patna-Dinapur SUA consisting of urban components and 59 rural components have a population of 1,170,768 and 92,028 with an area of 137.17 Km^2 and 68.33 km^2 respectively in 1991. Patna Municipal Corporation with two outgrowths of Pataliputra Housing Colony and Digha Mainpura is the core town of this SUA. The occupational structure of this SUA in 1981 and 1991 is as givan below % of the main working population:-

	1981	1991
1. Persons engaged in primary Sector (agricultural activitis livestock, forestry fishing etc mining and querries	10.55%	11.87%
2. Persons in secondary sector (Manufacting, processing servicing or repair in household and non-household industry imp, and industrial Categories).	2.16%	11.66%
3. Persons in teritary sector (Trade, Commerce, Transport, Storage, Communication, some Industrial work etc.	87.29%	76.47%
Large numbers of people migrate to this city for education government and other employment and medical treatment.		

Source: Census of India, 1991. Genaral Population Tables, Bihar Series 5, Part II- A, Published, 1998.

